To Brother and Sister Daniel Hess

May you receive inspiration from
President Lee's sermons as you
read his latest book.

May the Lord bless you and
keep you always in His loving
care.

Sister Harold B. Lee

March 1975.

# Ye are the Light of the World

# Ye are the Light of the World

Selected sermons and writings
of President Harold B. Lee

Published by Deseret Book Company,
Salt Lake City, Utah, 1974

Lithographed by

DESERET PRESS

in the United States of America

Ye are the light of the world. A city that
is set on an hill cannot be hid.

Neither do men light a candle, and put it
under a bushel, but on a candlestick;
and it giveth light unto all
that are in the house.

Let your light so shine before men,
that they may see your good works,
and glorify your Father which is in heaven.
                          —Matthew 5:14-16

## PRESIDENT HAROLD B. LEE
### PROPHET, SEER, AND REVELATOR

*As sons and daughters of the living God, we stand united in tribute to the living prophet. Since Eden, man has called His chosen servants—men of faith and wisdom who rise above the sins of the world by mastering themselves, their lives perfected in virtue by earthly trial; so are prophets raised up in the necessity of time to join this line of inspired men.*

*People of all nations cry for leadership—not leadership of oppression or bondage, but the divine leadership of Christ's church, where men are foreordained to lead God's children from sin into celestial glory. That leadership requires years of preparation and celestial refinement. For possession of those keys of peace in this last dispensation of time, the keys that unlock modern miracles and usher in Christ's Millennial reign, a man must be chastened of God.*

> *given life in a small world where the things of man*
> *were smaller still*
>
> *raised up at first by candlelight and always by gospel light*
> *to be a man while still a child of God*
>
> *made strong by a loving father's design*
> *tempered and mellowed by youth and placed before mountains*
> *on which to strengthen his feet*
>
> *then given a burden to bear alone with the light*
> *of an earlier life to show the way*
>
> *encircled again*
> *given future light*
> *and a call from an earlier home*

*Called from the simplicity of farms and fields to stand in the upper rooms of the temple, where the veil is thinnest, comes such a man, whose life is a testimony that speaks the praises of God. This is a man who is more than a man, a man bearing Israel's prophetic inheritance, one of God's choicest sons. Thanks be to God that we live in a prophet's time, when his inspired leadership draws us closer to standing in those Holy Places where we prayerfully await Christ's second coming.*

(From a plaque presented to President Harold B. Lee by the Associated Students of Ricks College, Rexburg, Idaho, October 26, 1973)

# FOREWORD

President Harold B. Lee was born March 29, 1899. He served as president of Pioneer Stake from 1930 to April 6, 1941, when he was ordained an apostle and set apart as a member of the Council of the Twelve. In 1970 he was ordained president of that quorum and set apart as first councilor to President Joseph Fielding Smith. In July of 1972 he became the prophet, seer, revelator, and president of the Church. He passed on to a great reward December 26, 1973.

Although he served a shorter time as president of the Church than any of his predecessors, his contributions to it were great.

He was no ordinary man. His influence in its councils was effective from the beginning. It continued to increase until the day of his passing.

He understood and loved the underprivileged. Addressing them, he said:

I have come to know you intimately. Your problems, thank the Lord, have been my problems, because I know as you know what it means to walk when you have not the money to ride. I know what it means to go without meals to buy a book to go to the University. I thank God now for these experiences. I have loved you because of your devotion and faith. God bless you that you won't fail. (General conference address, April 6, 1941.)

In helping them, he made one of his greatest contributions, developing and directing the Church welfare program. He made other monumental contributions in the home teaching and family home evening programs and in Church correlation.

All the programs of the Church operative during the nearly thirty-three years he served as one of the General Authorities bear the mark of his prophetic genius.

The spirit in which he pursued his labors is revealed in the following quotation from the address he gave at the general conference in which he was first sustained as a member of the Quorum of Twelve Apostles, April 6, 1941.

"On April 20th, 1935," he said, "I was called to the office of the First Presidency. . . . My humble place in this [welfare] program at that time was described. I left there about noon . . . [and] drove . . . to the head of City Creek Canyon. I got out, after I had driven as far as I could, and I walked up through the trees. I sought my Heavenly Father. As I sat down to pore over this matter, wondering about an organization to be perfected to carry this work, I received a testimony, on that beautiful spring afternoon, that God had already revealed the greatest organization that ever could be given to mankind and that all that was needed now was that that organization be set to work and the temporal welfare of the Latter-day Saints would be safeguarded." (Ibid.)

He believed that the basic fundamental revelations made provision for the solution of all our problems. He began his search for every solution by finding out, through prayer and searching the revelation, what the Lord had to say on the subject.

He loved the youth with a divine compassion. He sorrowed over the rebellious and unrepentant and rejoiced over the returning prodigal.

During 1945 he delivered a series of radio addresses, titled *Youth and the Church*—which was later published in book form—in which he developed the thesis that the sure solution to youth's problems is to be found in the gospel of Jesus Christ. In the final chapter he writes: "During the preparation of this book, I have lived intimately with the problems of youth. I have tried to lead you to see and understand how the restored principles, powers, and ordinances of our glorious gospel dispensation may be applied to the lives of the youth of today." (*Youth and the Church*, p. 233.)

President Harold B. Lee was one of the most powerful men in modern Israel. The source of his strength was in his knowledge that he himself lived in the shadow of the Almighty. To him, his Heavenly Father was a senior partner, daily giving him guidance. Few indeed have had contacts with heaven as direct and regular as did he. He knew that the gospel of Jesus Christ is eternal truth.

"The dispensation in which you and I live," said he, "is intended to be a demonstration of the power and effectiveness of the gospel of Jesus Christ to meet [our] everyday problems here and now." (General conference address, October 1941.)

This conviction came to him out of his own experiences, as witness the following:

I know there are powers that can draw close to one who fills his heart with . . . love. . . . I came to a night, some years ago, when on my bed, I realized that before I could be worthy of the high place to which I had been called, I must love and forgive every soul that walked the earth, and in that time I came to know and I received a peace and a direction, and a comfort, and an inspiration, that told me things to come and gave me impressions that I knew were from a divine source. (General conference address, October 1946.)

In responding to his call to the Council of Twelve, he said:

Since nine o'clock last night I have lived an entire lifetime in retrospect and in prospect. . . . Throughout the night, as I thought of this most appalling and soul-stirring assignment, there kept coming to me the words of the Apostle Paul, . . . 'Let us therefore come boldly unto the throne of grace, that we may obtain mercy, and find grace to help in time of need.' . . . Therefore I shall take the word of the Apostle Paul. I shall come boldly unto the throne of grace, and ask for mercy and His grace to help me in my time of need. With that help I cannot fail. Without it I cannot succeed. (General conference address, April 1941.)

Humility before God and fearlessness before men was the key to his character. His ministry was characterized by an uncommon originality and daring. He was not hampered or restricted by worldly learning nor the ways of men. We who sat with him daily were frequently startled by the scope of his vision and the depth of his understanding. With forthrightness, he separated the wheat from the chaff and came directly to the truth.

The title of this book, *Ye Are the Light of the World,* was well chosen. It was taken from that portion of the Sermon on the Mount which reads:

Ye are the salt of the earth: but if the salt have lost his savour, wherewith shall it be salted? it is thenceforth good for nothing, but to be cast out, and to be trodden under foot of men.

Ye are the light of the world. A city that is set on an hill cannot be hid.

Neither do men light a candle, and put it under a bushel, but on a candlestick; and it giveth light unto all that are in the house.

Let your light so shine before men, that they may see your good works, and glorify your Father which is in heaven. (Matthew 5:13-16.)

President Lee with all his "heart, might, mind and strength" (D&C 4:2) sought to induce people to implement this charge of the Master.

Each of the messages in this book reflects the power and spirit of President Harold B. Lee.

President Marion G. Romney
Second Counselor in the First Presidency

# CONTENTS

# THE POWER
# OF EXAMPLE

# That Thy Light May Be a Standard Unto the Nations

This day, in this dispensation of the fulness of times, it is for us and for the world to see the fulfillment of the prophecies of the prophets Isaiah and Micah, in which they said:

> And it shall come to pass in the last days, that the mountain of the Lord's house shall be established in the top of the mountains, and shall be exalted above the hills; and all nations shall flow unto it.
>
> And many people shall go and say, Come ye, and let us go up to the mountain of the Lord, to the house of the God of Jacob; and he will teach us of his ways, and we will walk in his paths. . . . (Isaiah 2:2-3.)

In another commandment in a revelation given to us, the Lord said, in an injunction that we must never have absent from our minds:

> Verily I say unto you all: Arise and shine forth, that thy light may be a standard unto the nations;
>
> And that the gathering together upon the land of Zion, and upon her stakes, may be for a defense, and for a refuge from the storm, and from wrath when it shall be poured out without mixture upon the whole earth. (D&C 115:5-6.)

It was with a similar meaning in mind, no doubt, that the Master in his day declared:

> Ye are the light of the world. A city that is set on an hill cannot be hid.
>
> Neither do men light a candle, and put it under a bushel, but on a candlestick; and it giveth light unto all that are in the house.
>
> Let your light so shine before men, that they may see your good works, and glorify your Father which is in heaven. (Matthew 5:14-16.)

The Apostle Paul added another note to the urgency of these previous injunctions when he urged the people in his day to be awake and alert to the demands of their day, and this might well apply to us today. Said he: ". . . knowing the time, . . . now it is high time to awake out of sleep: for now is our salvation nearer than when we believed. The night is far spent, the day is at hand: let us therefore cast off the works of darkness, and let us put on the armour of light." (Romans 13:11-12.)

The writer of Proverbs defined the spirit of man as "the candle of the Lord" (Proverbs 20:27), while another prophet gave meaning to this profound thought when he said, ". . . there is a spirit in man: and the inspiration of the Almighty giveth them understanding" (Job 32:8).

By this I feel that the prophet is trying to help us understand that the spirit of man can become the candle of the Lord, and through the spirit of men may the candles of the Lord light the world in its entirety.

How can we arise and shine forth?

From time to time editors and religion writers have visited our conferences. One of the nation's leading religion editors, not a member of the Church, spent some time with us at June Conference, during which time he witnessed the beautiful spectacle of our MIA dance festival; saw a demonstration performance in which a bishop and his ward council discussed ways to aid in various family problems; attended performances featuring the singing of

4

youthful voices; and observed outdoor and indoor social activities that were opened and closed with prayer. After he returned to his home in New York City, I was anxious to get an appraisal from this man who probably has studied more religions and understands more about the religions of all people than any other man I know. He was asked to give a "post-mortem," as it were, upon his experiences at the youth conference he had just attended.

He said that at first he was surprised when he arrived in Salt Lake City to find that the conference wasn't overrun with young people. I replied, "This conference isn't primarily for young people; it is for youth leaders. There are many young people who participate in the conference events, but this is a conference of youth leaders."

After discussing some of the activities he had witnessed, he said, "I think I can sum up my impressions of what you are doing by saying that the plan of the Church is to teach your young people so many good things that they don't have time for bad things."

Another time a young couple from the South came to see us. They had been investigating the Church; they had been studying its principles. A student of theological matters, he had heard the missionaries bear witness. He wanted to know the truth as well as to see the Church in action, and he wondered if I could suggest a time for him to come when he could have this look at the Church. I said, "Come to a youth conference. There you will see what is being attempted in this day to reach our youth and to show the world how we go about solving the problems that are extant among youth today."

As I think about contentment in the lives of young people, Goethe's famous nine-point checklist of essentials to human contentment come to mind. These points are: health, wealth, strength, grace, patience, charity, love,

5

faith, hope. And, of course, we would add, "Make goodness popular in your lives, and gain that eternal joy which springs from keeping your hands clean and your hearts pure."

What are some of the standards given by the Lord for his church, and for the world, if they should seek to it? I mention the home as the most basic and vital of all God's institutions. The key to our whole correlation program was given to us when the First Presidency declared one of the most fundamental principles on which we were to build: "The home is the basis of the righteous life, and no other instrumentality can take its place nor fulfill its essential functions. The utmost the auxiliaries can do is to aid the home in its problems, giving special aid and succor where it is necessary."

With that in mind, then, every activity in the Church should be so planned as to strengthen—not to subtract from—the functioning of a well-ordered home. If parental leadership is weak, the priesthood home teachers and auxiliaries must give the necessary guidance. This means in essence that every event sponsored by the Church must be planned with this in mind, with particular emphasis on the importance of urging every family to observe faithfully the weekly home evening, and urging and aiding fathers who hold the holy priesthood in assuming their proper role as the heads of their households.

The thought-provoking and wise comments of Dr. Henry C. Link, from an article in the *Reader's Digest,* are most appropriate:

> A happy family life is probably the principal factor in the security of adults, as it is in the security of children. Much has been written about marital security, yet most discussions of what makes a happy marriage place little emphasis on the necessity of having children. Wars can come, jobs can go, money can run out, but if father, mother and children stand by each other, hope and happiness may survive.

In the midst of social unrest and so-called minority group disturbances, there are some disturbing tendencies among us today. I mention only three, but the list could be greatly expanded.

First, there is the dangerous temptation or tendency to compromise Church doctrines and standards in order to satisfy worldly pressures to change things that, in the final analysis, only God can change; and that tendency is among some of our leaders in the Church today.

Second, we find a tendency of some in our Church schools and seminaries and institutes to challenge, under the guise of so-called academic freedom, the doctrinal purity and Church standards. Beware!

And third, there is a tendency to think that it is wholesome to encourage dissent against Church institutions and divinely appointed authority. Faith was never built by providing the dissenters with a forum to criticize the Church, its institutions, and its authority.

Some years ago a prominent doctor, who was the head of a major university, visited here among us for the purpose of studying social community life. Later one of our prominent Church leaders astounded me when he said, "Do you know what Dr. _____ said to me? He said, 'If you folks would do away with this principle of so-called continuous revelation, I could join your church.'" Then this member of our church with whom I was speaking made this astounding statement: "You know, I think we ought to do something about that."

To do away with the very principle upon which the kingdom was to be founded—the principle of revelation—would be to deny the divinity of the Church and Kingdom of God on the earth!

At a testimony meeting some time ago I heard a man of great prominence in Church work and in a scientific

7

field tell of an experience in his own family. His father had gone on a mission, but because of the death of a member of the family, he had been called home. While he was home he caught a severe cold, which resulted in complete loss of hearing, so he was unable to return to his mission. It was a trial of the faith of the family and the father. Why couldn't this man now have his hearing restored, when he had lost it while on a merciful errand and in the midst of this great missionary service?

About that time he was visited by some emissaries of the devil, the Godbeites, one of the splinter groups of that day. (They are among us today by other names, and they are doing and saying exactly the same; this is not a new phenomenon.) They were trying to influence people in high places. They came to this father who had been struggling with his faith, and that night, after they left, the father pondered what had been said, with his faith somewhat weakened by his experience. As he walked along and approached a light on the corner, he heard, with ears with which he had not heard for months and months, a voice that said, "Stick with the old ship; it will lead you safely through."

Today is the time for all of us to remember those words. "Stick with the old ship." The Church doesn't need anything new except as the Lord reveals his will through revelation. This church—this "ship"—guided as it is by divine leaders, will carry us safely through.

The Lord made this promise of protection to the early leaders of the Church: "Wherefore, let them bring forth their strong reasons against the Lord. Verily, thus saith the Lord unto you—there is no weapon that is formed against you shall prosper; And if any man lift his voice against you he shall be confounded in mine own due time." (D&C

8

71:8-10.) And that is just as true today as it was when this revelation was given to our early leaders.

Following the death of President Brigham Young, the Council of the Twelve sent out a message to the Church that I think bears repeating today:

> Latter-day Saints should so live that they will know the voice of the true shepherd and not be deceived by pretenders. This is a privilege of every member of the Church, and the Latter-day Saint who does not live so as to have revelations of Jesus constantly with him stands in great danger of being deceived and falling away. All signs which the Lord promised to send in these last days are making their appearance. They show that the day of the Lord is at hand. A great work has to be done, and there is but little time in which to accomplish it. Great diligence is therefore required. Let us not slacken our diligence or give way to doubt, unbelief or hardness of heart, but be strong in the Lord and cry unto him unceasingly to give us the power to build up his Zion upon the earth, and to help establish a reign of righteousness, peace and truth. Let us build each other up in the most holy things, cultivating love, meekness, lowliness of heart, charity, patience and long suffering, bearing with each other's faults; and yet avoiding the very appearance of evil, so that others seeing our good works may be led to glorify God.

"Ye fearful Saints, fresh courage take;/ The clouds ye so much dread/ Are big with mercy and shall break/ In blessings on your head." (Hymn 48, "God Moves in a Mysterious Way.")

The Master prayed for his disciples, "I pray not that thou shouldst take them out of this world [the world of sin, he meant], but that thou shouldst keep them from evil." (John 17:15.) So today, we don't pray to have our youth and our people taken from out of the world, because they shall be as a leaven to the world. But we do pray to God, with all our power, that while they are in the world, they may be kept from evil. I bear you my solemn testimony— to you who may be wavering and who haven't yet developed a testimony—that this is the Lord's work. I know that Jesus Christ lives, and that He is closer to this church and appears more often in holy places than any of

9

us realize. The time is hastening when He shall come again to reign as Lord of Lords and King of Kings. You parents and all who lead youth, don't neglect to bear your testimony to them so that they may have something to cling to when turmoil comes in their lives and the temptations and the fires of Satan are burning hot in their lives. Through your lives and your actions, reflect the light of truth from heaven to all the world. "Let your light so shine . . . that they may see your good works, and glorify your Father which is in heaven."

# 2

# Ye Are the Salt of the Earth

In the beautiful Sermon on the Mount the Savior said: "Ye are the salt of the earth: but if the salt have lost his savour, wherewith shall it be salted? it is thenceforth good for nothing, but to be cast out, and to be trodden under foot of men." (Matthew 5:13.)

You will note that the Master personalized the "salt" of His illustration: "if the salt have lost his savour." He was speaking to His disciples and trying to impress the greatness of their mission. The Savior's disciples are the salt of society in every dispensation. Salt preserves food from corruption and seasons it, making it wholesome and acceptable; in like manner the Master's disciples are to purify the society in which they move, setting a good example and counteracting every corrupt tendency. They are to be, as He put it in another parable, the kingdom of heaven, which "is like unto leaven, which a woman took, and hid in three measures of meal till the whole was leavened." (Matthew 13:33.) The Apostle Paul added to that concept these words: "Know ye not that a little leaven leaveneth the whole lump?" (1 Corinthians 5:6.) "For this purpose their Christianity must be genuine. Men must feel that they are different from the world, and have a savour of their own." (J. R. Dummelow, *The One Volume Bible Commentary*, New York: Macmillan, 1974, p. 64.)

I have sought to find out in what sense salt and individuals might be on parallel ground. A dictionary states this interesting definition of savor: "Anything that gives loveliness, freshness, or pungency to anything, even spiritual emotion, vigor, may be said of one who has not lost his savor." The loss of savor, by contrast, means one who is insipid; who has willful barrenness, a dull life, and is without flavor. The salt that has lost its savor is the Christianity that is worldliness under a different name.

There are revelations that seem to spell out another aspect of this text. The Lord said:

When men are called unto mine everlasting gospel, and covenant with an everlasting covenant, they are accounted as the salt of the earth and the savor of men;

They are called to be the savor of men; therefore, if that salt of the earth lose its savor, behold, it is thenceforth good for nothing only to be cast out and trodden under the feet of men. (D&C 101:39-40.)

The most revealing point is this: "For they were set to be a light unto the world, and to be the saviors of men; And inasmuch as they are not the saviors of men, they are as salt that has lost its savor, and is thenceforth good for nothing but to be cast out and trodden under foot of men." (D&C 103:9-10.) In other words, we have lost our savor when we are no longer the saviors of men.

"Ye are the light of the world; a city set upon a hill." What does that mean? Well, a commentary on this scripture says:

. . . the disciples are to be the light of the world, being the representatives of Him who is the world's true Light. They are to enlighten it as its teachers and also by the examples of their lives . . . . they are contemplated not as individuals but as a visible Society, or Church. The old city set on a hill was Jerusalem. This was shortly to be trodden under the foot of men as having lost its savour. (Dummelow, *op. cit.*)

Just so today, any Latter-day Saint in Church circles, in military service, in social life, or in the business community is looked upon not just as an individual, but as the visible Church today. Someone has said: "Be careful how you act, because you may be the only Standard Church Works some people may ever read." The Lord here warns us that the standard of living in the Church must be visibly higher than the standard of living in the world. A church that tolerates a corrupt ministry or laxity of life among its communicants is not bearing its witness as the church of Jesus Christ before the world.

One of the last teachings the Master left to His disciples here on this continent, just before He was to leave them for the last time, was this: ". . . Behold, I am the light; I have set an example for you." Then he said, "Therefore, hold up your light that it may shine unto the world. Behold I am the light which ye shall hold up—that which ye have seen me do. . . ." (3 Nephi 18:16, 24.) There is another related scripture that is rather ominous for our day. The Lord warned us: "Woe unto you, when all men shall speak well of you! for so did their fathers to the false prophets." (Luke 6:26.) This is a warning to all who would teach the gospel to court popularity by speaking smooth words.

The story is told by Plutarch of a prominent Athenian, Phocian. Once when he was delivering a public speech and making a good impression and saw that all his hearers were equally pleased with what he said, he turned sharply to his friends and said, "Surely I have forgotten myself, and said something wrong." Another philosopher

13

said, when someone announced to him that all men were praising him, "Why, what evil have I done?"

President Joseph F. Smith, speaking of this same subject, said, "There are at least three dangers that threaten the Church within, and the authorities need to awaken to the fact that the people should be warned unceasingly against them. As I see these, they are the flattery of the prominent men in the world, false educational ideas, and sexual impurities."

I heard President Heber J. Grant say many times, "When certain men start to praise me or applaud me or speak well of me, I say to myself: 'Heber Grant, you must not be doing your duty or such men would not praise you.'"

Sometimes it is the mark of distinction to have men of ill repute not say good things about you.

What the Lord meant when He counseled His disciples to "beware" when all men shall speak well of them is suggested by another statement: "Behold, I send you forth as sheep in the midst of wolves: be ye therefore wise as serpents, and harmless as doves. But beware of men: for they will deliver you up to the councils, and they will scourge you in their synagogues." (Matthew 10:16-17.)

Truly our worst enemies are they of our own household. When flatterers meet, someone said, "the devil goes to dinner." Cooper said it this way: "The lie that flatters, I abhor the most." Someone else stated: "The only benefit of flatterers is that by hearing what we are not, we may be instructed in what we ought to be."

One of our brethren told me of an incident that occurred once when he and his family were eating in a restaurant. A family in a stake where he had been the visiting authority came over to shake hands with him, and they used superlatives to say that he was the most wonderful,

14

the greatest, the most powerful, and so on. After they had left, he made some comment about these statements, and his sweet daughter said, "That's all right, Daddy, if you don't begin to believe it yourself." Beware when men shall speak well of you, and remember that ofttimes your foes will be those of your own household.

"What and if ye shall see the Son of man ascend up where he was before?" the Master said. "Therefore said I unto you that no man can come unto me, except it were given unto him of my Father." (John 6:62, 65.) Recall the lament of the Master as some of them turned from Him. John writes:

> From that time many of his disciples went back, and walked no more with him [for Jesus knew from the beginning who were they who believed not and who were they who would betray Him].
>
> Then said Jesus unto the twelve, will ye also go away?
>
> Then Simon Peter answered him, Lord, to whom shall we go? thou hast the words of eternal life.
>
> And we believe and are sure that thou art that Christ, the Son of the Living God.
>
> Jesus answered them, Have not I chosen you twelve, and one of you is a devil?
>
> He spake of Judas Iscariot the son of Simon: for he it was that should betray him, being one of the twelve. (John 6:66-71.)

Joseph Smith was betrayed by some of his chosen leaders. Remember Brother Law, William E. McLellin, John C. Bennett, and others. Here again the Prophet Joseph Smith has given us the key interpretation to explain why apostates become persecutors:

> There is a superior intelligence bestowed upon such as obey the Gospel with full purpose of heart, which, if sinned against, the apostate is left naked and destitute of the Spirit of God. . . . When once that light which was in them is taken from them, they become as much darkened as they were previously enlightened, and then, no marvel, if all their power should be enlisted against the truth, and they, Judas like, seek the destruction of those who were their greatest benefactors. (*Teachings of the Prophet Joseph Smith*, p. 67.)

15

Today the greatest enemies we have are those who, for flattery of the world, would betray the Savior by denying His prophets and making light of Church pronouncements on vital issues that strike at the very foundation of the Lord's work. Such we have among us today—make no mistake.

When the welfare program was being structured and some of us were trying to assist, President Heber J. Grant made one of the saddest comments a president of the Church could make. I was invited to the office of the First Presidency, and as we presented the outline of the plan that was proposed, President Grant, who had listened in silence for quite some time, said, "Well, there is just one thing wrong with it. It won't work." President David O. McKay, his counselor, asked, "Why won't it work, President Grant?" And he said, "I am afraid it won't work because we can't trust the membership of this church to follow our leadership. See what they did when I pleaded with them to vote against the repeal of the liquor amendment. Until the Saints learn to follow our counsel, there is not much we can do about it."

May I refer to two incidents in the Bible concerning the apostles. As they withdrew to Caesarea Philippi for a rest, the Master called upon them to give something of a missionary report. He asked: "Whom do men say that I the Son of man am?" Then, turning to Peter, He said, "But whom say ye that I am?" and Peter answered, "Thou art the Christ, the Son of the living God." The Master then answered, "Blessed art thou, Simon Barjona: for flesh and blood hath not revealed it unto thee, but my Father which is in heaven." (Matthew 16:13-17.) Peter had received a revelation from heaven. It was a tremendous day for him. But in only another year or so, there was a sad day when the Master turned to Peter and rebuked him and said,

"Simon, Simon, behold, Satan hath desired to have you, that he may sift you as wheat: But I have prayed for thee, that thy faith fail not: and when thou art converted, strengthen thy brethren." (Luke 22:31-32.)

Often new missionaries, when they start to bear testimony, hear the adversary say to them, "You don't know the gospel is true; you don't know Joseph Smith was a prophet; you don't know that Jesus is the Savior of the world." This doubt keeps hammering at them until finally they call their mission president and say, "I can't go on bearing testimony because I have no testimony."

How does one gain a testimony? The Master gave the answer when someone asked Him how one may know whether what He spoke was of God or of man. He said, "If any man will do his will, he shall know the doctrine, whether it be of God, or whether I speak of myself." (John 7:17.)

To the new missionary faced with doubts about his testimony, his mission president probably quoted this scripture and then said, "Now, son, do you have unclean thoughts? Are you and your companion having disagreements? Do you have some ugly habits? Are there situations now that you are neglecting in your work? Are you failing to put your heart and soul into it?" He may have said, "What you have to do is to clean up your own house, your temple. If you want the Holy Ghost to bear witness to your soul, you will have to look to your spiritual housekeeping and you will have to keep the commandments of the Lord."

It was Cyprian, the defender of the faith, who made this impressive statement in explaining how he received his testimony. He said: "Into my heart, purified of all sin, there entered a light which came from on high, and then

17

suddenly and in a marvelous manner, I saw certainty exceed doubt."

I recall meeting a young missionary in Chicago who was having doubts about his testimony. After explaining to him some of the scriptures to which I have previously referred, I then told him of Lorenzo Snow's testimony. President Snow had been intellectually convinced, but he didn't have that spiritual certainty that he wanted. He struggled day after day, and each night he would pray for direction. Then one night, while he was praying, it seemed as though he were being enveloped by a heavenly element that immersed him as completely as when he was baptized of water. He heard the rustling of what sounded like silken robes, and with all his soul he knew, because the flood of spiritual light had come upon him.

In Los Angeles some time later, I mentioned this experience with the young missionary in Chicago. After the meeting a young man came up to me and said, "President Lee, you probably won't recognize me, but I think you were impressed to repeat that incident because of me. I am that missionary, and I have slipped so badly away from my old moorings that I must start all over again to find from the Spirit the testimony that I gained when I put into practice the teachings that you told me the Lord had said we must do if we would gain a testimony."

In other words, we can fall out of a testimony or fall from grace, just as we fall into grace. Oh, how important it is that we receive the witness of the Spirit! The Prophet Joseph Smith said, "No man can receive the Holy Ghost without receiving revelations. The Holy Ghost is a revelator." (*Teachings of the Prophet Joseph Smith,* p. 328.)

When I visited the New England Mission a few years ago I found we were having some difficulties with our missionary work. We weren't making too much headway in

18

some parts, and so I made it a practice to talk with some investigators and those who had been recently converted and to ask them all the same question: "What was it that attracted you to the Church?" I received a startlingly similar answer from almost everyone with whom I talked: "When we attend Latter-day Saint meetings and hear the missionaries talk, they seem different. Their faces just seem to shine when they explain the principles of the gospel."

Several years ago Sister Lee and I went to Hong Kong to check up on our members there. When we arrived, a group was waiting at the airport to receive us, and there were two men in the group who were seemingly the leaders and the ones most interested in wanting to help us. They were eager to see if there was anything they could do to make our stay comfortable. As we inquired about them, we found to our surprise that both of these men were Catholics—one a man whose family is still in Shanghai and the other a man who was educated at a Catholic university in Hawaii.

These men wanted to be in our company. They were with us almost constantly. They were solicitous of our welfare, and we didn't know, since they were both businessmen, whether or not there was some selfish purpose in it. Finally, on our last night there, they invited us to one of their homes for a Christmas dinner. After the meal had been finished and some had retired to the living room to visit, these two men remained at the table and began to ask questions. We talked about the gospel; we talked about the restoration of the priesthood, and of the descent from Peter as claimed by the Catholic Church or the descent from Peter as claimed by the Latter-day Saints as being the only foundation stone upon which a church could claim divine authority. It either had to be by succession, passed down as the Catholics claim, or it had to be by a restoration through Peter, who held the keys, as the Latter-day Saints claim. There was no middle ground. After we had talked for about an hour, one of them said, "Brother Lee, we will have to say to you frankly that somehow your men have seemed different from the ministers of our own church. We see something different about them."

We next arrived in the Philippine Islands from Hong Kong late at night. We had had anxieties about the troubles of getting through customs, immigration, and so on. To our surprise we found somebody taking our bags and getting us through customs and through immigration with the speed the like of which I have never witnessed before. Again we were surprised when we found that the persons who had been our helpers were not members of the Church, and the man who had directed the whole thing was a wealthy man—one of the wealthiest men, I suppose, in the Philippine Islands—who had brought his assistant down to help us get quickly to our hotel because he knew we would be tired. While we were there he placed his car and chauffeur at our disposal. Before we left he said, "I was a colonel in World War II, and I was so impressed by the returned missionaries of your church that I met in the military service."

Wherever we went, up and down Korea, Japan, Okinawa, the Philippines, and Guam, it was all the same. We were accorded great courtesies and privileges—not because of who we were as individuals, but because of the kind of ambassadorial life of our splendid missionaries and military men who had kept the faith.

Now, why are they different? Turn to section 88 of the Doctrine and Covenants and read from verse 67 and you will find this promise of the Lord: "And if your eye be single to my glory, your whole bodies shall be filled with

20

light, and there shall be no darkness in you; and that body which is filled with light comprehendeth all things."

What is the glory of God? The glory of God is to bring to pass the immortality and eternal life of man. And that man or that woman who has his eye ever fixed upon that eternal goal of eternal life is rich indeed, because his whole soul is charged with a fire that comes to him who has kept his life worthy.

Now the negative is just as true as the affirmative of this kind of missionary work. The Apostle Paul came back to the Corinthians, some of whom apparently had been baptized under his direction, and he found some who had been baptized sitting at the tables where idols were being worshiped. He chastiseth them with these words:

> But take heed lest by any means this liberty of yours become a stumbling-block to them that are weak.
>
> For if any man see thee which hast knowledge sit at meat in the idol's temple, shall not the conscience of him which is weak be emboldened to eat those things which are offered to idols;
>
> And through thy knowledge shall the weak brother perish, for whom Christ died?
>
> But when ye sin so against the brethren, and wound their weak conscience, ye sin against Christ. (1 Corinthians 8:9-12.)

There is never a man or a woman of station in this church who falls below the standards he is expected to live without dragging down with him many who have had faith in him. He has wounded their conscience; he has dragged down those of weaker faith, and many count the day of their disaffection in this church when someone in whom they had faith fell below that standard they expected him to maintain.

"By their fruits shall ye know them."

President J. Reuben Clark, Jr., one time said something like this: "During my long stay in the East I saw

21

many of our members of the Church come and take positions of leadership, although they weren't especially bright as compared to others over whom they seemed to take leadership; and as I watched them, I began to wonder what it was that makes these people different. As I have pondered it since, I have concluded that it is because they have two things: These men hold the holy priesthood of God and honor it, and they possess the power of the Holy Ghost as baptized members of the Church. It is that and nothing more, plus fidelity to duty, that makes men who will, be strong."

I remember a story told by one of our servicemen once. He was invited to an officers club where a drinking party was going on, and the men were conducting themselves in a rather riotous manner. He noticed one apart from the rest who seemingly wasn't interested in what was going on, and so he sidled off to this man who, like himself, was not partaking, and said, "You don't seem to be very much interested in this kind of party." This young man straightened himself to his fullest height and said, "No, sir, I don't engage in this kind of a party because, you see, I am a member of the Royal House of England." And our Latter-day Saint officer said, just as proudly, "Neither do I, because I am a member of the Royal House of God."

To help us appreciate the positive aspects of living with the Spirit, let me cite one story of a tragedy that has occurred many times.

Several years ago one of our respected men whom we had heralded in high places had to be excommunicated because he had defiled one of his students, a young girl. Some time later he came to my office. He said that he had been sitting in a stake conference a few months before and one of the General Authorities assigned to the conference had told what a terrible condition it was to have lost the Spirit of the Lord after once having had it. This man said to himself, as he sat there, "How does he know what it is to lose the Spirit of the Lord unless he has sinned as I have?" As he walked home after the conference, he reasoned that maybe the General Authority had had experiences with those who have lost the Spirit, or perhaps someone in a position similar to his might have revealed to the General Authority the fear one experiences if he loses the Spirit of the Lord, once having had it. Being somewhat gifted in writing, he wrote down his feelings. He handed his writing across my desk, and I there read the saddest words I have ever read from the pen of man. He had written:

When I was enjoying the Spirit of the Lord and was living the gospel, the pages of scripture would stand open to me with new understanding and the meaning of the pages of scripture would just leap into my soul. Now since the sentence of excommunication, I no longer read with understanding; I read with doubt the passages that before I thought I understood clearly. I formerly enjoyed performing the ordinances of the gospel for my children, to bless my babes, to baptize them, to confirm them, to administer to them when they were sick. Now I must stand by and witness some other man performing those ordinances. I used to enjoy going to the temple, but today the doors of the temple are closed against me. I used to complain a bit about the contributions the Church asks, paying tithing, paying fast offerings, contributing to this and contributing to that, and now as an excommunicant, I am not permitted to pay tithing; the heavens are closed to me now because I can't pay tithing. I shall never in all my life complain again of the requests of the Church to make sacrifice of my means. My children are very kind to me, but I know that deep down in their souls, they are ashamed of the father whose name they bear.

That is the sad story of a man who has enjoyed the Spirit and then through his sinning has lost it.

Keep yourself growing in the faith as you seek secular learning. You show me one who has grown so sophisticated as to want to reform the Church of its practices or its standards or who declares revelations of the Lord as merely "church policy," and I will show you one who is wavering

23

in the faith or one who has lost it. To use the Apostle Paul's phrase, "he is but seeing through a glass darkly."

"O that cunning plan of the evil one!" Nephi wrote. "O the vainness, and the frailties, and the foolishness of men! When they are learned they think they are wise, and they hearken not unto the counsel of God, for they set it aside, supposing they know of themselves, wherefore, their wisdom is foolishness and it profiteth them not. And they shall perish. But to be learned is good if they hearken unto the counsels of God." (2 Nephi 9:28-29.)

In every dispensation, the Lord has given us instructions through prophets—the instructions as to how we shall be able to judge between what is right and what is wrong. He said it to the Book of Mormon people, and you will find it in the seventh chapter of Moroni. He said it in our day, and it is recorded in the fiftieth section of the Doctrine and Covenants. He also said it in the Master's day.

Bernard Baruch, who counseled several of our presidents of the United States, made a wise statement when he said: "If there was any key to this process of growing up, it lay in the systematic efforts I made to subject myself to critical self-appraisal. As I came to know myself, I acquired a better understanding of other people." To learn to make a critical self-appraisal is the key to the process of growing up safely and, in that process, to learning to understand other men.

We should accept every opportunity to bring the knowledge of the gospel to others—to our inactive Church member associates, to our nonmember friends in college, military service, and business, to our neighbors and friends.

The Lord gave this revelation to the Prophet: "For there are many yet on the earth among all sects, parties, and denominations, who are blinded by the subtle craftiness of men, whereby they lie in wait to deceive, and who are only kept from the truth because they know not where to find it." (D&C 123:12.) You remember how the Lord scolded some of the brethren when they were riding swiftly down the Mississippi River. He said, "But verily I say unto you that it is not needful for this whole company of mine elders to be moving swiftly upon the waters, whilst the inhabitants on either side are perishing in unbelief." (D&C 61:3.)

These are matters to which the elders should attend. We who have borne testimony as elders in the faith, defenders of the faith, returned missionaries, sometimes have allowed ourselves to slip into careless habits. It is for us now to start this same process of rebuilding as was necessary in the beginning.

As one who is expected to bear solemn testimony, I exercise the opportunity of declaring to you my sacred testimony. When the call to the apostleship came, it was on a Saturday night of general conference. I was called to the front of the Tabernacle to meet the president of the Church, and I walked into the General Authorities' room and found him crying. He put his hands on my shoulders and told me that I had been named to be a member of the Council of the Twelve. I said to him, "Oh, President, do you think I am worthy of that?" As quick as a flash, he said, "If I didn't think so, my boy, you wouldn't be called."

Then I spent a night I shall never forget. There was no sleep that night. All my life seemed to be coming before me, as in a panorama. I could have told you every person who had any ill will toward me. I could have told you every person against whom I had any ill will, and the feeling came that before I was worthy to accept that call as an apostle of the Lord Jesus Christ, I had to love and forgive every soul that walked the earth. Then when I began to fear the experience of standing in the Tabernacle with so

25

many listening, I found the Spirit directed my words. I don't know what I said; it wasn't anything I had prepared.

On the following Thursday I walked into the room where I was to be ordained. There were twelve chairs in a semicircle, with three chairs in front for the First Presidency. As I thought of the men who had sat in those chairs, and I now was being invited to sit as one in that circle, it was an overwhelming, shattering feeling. Am I worthy, can I measure up, can I reach the goal or attain the spiritual heights that such a position requires?

Well, that day passed, ordination came, and then one of the Twelve came to me and said, "Now we would like you to be the speaker at the Sunday night service. It is for Easter Sunday. As an ordained apostle, you are to be a special witness of the mission and resurrection of the Lord and Savior Jesus Christ." That, I think, was the most startling, the most overwhelming contemplation of all that had happened.

I locked myself in one of the rooms of the Church Office Building and took out the Bible. I read in the four Gospels, particularly the scriptures pertaining to the death, crucifixion, and resurrection of the Lord, and as I read, I suddenly became aware that something strange was happening. It wasn't just a story I was reading, for it seemed as though the events I was reading about were very real as though I were actually living those experiences. On Sunday night I delivered my humble message and said, "And now, I, one of the least of the apostles here on the earth today, bear you witness that I too know with all my soul that Jesus is the Savior of the world and that he lived and died and was resurrected for us."

I knew because of a special kind of witness that had come to me the preceding week. Then someone asked, *"How* do you know? Have you *seen?"* I can say that more powerful than one's sight is the witness that comes by the power of the Holy Ghost bearing testimony to our spirits that Jesus is the Christ, the Savior of the world. To that, I bear testimony, with the admonition to every one of you who read my words now to hold fast to the iron rod. Don't lose your course in the mists along the path that would lead to certain destruction. If you have found your faith wavering and you are not as sharp on testimony as you might be, then pray, study, and put your life in order, because the most precious possession you and I have in this world is the knowledge and testimony and witness that the Holy Ghost bears to us that these statements are true.

# 3

# Doing the Right Things for the Right Reasons

We live in a day when in every phase of life we are trying to find new incentives—in missionary work, in industrial activities, in sales work, in school work, in church work. Incentives seem to be of prime importance. As I have thought of incentives, perhaps the greatest of all is found in what the Lord said: "Think not that I am come to send peace on earth: I came not to send peace, but a sword." (Matthew 10:34.)

There is also the angels' announcement: "Peace on earth to men of good will," as one gospel writer has interpreted it. The purpose of our existence is to gain peace. And this is gained in the way the Master explained to His disciples when He said, ". . . in me ye might have peace" by overcoming the world. (John 16:33.)

In the first visitation of the Father and the Son to the youthful Joseph Smith, the Lord, speaking of the world in which we live, said, "They draw near to me with their lips, but their hearts are far from me." (Joseph Smith 2:19.)

In placing these words with the two scriptures quoted

above, I find a clearer meaning of the Lord's words; the people were not doing the right things for the right reasons when they were merely drawing near the Lord with their lips but their hearts were far from Him. One of the severest words the Master used all through his ministry was the word *hypocrite*. He said, "Wo unto you, . . . hypocrites" (Luke 11:44), which I am sure is described by His statement and the phrases that follow it: "They draw near to me with their lips, but their hearts are far from me, they teach for doctrines the commandments of men, having a form of godliness, but they deny the power thereof." (Joseph Smith 2:19.)

Now let me give you some examples from the scriptures to illustrate the Master's declaration. Matthew records Him saying something about things the people were doing but for the wrong reasons. He said: "Moreover when ye fast, be not, as the hypocrites, of a sad countenance: for they disfigure their faces, that they may appear unto men to fast. Verily I say unto you, They have their reward." (Matthew 6:16.)

Now we have some parallels to that today. We have men in politics, for example, who have announced how much tithing they paid the previous year as a sort of political boon to their candidacy. This is supposed to be a carefully concealed matter, but these politicians publicize it for the purpose of gaining favor among Church people who would be impressed by the amount and the faithfulness of their so-called tithing. We have the spectacle of certain politicians who, when they are going to church, whatever denomination it may be, notify the photographers and the press that they are going to church that morning, so the newspapers all over the country will publish the fact that they have gone to church. That always sounds good to Christian people.

29

We have people who pray in private places and then publicize the fact that they pray. We sometimes are more concerned about publicizing ward teaching and sacrament meeting attendance for the sake of comparative statistics than about improving the spiritual qualities of our performance. We sometimes publicize convert baptisms to make a record rather than concern ourselves principally with the salvation of human souls. I fancy that the Master, if He were among us, would say of all such, "Moreover when you fast, when you pray, when you worship, when you pay tithing, when you do your ward teaching, when you attend sacrament meeting, when you baptize, be not as the hypocrites. Verily, if you publicize it and dramatize it, you have your reward already." This is but another way of repeating what the Master previously warned.

Let me give you another example. The Master said,

How wilt thou say to thy brother, Let me pull out the mote out of thine eye; and, behold, a beam is in thine own eye?

Thou hypocrite, first cast out the beam out of thine own eye; and then shalt thou see clearly to cast out the mote out of thy brother's eye. (Matthew 7:4-5.)

You cannot tell me the Master did not have a sense of humor when he said that. Here you have a great big boulder in your own eye and yet you are trying to pull a little tiny splinter out of your neighbor's eye.

I remember sitting with a group of men after a 24th of July parade in Salt Lake City and hearing someone say to President David O. McKay, "President McKay, didn't that shock you—the immodesty of those girls who rode the floats? My, wasn't that a spectacle?"

President McKay listened patiently and then said, "Well, you know, I never noticed it. I thought it was beautiful. I never noticed any such immodesty."

30      After the election of John F. Kennedy as President of

the United States, someone said, "President McKay, doesn't it worry you that a Catholic has been elected President?" And do you know what he replied? "You know, all I thought about an election day was how wonderful it is that in this great country everybody can go to the polls and vote for a Catholic or a Quaker just as they please and not have to worry about it." You see how we can think higher about the many things about which we are so ready to judge. He was not seeking to dig out the little sliver or the little tiny speck in a neighbor's eye. He was not concerned about that. He was only concerned about his own reaction to these things.

The sixth beatitude, you remember, says, "Blessed are the pure in heart: for they shall see God." (Matthew 5:8.) Now there were a lot of people in the days of the Master who did not accept Him as the Son of God. There were some who said, "Oh, He is just the son of Joseph, the carpenter." Others said, "He is a Prince of Beelzebub," which means the son of the devil. When He performed some of these miraculous things they said, "He is a winebibber," meaning he had just been drinking strong wine. There were only a very few who could say, "Thou art the Christ, the son of the living God." (Matthew 16:16.) Why couldn't everybody see Him as the Son of God?

We sing, "I wish I could have been with Him then, when He took little babes in His arms." A lot of our people would not have accepted Him any more then than they can accept the doctrines that come from the teachers of righteousness inspired by that same Savior. When we cannot accept those who represent Him here, it would not be a bit easier to accept the Master Himself, were He to appear.

What does it mean to be "pure in heart"? Someone has described it as follows:

It stands for man's immortal soul when we speak of heart. It is pure

31

when it contains no admixture of other substance. Benevolence is pure when it contains nothing of self-seeking. Justice is pure when it contains nothing of partiality. Love is pure when it has no lust. A man's heart is pure when it loves only the good, when its motives are right, and when all its aspirations are after the noble and true. Purity is here not synonymous with chastity, but it includes it.

Just as the liar does not understand truthfulness and does not recognize it when he encounters it, so the unholy person does not understand sanctity and cannot understand God. But those who cleanse their hearts understand God in proportion to their purity and one day they shall be cleansed from all sin and shall see Him face to face.

We must be careful not to be so concerned about picking the speck out of our neighbor's eye when we have a great big two-by-four in our own.

Again the Master said,

Thou hypocrite, doth not each one of you on the sabbath loose his ox or his ass from the stall, and lead him away to watering?

And ought not this woman, being a daughter of Abraham, whom Satan hath bound, lo, these eighteen years, be loosed from this bond on the sabbath day? (Luke 13:15-16.)

I remember a sister who came into my office from a foreign country. She was working in the bishop's storehouse in Logan, Utah. She had gone storming in to Elder Joseph F. Merrill of the Council of the Twelve and said, "Why, Brother Merrill, they are distributing pork from the bishop's storehouse up there where I have been working, and it is summertime." Elder Merrill very wisely said, "Go in and talk that over with Brother Lee."

So she came in to me and repeated her comment, since I was at that time working with the welfare program. I asked, "Why are you so much disturbed about that?"

"Why," she said, "the Lord said we should not eat pork or meat in the summertime."

I said, "Oh, where did he say that? I haven't read that."

32

"Why, in the Word of Wisdom."

I said, "Not in my Doctrine and Covenants, it doesn't say that. Will you open the Doctrine and Covenants and read me what you have just said?"

Well, she tried to justify what she had said. I suggested that she read section 49 of the Doctrine and Covenants, and told her I was not sure what a famine was as mentioned in section 89. We should eat meat sparingly, yes, as the Lord counsels. But when we reach a hard and fast conclusion contrary to what the Lord has said, be careful.

I find some of our brethren who are engaged in leadership positions justifying their neglect of their families because they say that they are engaged in the Lord's work. I say to them, "My dear brother, do you realize that the most important part of the Lord's work that you will do is the work that you do within the walls of your own home? That is the most important work of the Lord. Don't get your sense of values mixed up."

I remember a woman who came into my office heartbroken because her husband had said to her, "When you married me, you agreed to obey the law of your husband." She said, "He insists that I sign my name to a mortgage. He has no sense about money, and I know that if I sign the paper, I will lose my home. My son also has some savings that I am keeping while he is in the service, and my husband insists that I give them to him also so that he can use the money to pay some of his debts. When I refuse to, he says, 'You have agreed to obey the law of your husband.'"

Well, I said to her, "Let me tell you something that Brigham Young said. He said, 'I have never counseled any woman to follow her husband to hell.' Now, you are bound to the law of your husband only so far as he keeps the law of God and no further."

Oh, how many are like these folks who complained    33

about healing someone on the Sabbath day, and yet they lead their own ox away to the water?

Yes, we are like that today.

Again the Lord said, "O ye hypocrites, ye can discern the face of the sky; but can ye not discern the signs of the times?" (Matthew 16:3.)

When I was on my mission, a group of us missionaries went with our mission president once to Carthage Jail. Impressed by the atmosphere of the place where the Prophet and his brother Hyrum met their martyrdom, we asked him to recount the incidents that led up to the martyrdom. I was deeply impressed when the mission president said this: "When the Prophet Joseph Smith died, there were many who died spiritually with him. So has it been with every change of administration in the kingdom of God. When Brigham Young died, there were many who died with him spiritually, and so with John Taylor, and the passing of every President of the Church."

For example: President John Taylor was alleged to have had a revelation on plural marriage that nobody knew about except certain individuals. Writing about that in an official statement to the Church, the First Presidency said:

It is alleged that on September 26th and 27th of 1886, President John Taylor received a revelation from the Lord, the purported text of which is given in publications circulated apparently by or at the instance of the same organization. Furthermore, since this pretended revelation, if ever given, was never presented to and adopted by the Church nor by any council of the Church, and since to the contrary an inspired rule of action, the Manifesto, was subsequently given to the pretended revelation, presented to, and in effect was directly opposite to the interpretation given to the revelation, it carries no validity nor binding effect and force upon Church members, and action under it would be unauthorized, illegal and void. The second allegation made by the organization and its members as reported is to the effect that President John Taylor ordained and set apart several men to perform marriage ceremonies (inferentially polygamous and plural marriage ceremonies), and gave to those so allegedly authorized the power to set others apart to do the same thing. Furthermore, any such action would have been illegal and void because the Lord has laid down without qualification the principle that there is never but one on the earth at a time on whom this power and the keys of this priesthood are conferred. The Lord has never changed this rule. (Official Statement of the First Presidency, June 17, 1933, p. 17.)

Now that is exactly what is happening in our day. People are still trying to imagine what John Taylor would have done in the days of President David O. McKay. They are like the ones the Master talked about. They can discern the face of the sky, and they can predict the weather, but they forget that there is a prophet today.

Sometimes we die spiritually and cut ourselves off from pure spiritual light and forget that today, here and now, we have a prophet who alone holds the keys. We are like those folks who discern the face of the sky but forget to see the signs of the present time.

President Heber J. Grant used to say, "We sing 'We Thank Thee, O God, for a Prophet,' but we ought to add the postscript, 'provided that he leads in the way we want to go.' " That is about the way it is sometimes.

The people said to the Master, "Tell us therefore, What thinkest thou? Is it lawful to give tribute unto Caesar, or not?" And the Master said, "Render therefore unto Caesar the things which are Caesar's; and unto God the things that are God's." (Matthew 22:17, 21.)

One of our brethren related this significant incident:

A man who was very bitter about the welfare program was in the grocery business. Needy people had previously been patronizing his store, and the bishop was having to pay their bills out of the fast offerings, and now we were taking care of their needs at the bishop's storehouse. He said he was not going to come to church or pay his tithing, and that we were ruining his business. Well, shortly

35

thereafter, the man was taken seriously ill and was taken to the Veterans Hospital. His stake president went up there to see him. As he was about to leave, this man asked the president if he would administer to him and give him a blessing. The president said, "No, I don't think it would be wise to administer to you, because you see, if I should bless you and you should get well you would be depriving the doctors and hospital of their profession of taking care of you for a longer period. No, it wouldn't be right for me to do that."

The man said, "All right, I know what you are trying to teach me. I repent."

During political campaigns some members say, "Why doesn't the Church tell us how we should vote?" If the Church did that, we would have a lot of Democrats or Republicans who would want to apostatize. We believe in being subject to kings, presidents, rulers, and magistrates. We are told that if we obey the laws of God, we will have no need to break the laws of the land. When people ask me whom to vote for, I tell them to read Mosiah 29 and section 134 of the Doctrine and Covenants, to pray about it, and then they will know whom to vote for in any given election. It is just as simple as that.

President Grant used to say to us time and again: "Brethren, keep your eye on the President of this Church. If he tells you to do anything and it is wrong and you do it, the Lord will bless you for it. But you don't need to worry; the Lord will never let his mouthpiece lead this people astray."

There are a few other things that we do for the wrong reasons.

Some people have had unique testimonies, and to draw attention, they go around bearing them again and again everywhere they go. Some have even published them and had them broadcast throughout the Church. They tell of dreams and of administrations when they have been healed. These are wonderful blessings, but why do they think they have to publicize them all over the Church?

I have seen men, ambitious for recognition, who have set up little organizations of their own to criticize and find fault with the Church. I am sure, knowing the early history of some of these young men, that they have been disappointed because they have not been called to positions that they have thought their abilities and desires have warranted. They are just like the little child who, when his mother speaks too long on the phone, tips over the ink bottle on the rug to draw attention to himself.

So we have people doing right things for the wrong reasons. Some go on missions under the pressure of parents or Church leaders or a sweetheart. They go to the temple to be married to a mate who would not be married out of the temple, yet are not willing to accept the responsibility of promises made in the temple. They do the right things, but for the wrong reasons.

Singleness to God means the goal of eternal life. In the choice of your vocation, which will be most likely to help you on your road to eternal life? It is the same with your church activity, your choice of company, your home, your mate.

A truth of the gospel is not a truth until you live it. You do not really believe in tithing and it is not a truth of the gospel to you until you pay it. The Word of Wisdom is not a truth of the gospel to you until you keep it. The Sabbath day is not a holy day unless you observe it. Fasting and paying fast offerings, consecrating your fast, are not truths of the gospel unless you live them. Temple marriage does not mean anything to you unless you have a temple marriage. A friend is not a friend unless you defend him. A sweetheart is not a true sweetheart if he betrays his companion. Someone has said, "A home is a roof over a good woman," but a home is not a home unless there is a good woman to put a roof over.

You are only a true Latter-day Saint when the conduct of your life has not prevented others from coming into the Church or being active in the Church. Let us not come under that condemnation of the Master when he said, "Ye hypocrites." Let us be true. Let us not just serve with our lips, but also with our hearts, minds, might, and strength.

# 4

# Zion Must Be Strengthened

*I* recall a remark that was once made to Elder Lorenzo H. Hatch and myself, as we waited in Las Vegas, Nevada, for a late, delayed train. We chanced to be in conversation with a life insurance salesman who is reputed to be one of the outstanding salesmen in America. He expressed a sentiment that has intrigued me and made an impression upon me. He said, "If you ever want to stir a man into action, you want to back up the hearse and let him smell the flowers prepared for his own service."

At first that seemed to be a terribly gruesome thought, but as I thought about it, it seemed to me that it was really but a crude way of stating a great eternal truth that has been thundered to us by the prophets from the beginning. All through the scriptures we have had counsel given us that all that we do should be done with an eye single to the glory of God, which glory, the Lord declared to Moses, is to bring to pass the immortality and eternal life of man, that very reminder that death draws nearer each day that we live.

The great prophet Amulek bore testimony to this principle:

> For behold, this life is the time for men to prepare to meet God . . . [and] to perform their labors.
>
> . . . for after this day of life, which is given us to prepare for eternity, behold, if we do not improve our time while in this life, then cometh the night of darkness wherein there can be no labor performed.
>
> For behold, if ye have procrastinated the day of your repentance even until death, behold, ye have become subjected to the spirit of the devil, and he doth seal you his; therefore, the Spirit of the Lord hath withdrawn from you, and hath no place in you, and the devil hath all power over you; and this is the final state of the wicked. (Alma 34:32-33, 35.)

It was this very reminder that the Angel Moroni gave to the Prophet Joseph Smith, which he records in that famous Wentworth letter when he quoted the Angel Moroni as saying that "preparatory work for the second coming of the Messiah was speedily to commence; that the time was at hand for the gospel in all its fulness to be preached in power, unto all nations, that a people might be prepared for the Millennial reign." (*History of the Church,* vol. 4, p. 537.)

In making that preparation, the Lord has defined certain great responsibilities for His church. He said that as one of the signs of His coming, the gospel of the kingdom was to be preached unto all the world for a witness unto all nations, and then should the end come, with the destruction of the wicked. (See Matthew 24:14.) That witness, we have understood, was to be a witness of the mission of the Messiah. It was to be a witness of the divinity of His mission. It was to be a witness that the gospel of Jesus Christ had been restored in all its fulness, in this the dispensation of the fulness of times.

But there was something else that we were supposed to witness that is also spoken of in the revelations. Alma spoke

40    of this to his people who were about to be baptized. As a

part of the covenant they were about to enter, he said that they were to stand as witnesses of God at all times and in all things, and in all places in which they might be, even until death. (Mosiah 18:9.)

I have remembered a statement that was made by an official of the United States Steel Corporation after I had spent an hour or two at Welfare Square with him and a group of officials from his company. He said, "This is a practical demonstration of the gospel of Jesus Christ, in giving aid to the needy and the less fortunate." That was a new concept to me, that in the welfare program we were standing as witnesses before the world of the divine way by which the Lord's work is to be done.

So, we witness in our missionary work the magnificent spectacle of young men and young women, for the most part, going to all the ends of the earth and, by their unselfish services, standing as witnesses at all times and in all places of the divine responsibility upon the Church to teach the gospel.

In making sacrifice, in the payment of our tithes, in fasting and paying our fast offerings, and in raising money to pay for meetinghouses and temples, again we are witnessing that the law of sacrifice is required of all true Saints if we would claim kinship to Him who gave His life that such might be.

In our social conduct, in our dancing, in our play, we must never forget that we are witnessing also that we are His special witnesses of the divinity of the organizations that sponsor our play.

Every person in military service, every person in his social conduct, every businessman in his dealings with his neighbor, is a witness as to whether or not this work in which he believes is divine. The Church rises or falls on the tide of these personal witnesses.

Some time ago I sat in fast meeting in the South Eighteenth Ward in Salt Lake City and heard a lovely girl in her mid-twenties stand to bear her testimony. It was a thrilling testimony. She told about living on a farm in a little country district where at four o'clock in the morning she went out with her father to milk the cows. And as she and her father went toward the barn, her father took her by the hand and said, "My girl, you are the product of the Church of Jesus Christ and you are also the product of a true Latter-day Saint home. If you fail, so far as you are concerned the Church has failed and your home has failed." That girl from that time has realized that she, as a member of the Church of Jesus Christ, is a witness of it to all the world either for good or for bad.

Oh, the majesty of Joseph sold into Egypt, who shamed the beautiful but apparently unloved wife of Potiphar, when she would have tempted him to a serious sin and he said, "My master trusts me, and thou art his wife. How can I do this great wickedness and sin against God?" (Genesis 39:8.) He too felt his great responsibility in being a true witness of the divine truths he professed to believe.

I heard a lovely Japanese missionary in Kamuela on the island of Hawaii a few years ago make what I think was a personal application of that principle. There were few missionaries in that day, the war was not yet ended, and this young lady and her companion were two of the only four missionaries on that island. We had in the audience eighty-five United States Marines, all Latter-day Saints, who were being trained there for an invasion off Japan, the homeland of these two lovely missionary girls, whose families now lived in Hawaii. Our sister missionary was called to speak before that audience. Tremblingly she stood at the pulpit, and this is what she said: "When my father came to me and told me that they wanted me to go on a mission, I said to him, 'No, Father, I can't go on a mission.' " He pressed her as to why, and she said, "Oh, I just can't." But he urged further, and then she said, "I can't go because if I go out into the mission field, I'll be expected to preach certain principles of the gospel, principles that my own father and my own family are not living."

The father asked, "What are we not doing that you'd have to preach?"

"Well," replied his daughter, "I'll be expected to teach the law of sacrifice. You're not paying your tithing. I'll be asked to teach about family prayer, and we never have family prayers. I'll be expected to teach the Word of Wisdom; we're using coffee and tea in our home. I'll be expected to teach the importance of giving service in the Church, and you are shunning that service. No, Father, I can't go out and be a hypocrite."

I think that father spent a sleepless night. "The next morning," the Japanese sister said, "Father came to me and said, 'You go, my dear, and your father will try to live as his daughter will preach.' "

Two days later I met her in Honolulu at a missionary conference, and she had just been home for the first time in nearly two years. During the course of the conference I whispered to her, "How did you find things at home?"

She smiled and tears were in her eyes as she said, "It's all right. Father is living the commandments, and I'm happy."

The youths whom we send out as missionaries and to military service will rarely ever be stronger than the kind of homes and environment from which they come. The challenge of this time is to see that Zion is increased in holiness. We must increase in beauty. Our homes, our quorums, our wards, and our stakes must be strengthened. Zion must arise and put on her most beautiful garments.

43

A short while ago I read wise counsel from a lovely mother, Susannah Wesley, mother of famed religious leader John Wesley. This was what this lovely mother said to her son, which was a criterion by which he could judge right and wrong in all the affairs of life:

> Would you judge the lawfulness or unlawfulness of pleasure? Then use this rule: Whatever weakens your reason, impairs the tenderness of your conscience, obscures your sight of God, takes from you your thirst for spiritual things, or increases the authority of your body over your mind, then that thing to you is evil. By this test you may detect evil no matter how subtly or how plausibly temptation may be presented to you.

Oh, I wish that every youth would use that rule and measure everything presented to him in order that he might choose the right. God grant that we may strengthen Zion within ourselves, that we might live nobly and prepare to present ourselves in honor at the close of our lives here, before Him whose name we bear as members of The Church of Jesus Christ of Latter-day Saints.

# 5

# Let Us Be As One

*A*s I have pondered the importance of the matter of unity and oneness of the Latter-day Saints, I have recalled some of the blessings we might enjoy if we were united as a people.

If we were united in paying our fast offerings and observing the law of the fast as fully as the Lord has taught it, and if we were united in carrying out the principles of the welfare program as they have been given to us by our leaders today, we would be free from want and distress and would be fully able to care for our own. Our failure to be united would be to allow our needy to become the pawns of politicians in the public mart.

If we were fully united as a people in our missionary work, we would rapidly hasten the day when the gospel would be preached to all people without and within the boundaries of the stakes of Zion. If we are not united, we will lose that which has been the lifeblood and which has fed and stimulated this church for a generation.

If we were fully united in keeping the law of sacrifice

and paying our tithes as we have been taught today, we would have sufficient to build our temples, our chapels, our schools of learning. If we fail to do that, we will be in the bondage of mortgage and debt.

If we were united as a people in electing honorable men to high places in our civil government, regardless of the political party with which we have affiliation, we would be able to safeguard our communities and to preserve law and order among us. Our failure to be united means that we permit tyranny and oppression and taxation to the extent of virtual confiscation of our own property.

If we were united in supporting our own official newspapers and magazines which are owned and operated by the Church for our Church members, there would always be in this church a sure voice to the people. But if we fail to be united in giving this support, we permit ourselves to be subject to abuse, slander, and misrepresentation without any adequate voice of defense.

If we were united in safeguarding our youth from promiscuous associations that foster marriages out of the Church and out of the temples, by having socials and recreation activities as a united people, as has been the practice from our pioneer days, we would be building all our Latter-day Saint homes on a sure and happy foundation. Our failure to be united in these things will be our failure to receive eternal blessings that otherwise could be ours.

If we were united in safeguarding the Church from false doctrines and error and in standing as watchmen upon the tower as teachers and leaders in watching over the Church, then we would be free from those things that cause many to stumble and fall and lose their faith. If we are not thus united, the wolves among us will be sowing the seeds of discord, disharmony, and all that tends to the destruction of the flock.

If we were united in our temple work and in our genealogical research work, we would not be satisfied with the present temples only, but we would have sufficient work for temples yet to come, to the unlocking of the doors of opportunity to those beyond who are our own kin, and thus would ourselves become saviors on Mount Zion. Our failure to be united will be our failure to perpetuate our family homes in eternity.

So we might multiply the blessings that could come to this people if they were fully united in the purposes of the Lord.

The importance of unity was prayed for by the Master of us all. In that last great prayer—you will recall it—He prayed:

> . . . I come to thee. Holy Father, keep through thine own name those whom thou hast given me, that they may be one, as we are.
>
> Neither pray I for these alone, but for them also which shall believe on me through their word;
>
> That they all may be one; as thou, Father, art in me, and I in thee, that they also may be one in us: that the world may believe that thou hast sent me. (John 17:11, 20-21.)

The purpose of unity in the Church has been expressed by the Lord both from a positive standpoint, as herein expressed, and also in a negative way as given in a revelation at the beginning of this dispensation. The positive purpose of the unity of Saints here is clearly suggested: "that the world may know." May know what? That this is the church and kingdom of God on the earth to whom Jesus, the Christ, was sent.

If we are not united, we are not His. Here unity is the test of divine ownership as thus expressed. If we would be

47

united in love and fellowship and harmony, this church would convert the world, which would see in us the shining example of those qualities which evidence that divine ownership. Likewise, if in the Latter-day Saint home the husband and wife are in disharmony, are bickering, and divorce is threatened, there is evidence that one or both are not keeping the commandments of God.

If in our wards and our branches we are divided, and there are factions not in harmony, it is but an evidence that something is wrong. If two persons are at variance, arguing on different points of doctrine, no reasonable, thinking persons would say that both were speaking their different opinions by the Spirit of the Lord.

In the writings of the Apostle Paul to the Ephesian saints, after describing the nature of the church as it was organized in his day, he said this organization was given for the purpose of the "perfecting of the saints, . . . till we all come in the unity of the faith." (Ephesians 4:12-13.) When men receive the Spirit of God by living righteously, truth and error begin to disappear.

If it is so important, then, that this people be a united people, we might well expect that upon this principle the powers of Satan would descend for their greatest attack. We might well expect also that if there be those of apostate mind among us, they would be inclined to ridicule and to scorn this principle of oneness and unity as being narrow-minded or as being unprogressive. We would likewise expect that those who are enemies would also seek to fight against that principle.

Recently some arguments were handed to me that were presented before a congressional committee in Washington, D. C., in 1888, by a former mayor of Salt Lake City, in which he said this about this same matter: "The theocratic tenet of the Mormon Church is a great evil, and

48

opposed to our American institutions. What is a theocracy?" Then he gave his own definition: "It is government by the priesthood through a direct authority from God. . . . The thing I wish to accomplish is to pass laws which will strike at the foundation of the theocratic system."

To put his words plainly, the thing he wished to strike at was the unity of the Latter-day Saints, who believe in a government through a direct revelation from God through His appointed agents.

The Lord has given a threefold plan by which this unity might be fully realized. Unity centers in heaven, even as the Master prayed, "Father, that we might be one." The Saints might become one with the Father and the Son, spiritually begotten by baptism and through the Holy Ghost even unto the renewing of their bodies as the Lord tells us, and thus "become the sons of Moses and of Aaron . . . the church and kingdom, and the elect of God" (D&C 84:34), and thus become adopted into the holy family, the church and kingdom of God, the Church of the Firstborn.

Then, besides those ordinances by which we are adopted into that oneness with the Father and the Son, He has given to us principles and ordinances all intended to the perfecting of His saints, that this same unity might be realized.

And finally, the Lord has given this generation another principle, that through His appointed authorities He would teach His laws and administer His ordinances, and through them He would reveal His will. On the very day this church was organized, He made this principle clear to the Saints when He said,

Wherefore, meaning the church, thou shalt give heed unto all his words and commandments which he shall give unto you as he receiveth them, walking in all holiness before me;

> For his word ye shall receive, as if from mine own mouth, in all patience and faith.
>
> For by doing these things the gates of hell shall not prevail against you; yea, and the Lord God will disperse the powers of darkness from before you, and cause the heavens to shake for your good, and his name's glory. (D&C 21:4-6.)

About a year later the Lord expressed that same thing in these words: "What I the Lord have spoken, I have spoken, and I excuse not myself; . . . whether by mine own voice or by the voice of my servants, it is the same." (D&C 1:38.)

That is a bold doctrine, those who are not members of the Church and those who are members of the Church who have no faith may think, but I would remind all such that it is also a bold doctrine when we declare that this is the Church of Jesus Christ, the only true church upon the earth. This could not be the Church of Jesus Christ except for that other defined principle of revelation through the prophets of the Lord.

May I test your unity as Latter-day Saints? Have you received a witness of the Spirit to your souls testifying that this is the truth; that you know this is the church and kingdom of God; that you have received by baptism and by the laying on of hands the power of the Holy Ghost by which that unity of testimony might be accomplished? Have you that testimony in your souls?

Do you believe that the men whom we have sustained as prophets, seers, and revelators are the men through whom the channels of communication from our Heavenly Father are open? Do you believe as Enos, the grandson of the great prophet Lehi, declared in his writing when he said he went into the mountain and prayed and "the voice of the Lord came into my mind" (Enos 1:10)—do you believe that the voice of the Lord comes into the minds of these men? If you do, then you believe what the Lord said

50

that "whatsoever they shall speak when moved upon by the Holy Ghost shall be scripture, shall be the will of the Lord, shall be the mind of the Lord, shall be the word of the Lord, shall be the voice of the Lord, and the power of God unto salvation." (D&C 68:4.)

There are some who are prone to say, "We will follow their counsel in spiritual matters but not in temporal affairs. If they counsel us in other than that which pertains strictly to the spiritual welfare of the people, we will not follow them." Have any of you ever heard such comments?

As I have labored among the brethren and have studied the history of past dispensations, I have become aware that the Lord has given tests all down through time as to this matter of loyalty to the leadership of the Church. I go back into the scriptures and to such stories as David's loyalty when the king was trying to take his life. He wouldn't defile the anointed of the Lord even when he could have taken his life. I have listened to the classic stories in this dispensation about how Brigham Young was tested, how Heber C. Kimball was tested, how Willard Richards and John Taylor were tested in Carthage jail, how those in Zion's Camp were tested—and from that number were chosen the first General Authorities in this dispensation. There were others who didn't pass the test of loyalty, and they fell from their places.

I have been in a position since I was called to the Council of the Twelve to observe some things among my brethren, and I want to say to you: Every man who is my junior in the Council of the Twelve I have seen submitted, as though by Providence, to these same tests of loyalty, and I have wondered sometimes whether they were going to pass the tests. The reason they are here today is because they did, and our Father has honored them.

It is my conviction that every man who will be called      51 to high place in the Church will have to pass tests not devised by human hands, tests by which our Father numbers them as a united group of leaders willing to follow the prophets of the living God and to be loyal and true as witnesses and exemplars of the truths they teach.

Brigham Young in his day was invited into a group of some of those who were trying to argue against the principle of unity. After he learned that they were trying to "depose," as they said, the Prophet Joseph Smith, he stood before them and said something like this: "You cannot destroy the appointment of a prophet of God, but you can cut the thread which binds you to a prophet of God and sink yourselves to hell."

It was that kind of fearlessness which was manifest in him that made him the peerless leader he was to become. It is that same kind of courage—though not always popular—but the kind that has been demanded of every man whom our Father would honor with high places of leadership.

I heard President George Albert Smith speak after some scurrilous articles had been written about the Prophet Joseph Smith. He said this, and to me it was the ringing voice of a prophet speaking:

> Many have belittled Joseph Smith, but those who have will be forgotten in the remains of Mother Earth, and the odor of that infamy will ever be with them; but honor, majesty, and fidelity to God exemplified by Joseph Smith and attached to his name will never die. (General conference address, April 1946.)

I paraphrase those words today and make them meaningful to us: "Many there are today among us who would belittle George Albert Smith, and J. Reuben Clark, Jr., and David O. McKay, but those who do will be forgotten in the remains of Mother Earth, and the odor of their infamy will ever remain with them, but honor, majesty, and fidelity to God exemplified by the First Presidency and attached to their names will never die."

# 6

# Wells of Living Water

W hen our pioneer fathers came to this semiarid country, they settled on the mountain streams without the benefits of which they could not have made their homes or established communities. They organized themselves into irrigation companies in order that the water so vital to their welfare might be properly distributed, each man receiving shares according to his need. They built ditches and canals; they constructed reservoirs to hold back the spring run-off for late summer use. They gave special attention to the securing of culinary water that they might have from the mountain springs the purest of the water for human use. They were aware of the fact that if they carried this water long distances in open ditches, there was danger of pollution; that disease and epidemic might result unless a special care be given. With that in mind they safeguarded the channels and later constructed pipelines that were placed below the level of the ground to protect from heat and frost.

  To enjoy the benefits of this system, it was necessary

that they work together, each man receiving an assessment that he was expected to pay either in labor or in money, and for the maintenance of such a system each was required to pay his annual dues. Those who refused to accept such obligations were penalized by the company's refusing to deliver the water to which they were therefore not entitled.

Just as water was and is today essential to physical life, just so is the gospel of the Lord Jesus Christ essential to the spiritual life of God's children. That analogy is suggested by the words of the Savior to the woman at the well in Samaria, when He said: ". . . whosoever drinketh of the water that I shall give him shall never thirst; but the water that I shall give him shall be in him a well of water springing up into everlasting life." (John 4:14.)

Great reservoirs of spiritual water, called scriptures, have been provided in this day and have been safeguarded that all might partake and be spiritually fed, and that they thirst not. That these scriptures have been considered of great importance is indicated by the words of the Savior: "Search the scriptures; for in them ye think ye have eternal life: and they are they which testify of me" (John 5:39); and the experience of the Nephites in being sent back to procure the brass plates that contained the scriptures so vital to the welfare of the people. The use of the scriptures was suggested in the statement of Nephi when he said, ". . . for I did liken all scriptures unto us, that it might be for our profit and learning." (1 Nephi 19:23.) And again, when Laban forbade their use of scriptures, the angel declared it were better that one man should perish than that a whole nation dwindle and perish in unbelief.

Through these generations the messages from our Father have been safeguarded and carefully protected, and mark you likewise that in this day the scriptures are the

55

purest at their source, just as the waters were purest at the mountain source; the purest word of God, and that least apt to be polluted, is that which comes from the lips of the living prophets who are set up to guide Israel in our own day and time.

The distribution system that our Heavenly Father has provided is known as the church and kingdom of God, which is to give aid to his great and divine purpose of bringing to pass the immortality and the eternal life of man, whereby eternal joy might come. But because of the free agency that our Father in his wisdom has vouchsafed to us, His children, the dangers of pollution are great. Ever beckoning with tinsel show and with gaudily wrapped packages, with neon signs beckoning on every hand, the devil has tried to entrap, and under the label of "pleasures" he has sought to dissuade mankind from a straight course that would lead to eternal happiness. Pleasure-mad crowds surge at the bargain counters of him who would thus destroy.

The priesthood quorums and the auxiliary organizations are the carefully guarded channels provided within the Church through which precious truths are to be disseminated. Some have speculated that the strength of this church lies in the tithing system; some have thought in the missionary system; but those who understand rightly the word of the Lord understand full well that the strength of the Church is, fundamentally, in neither of these. The strength of the Church is not in a large membership, but the real strength lies in the power and authority of the holy priesthood that our Heavenly Father has given to us in this day. If we exercise properly that power and magnify our callings in the priesthood, we will see to it that the missionary work shall go forward, that the tithing shall be paid, that the welfare plan shall prosper, that our homes shall be safe, and that morality among the youth of Israel shall be safeguarded.

Just as in the illustration of the water system, however, we have certain obligations that we must assume if we are to be blessed. The price we pay for these eternal blessings and the right to the use of this eternal stream of water is, first, to yield obedience to the laws and ordinances of the gospel, second, to render willing and unselfish sacrifice, and third, to assume responsibility and our obligation to serve our fellowmen whereby we might gain rights and titles to the blessings that our Heavenly Father has in store for us. Every faithful Church member can bear witness to the joy and extreme happiness that comes to one who has kept the law; but perhaps all of us can likewise bear witness to the anguish and the disappointment that come through lack of obedience and through our own negligence.

At a U.S. Army base near Corvallis, Oregon, I once listened to a young Latter-day Saint army doctor tell of an experience he had had on one of the islands just off Guadalcanal, where a raging battle was taking place. He said they had established a hospital base back away from the front line, where they were receiving the wounded that were now coming from that area. Because of their limited facilities and the great need of medical attention by so many wounded, it was necessary that someone look carefully over the men who were brought in so that those who were most seriously wounded might be attended to first, and his was the task of making this initial examination. As he leaned over to the boys who were conscious, he would whisper to them, ask them how they were feeling, and then ask each one, "To what church do you belong?"

On one occasion as he leaned close to the ear of one boy who was pretty badly wounded and asked him to what church he belonged, the boy whispered back, "I am a Mormon."

The doctor said, "Well, I'm a Mormon, too. I'm an elder in the Church. Is there anything you would like me to do for you?"

The boy, as he clenched his teeth, with resolute white face, replied, "I'd like you to administer to me."

The doctor said, "I took out my little bottle of consecrated oil, and there before the gaze of all, because there was no chance for privacy, I anointed his head with oil, and by the authority of the holy priesthood I blessed him that he might be made well. I took him into the hospital tent for the care that he so much needed, and returned to the other wounded men. By a strange coincidence I found that the next boy I approached was also one of our own Latter-day Saint boys, and I asked him the same question, 'What would you like me to do?' and he replied, 'I'd like a cigarette.' I said, 'I think I could get you a cigarette,' and as the boy started to smoke, I said to him, 'Son, are you sure there is nothing else you would like me to do for you now?' Tears filled the boy's eyes. He said, 'Yes, there is, doctor, but I'm afraid I am not entitled to ask for what's in my heart. I wonder if the Lord would have a blessing for me. Would you administer to me?' I said, 'We'll leave that for our Heavenly Father to judge. If you want a blessing, I shall be His servant in asking Him to give you that blessing.' "

I ask you, what is the condition of our youth today? What part have you played in preparing them to partake deeply of the streams of eternal life?

I have a treasured picture of a group of servicemen in New Guinea, holding a sacrament service on that battle-inflamed island. Their rifles are across their knees, which evidences the fact that they are on the alert and expecting attack at any moment.

From Midway Island in the Pacific came a letter about how our servicemen likewise gathered around to hold sacrament services. The writer of the letter indicated that they "felt that if the Church could come that close to us, we would feel better and our minds would be relieved."

And then I read how one of our Latter-day Saint men got the names of those of our members who had been killed in a campaign in Italy, finding out where they were to be buried or had been buried so that he might go and dedicate their graves. And as I read of this young man and his companions holding Sunday services in the olive groves of that place, their songs rending the Sabbath air, I remembered the words of our Father:

"And that thou mayest more fully keep thyself unspotted from the world, thou shalt go to the house of prayer and offer up thy sacraments upon my holy day." (D&C 59:9.)

Yes, these are Latter-day Saints, followers of the Savior, who have drunk deeply from the fountain of spiritual waters, and theirs will be a well of living water, springing up unto everlasting life.

# LOVE, HOME, AND FAMILY

# 7

# Preparing Our Youth

Wherever one travels in the Church today he is faced with deepening concern about the future of our Latter-day Saint youth. The concern is warranted, since the future of the Church is bound up in our youth. It is they who will soon be presiding over families, quorums, stakes, wards, and auxiliaries.

Clearly, what we do now, or what we do not do, by way of preparing them will affect their capacity to lead the Church and to love their families, the gospel, and their fellow Church members.

There is timely counsel for both old and young in the Apostle Paul's letter to Timothy: "Let no man despise thy youth; but be thou an example of the believers, in word, in conversation, in charity, in spirit, in faith, in purity." (1 Timothy 4:12.)

We love the youth of the Church; and we say to them, as Paul said to young Timothy, that they will be happiest if they are examples of the believers. The future of the Church is secure, but it will be even brighter if our youth

63

in their word and in their conversation show forth the charity and purity that can come only from one who is a believer.

If anyone questions the importance of the youth to the Church, he should note the following information prepared by the Church Historian's Office from a large statistical sample.

Over fifty percent of the members of the Church are age twenty-five or under. There are as many members of the Church from twelve to twenty-five years of age as there are from thirty-six years up. And if one wishes to view the years from sixteen through twenty-five—probably the years of greatest stress and most crucial decisions—that group comprises over twenty-three percent of the total membership of the Church.

You can sense from the statistics alone the immense challenge we all have, for this large group of young people will eventually serve and guide the kingdom during very critical years. We all must do a better job of preparing them than we are now doing.

It is becoming increasingly clear that the home and family are the key to the future of the Church. An unloved child, a child who has not known discipline, work, or responsibility, will often yield to satanic substitutes for happiness—drugs, sexual experimentation, and rebellion, whether it is intellectual or behavioral. Our intensified efforts around family home evening, which we have not only urged our members to hold, but concerning which we have supplied more and more help, hold much promise if we will but use these opportunities.

There is no better place than in the home to teach and learn about marriage, love, and sex as these can properly combine in a sanctified temple marriage. There is no better place to deal with the doubts of our young than where there is love—at home. Love can free our youth to listen to those whom they know they can trust. Our curricula, quorums, and classes should supplement the home, and where homes are seriously defective, we will have to compensate as best we can.

When Jesus said of the first and second great commandments, "On these two commandments hang all the law and the prophets" (Matthew 22:40), he uttered one of the greatest insights in the course of history. For it is on these commandments that we should not only build all our teachings, but it is also by their guiding light that we should direct our organizations and cultivate our correlation of programs.

Can a child come to love his neighbor unless he has known love himself? Can a young person who has never been trusted learn to trust? Can a boy who has never known work or responsibility see how those vital traits are needed to hold our whole society together? Can a girl who has not been a part of honest, candid discussions of gospel principles in her home cope with the criticisms of the world and the intellectual assaults on her religion? Can a young man who must ask his father to stay away from the son's temple marriage because his father smokes (even though the father had obtained a recommend) have full respect for a bishop who winks at this noncompliance in order to be "nice" to a family? Without experiencing a gospel principle in action, it is much more difficult to believe in that principle.

We must remember that in some of our young, the offense over adult hypocrisy is not always their desire to "get something on us," but a deep sense of disappointment. They truly want us to be what we pretend to be, because when we are, it is a testimony to them that we really believe.

We must be more willing to give our youth appropriate responsibility. God has often given special chores to selected young men. Much of the youthful boredom and restlessness stems from the lengthened years of study and dependency before full responsibility and opportunities for service occur; our young want to be doing things and achieving things. They must be prepared, of course, but there are many things they could be doing as they mature if we will match the opportunities for service in our church programs with the aspirations of our youth.

In a time that we have been told would be much as in the days of Noah, we must help our young to learn how to make right choices, to grow in justified self-esteem, especially when they can be under the direct influence of the home, where family love can make repentance both possible and significant. The environment of our young outside the home and Church will often be either empty, so far as values are concerned, or it will contain ideas that contradict the principles of the gospel.

It seems clear to me that the Church has no choice—and never has had—but to do more to assist the family in carrying out its divine mission, not only because that is the order of heaven, but also because that is the most practical contribution we can make to our youth—to help improve the quality of life in the Latter-day Saint homes. As important as our many programs and organizational efforts are, these should not supplant the home; they should support the home.

Unlike some in the world, we do not want to engage in worship of youth by imitating them and by being so anxious for them to like us that we compromise our own integrity and individuality. Nor do we want to be like others in the world who, because of the actions of a few young men and women, would forsake all the young. As in all things, the teachings of the Master must guide us. We must be wise, not naive. We must love even those who abuse and misuse us. We must be uncompromising as to principle, but quick to love and to forgive. We must be ready always to give others, including the young, reasons for our own deep commitment to the Savior and His kingdom.

May we so serve, love, and lead our young members to prepare them for today and for the future.

# 8

# The Purposes of Dating

*I* once received a letter from a young man in military service who introduced himself by saying, "If I may, let me tell you my story. I am a member of the Church now serving in the armed forces. Before I came into the service I met you and your wife when you visited the mission where I was stationed, and your counsel to the missionaries seemed to be wise and understanding. I have attended a church school for two years." He then described certain unclean habits in which he had indulged since he was eighteen years of age and recited the advice he had received from secular teachers, contrasted with that of Church leaders, as to the rightness or wrongness in his conduct. Then he wrote:

The second problem is our relations (my fiancee and I) with one another when we are together. I see her rarely, only when I am on leave, and our moments together are so few! Before we were engaged there was no problem, but now when we see each other we find it hard not to enjoy ourselves in a more intimate way. "Petting" is the term used, I believe, but this is our problem and our question: Is it wrong for us, as an engaged couple, to do this? We don't like to use the term "petting." It connotes to us the relation of a fellow and a girl who do it merely for the stimulation it brings—who do not love each other, but who "pet" for "fun," in a petting party.

We understand, I think, the teachings of the Church concerning immorality. But this is a thing that is hard for us to understand. When two people are very much in love and are engaged to marry in the temple, as we are, what makes it wrong, if anything? For those not in love we can see that it is wrong—but isn't it different with an engaged couple? Shouldn't it be? We realize the argument that is given that a couple should refrain from it, even though they are in love, because it might lead to the ultimate sin of immorality. We've heard people say, "Well, it could happen—just by accident." This we cannot accept. Any action in life is voluntary. Any couple who go all the way, we feel, go all the way because they want to, at the moment at least. It can't just happen, we don't believe.

And for this reason, because with us, at any rate, "petting" does not lead into temptation, we find it hard to see any wrong in what we are doing. Are we wrong?—and if so, why?

## In reply to that letter I wrote in part as follows:

My dear brother:

Since receiving your letter I have tried to think how I could answer it in such a way as to point out to you the seriousness of the wrong thinking you have indulged in to justify a conduct which has been condemned and advised against by our Church leaders for as long as I can remember. As a Church member you should have learned the great fundamental truths concerning the teachings of the gospel of Jesus Christ.

The purpose of the whole plan of salvation is "to bring to pass the immortality and the eternal life of man." The planting of a desire for sexual companionship is a God-given part of that plan, to be served sacredly and solely for the building of the frail footpath over which our Heavenly Father might send his spirit children to tabernacle here in mortality. For a child of God, and particularly one bearing the priesthood and having been active in the Church, to consider his God-given gift of creative powers as a mere plaything or that his association with his sweetheart is primarily for the satisfying of his lustful appetite is to play the game of Satan, who knows that such conduct is the sure way to destroy in one the refinement necessary to receive the companionship of the Spirit of the Lord.

You apparently have forgotten the Master's great Sermon on the Mount concerning this matter. There He said this: "You have heard that it was said by them of old time, Thou shalt not commit adultery" (and when He uses the word *adultery,* if you will read carefully His statement, He is talking about all unlicensed sexual relations), "but I say unto you that whosoever looketh on a woman to lust after her hath committed adultery with her already in his own heart." What he is trying to make plain to his hearers is that an evil act is preceded by an evil thought. One doesn't kill unless he becomes angry. One doesn't steal unless he covets. Just so, one doesn't commit sexual sin unless he has a filthy, adulterous, immoral thought.

When you tell me that you have practiced an unclean habit and you find yourself powerless to refrain therefrom, you are but bearing testimony that your mind is not clean and that you have found yourself powerless to control your own habits. Could it possibly be that you are shackled as Satan set out to shackle men after he was cast out of heaven for rebellion against the plan of free agency? Read again what the scriptures declared with regard to the mission of Satan: "And he became Satan, yea, even the devil, the father of all lies to deceive and to blind men and to lead them captive at his will, even as many as would not hearken unto my voice."

You have raised a question as to whether or not you are licensed to indulge in intimacies with your sweetheart after your engagement, more so than before your engagement. I suppose it would be a shock to one with your kind of thinking if I were to say to you that even after your marriage you are not to consider your wife as a mere plaything for the gratification of your lustful appetites. One who has that concept of marriage is doomed to an unhappy union. No pure Latter-day Saint woman with an understanding of the great mission of wifehood and motherhood could ever be happy with a man who thinks of her as a mere convenience because he happens to have been legally married to her.

I wish that this letter could convey to you something of the strong feeling that I have and the hope that by this medium I could bring you upstanding on this question which is so vital to your welfare and the happiness of your family and your home. I say to you with all the conviction of my soul that unless you change your thinking and correct your bad habits and walk a course directed by the teachings of the gospel of Jesus Christ, you are doomed to disappointment and to bitterness in the future years of your life.

My prayers are with you that you might humble yourself before it is too late and to correct these weaknesses within you before you consummate marriage; and that from now on, when you are in the presence of a pure young woman, you will safeguard her with the realization that even a man married does not own the woman he marries. She is to be as the Lord said in the beginning: "a help meet." She is to be your companion, your partner, your equal. Any man who thinks of his wife as less than that, in my judgment, has proved himself unworthy of a pure, sweet Latter-day Saint girl.

I thank the Lord that not all of our young men are guilty of the kind of thinking that is evidenced in the letter from which I have quoted. By contrast, a letter was addressed to me from a group of boys somewhere in the European Theatre in World War II:

> Here away from the people we have known and loved, God has found a new inlet to our souls through which He whispers truths we had been prone to forget. . . . We think we can speak for the greater percentage of Latter-day Saint servicemen all over the world when we say that through this new inlet God has given us through which he whispers truths, he has given us the true light of real beauty. A girl is beautiful when her virtue cannot be questioned; when her stability and faith in the Church are steadfast. A girl is beautiful when she is sincere and humble; when she looks upon a child with affection and upon a sufferer with compassion. She is beautiful because she has a smile and a cheerful word for her associates. Beauty does not lie in the face alone, but rather, it is measured by character and the sweetness of her disposition.

A young man with such ideals as therein expressed has demonstrated an understanding that he must bring into courtship and ultimate marriage a mind and body as pure and unsullied as that of his sweetheart who may later become his wife. He indeed is a superior person whose thoughts smell of the sunshine, whose passions are honest and pure, and whose association is inspiring and uplifting. It would be well for you young people to remember that one of the greatest handicaps you can have in ultimately finding a desirable companion in marriage would be to be labeled among the associates in your crowd as a "loose or easy girl," or as a "wolf" in whose company a young woman never feels herself free from ungentlemanly advance.

President J. Reuben Clark, Jr., a wise father, counseled:

> If you would be chaste as God commanded, then avoid conduct and practices that arouse the passions. A wise and pure boy or girl—one who wishes to be clean—will not "pet" or "neck" or "love play" nor practice any other undue physical familiarity by whatever name known. At best these are gross and provocative indiscretions—at worst they are the preludes to certain, and too frequently, planned transgressions. They are all unclean in the sight of

71

the Lord. If youth will abandon these, if it will decently reclothe itself and cultivate modesty, a largely lost virtue, it will be a long way on the road to chastity which will bring untarnished happiness and eternal joy in the hereafter. (General conference address, October 1949.)

Now, again, I would have you remember that the purpose of dating which leads to courtship and ultimately to marriage is a social process by which young people ultimately find their mates in marriage. It is a truism that we find our husband or wife among that company we frequent the most. This thought brings me to another subject I would like to have you consider concerning dating.

From the days of ancient Israel the Lord has commanded, "Remember the sabbath day, to keep it holy." (Exodus 20:8.) Any dating you do on the Lord's day should be done with a clear understanding of the kind of activities that would be in harmony with what the Lord has commanded.

For Latter-day Saints, to offer up "sacraments" in the house of prayer as the Lord commands means for you to present your devotions before the Lord in the form of songs of praise, prayers and thanksgiving, testimonies, and the partaking of the sacrament and the study of the word of God. In its most widely accepted usage it means for you to stand for any sacred right or ceremony whereby you affirm your allegiance to your Heavenly Father and His Son.

Any of the activities I have named—in the house of worship or in the home, listening to good music, reading good books, engaging in "fireside" discussions that are uplifting or that contribute to our learning—might be considered in harmony with the spirit of the Sabbath.

Certainly, participating in activities far afield of the house of prayer or in the home—for example, joyriding, beach parties, picnics, or going to places of public amusement—on the Lord's day would not conform to the

Lord's prescription for His one holy day as a memorial to the Lord where He commands us to rest from these worldly things for our temporal as well as our spiritual benefit.

Therefore, make your dates on the Sabbath, if you desire to associate together on that day, to include faithful attendance at Sunday School and sacrament meeting. Make it a day to become acquainted with each other's family in the home.

Now you might well ask: Why is the proper observance of the Sabbath of importance in dating? The Lord answers in one terse statement: "That thou mayest more fully keep thyself unspotted from the world." Don't trade a soul full of spiritual strength which might be yours to help you resist temptations with which you may be daily confronted for a thimbleful of worldly pleasure in which you might otherwise indulge.

Take time to be holy each day of your lives. Let your conscience guide you from error in the future. Let your conduct be in compliance with eternal laws which have been given to you for your spiritual welfare.

# 9

# The Role of Parents in the Home and Family

*A* woman has a dual role in life: as a wife and as a mother. I give her role as a wife priority for reasons borne out of my lifetime of experiences as a husband and father of two lovely daughters, as the grandfather of eight grandsons and two granddaughters, and now as the great-grandfather of wonderful great-grandchildren. Her role as a wife has priority, and yet as a mother she must set the stage, as it were, for the essential teamwork with her husband in the raising of their children.

About all I know about parenthood is that which I have learned over the years from the laboratory of my own home, when I witnessed, from my own beloved companions and my two lovely daughters, some of the secrets of successful motherhood and wifehood.

Recently I read a talk that had been given by one of my daughters to a group of mothers and daughters, in which she related an experience with her firstborn son, an experience that began to teach her the responsibility she had as a mother. In this talk she began, "Many years ago when our oldest son was a very little boy I found myself, one warm summer night after supper, frantically trying to finish bottling some apricots." I am sure that young mothers all know the scene. Everything has happened during the day to keep her from getting to that project and finishing it. And now with the baby settled for the night, her husband off to his meeting on time, and her little three- and four-year-olds all but finished getting their pajamas on and getting ready for bed, she thinks, now I will get to those apricots. She realizes that they are ripening fast, and they just are not going to last until morning.

This was the situation I found myself in that night, so I was beginning to peel them and pit them when my two little boys appeared in the kitchen and announced that they were ready to say their prayers. In desperation and not wanting to be interrupted for the umpteenth time, I said to them, very quickly, "Now boys, why don't you just run in and say your prayers alone tonight, and mother will just keep working on these apricots."

But David, the oldest, planted his little feet firmly in front of me and asked, not unkindly, "But mommy, which is more important, prayers or apricots?" Little did I realize then, as a young mother and a busy wife, that in my life ahead there would be many such dilemmas that I would be faced with, large and small, as I carried out this role as wife and mother in my home, and that my success in these responsibilities would be measured by the manner in which I was able to solve problems. This was my challenge then, and this, as I see it, is your challenge as wives and mothers today. How we meet that challenge is the big question of our lives.

My daughter's experience reminded me of an incident that occurred in the home of one of our stake Primary presidents, on the occasion when two Primary general board members were attending a conference and were being entertained in her home. She was preparing for an open house that evening, at which her Primary workers were to be introduced to these general board members. While she was working at the sink, polishing some of her silver pieces, getting ready for the evening's entertainment, her young son came running in with his piggy bank, shaking his money and saying to his mother, "Mother, how do I figure my tithing?"

Of all the times when this busy mother would not want to be interrupted, this was the time; but patiently she wiped her hands and sat down at the table and together she and her son shook out the pennies, the nickels, and the dimes, and she then proceeded to explain to her son how out of every dime or dollar one-tenth belongs to the Lord. After she had completed her lesson, the lad threw his arms around her neck and said to her, with a kiss, "Oh, thank you, mother, now I know how to pay my tithing."

As she resumed her work at the kitchen sink, the Primary general board members who had witnessed this little scene said to her, "My, that was wonderful that you took the time to talk with your little boy when you were so busy." The mother then said something that was very meaningful: "Well, you see, all my life I will have time to polish silverware, but this may be the only time I will ever have to teach my little boy this important lesson on tithing."

There you have an important lesson for motherhood. The time for a mother or father to teach a child is when the child has a question that needs to be answered.

In a talk to a group of young women on another occasion, one of my daughters was asked to address herself to the subject "How to Lift Your Husband." She gave expression to this question by quoting from Ralph Waldo Emerson, who had written, "If you would lift me, you must be on higher ground." That meant that if any woman would help her husband, she must lift herself on higher ground, above the degradation of temper, of nagging, of quarreling or the pettiness of life.

She had heard her father say on one occasion that coming home to mother is like entering a quiet room. Her

76

mother's priorities were first to her husband and then to her children. Her mother's selflessness in denying her personal desires came because she realized that taking care of the husband was the first on her list, even as her strength began to fail.

This mother realized that to be a supplement or a complement to her husband meant being his confidante, to whom he could unburden his thoughts with complete assurance that she would never repeat them.

She must, if she would support her husband, be an honest, loving critic, and must not constantly say, "You are absolutely perfect, darling; I worship at your shrine—you can do no wrong." Rather, she should tactfully commend and point out ways and means to improve. Yes, each mother will live again in the lives of her children, but her greatest success will be her husband's success. Her greatest reward will be when she can say, when her husband succeeds or when she has a child who excels, "I helped him along the way."

Someone has said that "a woman happy with her husband is better for her children than a hundred books on child welfare." If a woman can achieve this in her wifehood and motherhood and can say always that she linked arms with her husband in loving embrace, she can set the example for her children to follow after. They will see mother and father saying little endearments to each other in the home, instead of having to witness bickerings and quarrelings that will stay with them and will be a detriment as they grow up and have homes of their own.

In the home of successful parents there must be what might be called a reinforcement technique, in which father and mother both give of themselves and make themselves constantly strive not to disappoint, but have a positive approach; and in which a more perfect combination of

77

parents might be found in a mother who was firm beneath her gentleness and a father who was gentle beneath his firmness, which is a good formula for all parents to follow.

It is a successful mother who is never too tired for her daughters, when they return home from a party, and to go into their bedroom while they are preparing for bed and there, at the highest of their glee and joy, hear of their evening's entertainment, instead of waiting until the next day, when the moment has passed, to enter into their lives. It is a successful mother who, as her little children begin to ask questions about intimate things, does not push them away, but sits down and answers honestly up to the limit of her child's ability to understand, in order to satisfy the child's curiosity. That kind of confidence between mother and daughter will exist until courtship and then to marriage, as the mother wisely guides her daughters through the difficult periods of growing up through girlhood and womanhood and wifehood and motherhood.

Most important in a home is to have a father who doesn't shirk his responsibility to his sons when they seek and need answers to delicate questions and he too takes time to answer them.

I remember a doctor who traveled around the country giving lectures to businessmen. He told of an incident during his boyhood when, while he was playing at a neighbor's home with a friend, a little baby was born. The doctor came out of the bedroom carrying in his arms a little bundle—a tiny infant—which he uncovered and showed to these two small boys. The doctor said, "Do you know that you were just this size one day?" The lecturer said, "I shot out of that home and ran to my father's house, where he was just going into the yard, and I asked him, 'Daddy, where did I come from?'" And the father pushed him away by saying, "Now, my boy, that is something we don't talk about."

"That didn't answer my curiosity," the doctor said, "and I went out to the man who was spading the yard on our lot and asked him the same question. This man battered and bruised my little soul by telling me in the most unwholesome language about the beginning of life. The recollection of what he told me has lingered with me throughout my life and has continued to be something of a poison to me."

Now I realize that this takes teamwork. Sometimes a woman has to fight literally and spiritually for the opportunity of bringing father from his busy labors to draw close to his family as often as possible. But she mustn't despair, for therein can be built a strength that will be an example for those who follow after her.

That kind of testimony will guide our sisters over many, many difficulties if they really know that Jesus Christ lived and died for us and that our Heavenly Father is concerned about His children more even than we are or can comprehend, and even when they may be inclined to be discouraged and give up, our Heavenly Father is still trying to save His children.

At a stake conference in New Jersey, we listened to a remarkable talk by the stake president in which he impressed the vital importance of love in the home. He said, "Some of my greatest resources come from lessons learned in my youth from acts of love shown by my parents."

He then illustrated by relating an incident in his childhood home, when he found his father sitting by the bedside of his mother while she was critically ill.

She was asleep. He was just sitting there appearing to be doing nothing. I was so startled and I asked him what was wrong, why wasn't he in bed asleep. My father's answer was, "Nothing's wrong. I was just watching over her." Later I learned that he sat each night by her side during the crisis, watching over her, and thinking of this, I have often thought that true love is kind and never faileth. The memory of this act of love, the light of warmth of that occasion, has always had a special meaning to me. It made me feel safe and secure to see this strong and gentle man so concerned about those of his household. It gave me a deeper appreciation for my father and set a high standard for me to try to follow.

I have repeatedly said to brethren in our priesthood meetings that the most important work that they would ever do would be done within the walls of their own homes.

Richard L. Evans of the Council of the Twelve once said:

> Parents, take time to draw close to your children: let there be love at home; let there be tenderness and teaching and caring. God grant that we may never be too busy to do the things that matter most for home makes the man. Parents, see that your children are blessed with a home that shields them from turmoil and division; that within your home they feel secure, wanted, loved, and are taught important lessons of love. "Parents have the duty to govern their children," says Lyman Abbott. "The object of all good government is to prepare the subject for self-government."

I pray that our families in the Church can have many opportunities together, to stay together, pray together, work together, so that strong bonds will be formed. Then, if the children should stray away temporarily from the path of truth and duty, the strongest bond that can be forged in their minds will be their fear of losing their place in the eternal family circle.

# 10

# Family Home Evening

We have talked a lot about family home evening, but I suppose it is somewhat like Mark Twain is popularly credited with saying about the weather: "We talk a lot about the weather, but we don't seem to do anything about it."

However, we have never had absent from our minds the responsibilities the Lord has placed upon the parents in the home in the teaching of their children. You recall what He said:

> And again, inasmuch as parents have children in Zion, or in any of her stakes which are organized, that teach them not to understand the doctrine of repentance, faith in Christ the Son of the living God, and of baptism and the gift of the Holy Ghost by the laying on of hands, when eight years old, the sin be upon the heads of the parents.
>
> And they shall also teach their children to pray, and to walk uprightly before the Lord. (D&C 68:25, 28.)

The home evening program gives strength to the teaching of the family in the home.

From a letter sent out to the Church in 1915 over the

signatures of Presidents Joseph F. Smith, Anthon H. Lund, and Charles W. Penrose, I quote:

> . . . we advise and urge the inauguration of a "Home Evening" throughout the Church, at which time fathers and mothers may gather their boys and girls about them in the home, and teach them the word of the Lord. . . . This "Home Evening" should be devoted to prayer, singing hymns, songs, instrumental music, scripture-reading, family topics and specific instructions on the principles of the Gospel, and on the ethical problems of life, as well as the duties and obligations of children to parents, the home, the Church, society, and the Nation. (*Improvement Era*, June 1915, p. 733.)

Then, to those who would put this family home evening into practice, the First Presidency made this promise:

> If the Saints obey this counsel, we promise that great blessings will result. Love at home and obedience to parents will increase. Faith will be developed in the hearts of the youth of Israel, and they will gain power to combat the evil influences and temptations which beset them. (Ibid., p. 734.)

President Joseph F. Smith, in commenting about the responsibility of parents in teaching their children, said:

> Do not let your children out to specialists in these things, but teach them by your own precept and example, by your own fireside. Be a specialist yourself in the truth. Let our meetings, schools and organizations . . . be supplements to our teachings and training in the home. Not one child in a hundred would go astray, if the home environment, example and training, were in harmony with the truth in the gospel of Christ, as revealed and taught to the Latter-day Saints. (Joseph F. Smith, *Gospel Doctrine*, p. 302.)

About this same matter President Wilford Woodruff said: "Ninety-nine out of every hundred children who are taught by their parents the principles of honesty and integrity, truth and virtue, will observe them through life." (*Discourses of Wilford Woodruff*, pp. 267-68.)

And then from President Heber J. Grant:

> The Lord has said it is our duty to teach our children in their youth. . . . It is folly to imagine that our children will grow up with a knowledge of the

gospel without teaching. . . . I may know that the gospel is true, and so may my wife; but I want to tell you that our children will not know that the gospel is true, unless they study it and gain a testimony for themselves. Parents are deceiving themselves in imagining that their children will be born with a knowledge of the gospel. (Heber J. Grant, *Gospel Standards,* p. 155.)

Some definite steps have been taken to strengthen parents in carrying out this great God-given admonition of teaching the gospel in the home. A set of lessons, one for each week throughout the year, is given to parents, so they may teach the gospel to their family. These lessons can be adapted to fit every age in the home. These weekly home lessons help us correlate with the priesthood instruction and the Relief Society lessons. Thus, as fathers are taught in priesthood meetings, mothers in Relief Society meetings, and the family studies the gospel in the family home evening, all of this works together to assist parents in strengthening home relationships.

As I have thought of home night, I have thought of my own family. When our older daughter was to be married to a fine Latter-day Saint boy, the two mothers were talking to each other, and the mother of our older daughter said, "You know, from the time my little girl was born, I have been praying all my life that somewhere a mother would be preparing a son worthy to marry my daughter." And this other mother smiled and said, "Isn't that strange? This is my only son who is being married to your daughter, and ever since he was born, I, too, have been praying that somewhere there would be a mother preparing a daughter worthy to meet and to marry my son." That is the kind of home attention that will make us and our homes stronger today.

As I think of family home evening and its possible impact, the words of the prophet Micah come to mind:

But in the last days it shall come to pass, that the mountain of the house

83

of the Lord shall be established in the top of the mountains, and it shall be exalted above the hills; and people shall flow unto it.

And many nations shall come, and say, Come, and let us go up to the mountain of the Lord, and to the house of the God of Jacob; and he will teach us of his ways, and we will walk in his paths: for the law shall go forth of Zion, and the word of the Lord from Jerusalem. (Micah 4:1-2.)

I say to you Latter-day Saint mothers and fathers, if you will rise to the responsibility of teaching your children in the home—priesthood quorums preparing the fathers, and Relief Society the mothers—the day will dawn when the whole world will come to our doors and say, "Show us your way, that we may walk in your path."

# EDUCATION, LEARNING, TEACHING

# 11

# Plain and Precious Things

On a recent radio broadcast a commentator repeated the conclusions of some eminent scholars who had been asked to list fifteen of the best and most sought-after books in the world today. Six of them selected *The Adventures of Tom Sawyer,* but not one of them listed the Bible.

Now, while the reading of Mark Twain's boyhood adventure classic should not be discouraged, its overwhelming acceptance to the exclusion of the Bible indicates a potential danger in the changing values of the modern world.

While speaking at a youth conference in the East, I told of my concern when, as a young missionary, I observed the attitudes of various church leaders with whom I came in contact and their regard for the Bible. I believe that the problem of our missionaries in our day too might be not so much to prove that the Book of Mormon, the Doctrine and Covenants, and the Pearl of Great Price are indeed the word of the Lord, but that the Bible, which is generally accepted as the word of God, is being doubted as having been derived from the words of inspired prophets of past generations.

The radio commentator whom I mentioned before went on to denigrate the worth of the writings in the Bible, saying that the words recorded were not put down by highly educated scholars as we think of such historians in our day. They were fishermen, farmers, laborers, tax collectors, carpenters; and yet, the writings were precise and direct in documenting doctrines of the gospel and in narrating historical events through which the world of their day was passing.

Making an invidious comparison, the commentator cited the fact that the play-by-play broadcaster at a football or basketball game today goes into more detail and uses more words in one game than the early prophets used in narrating the entire story of the creation of the world.

As I contemplated these observations, I thought of the rare gems of sparkling wisdom that are to be found in the epistles of the apostle Peter, one who was of the ranks of the so-called common people. The secret and the explanation of the writings of these profound teachings are explained by this great but impulsive and strong-willed leader in these few but meaningful words: "For the prophecy came not in old time by the will of man: but holy men of God spake as they were moved by the Holy Ghost." (2 Peter 1:21.)

These prophet leaders have given us the simple, direct words of God as they were impressed upon them after much soul-searching; and sometimes because of a great crisis, they were under the influence of the greatest of all spiritual endowments, the gift of the Holy Ghost, one of the Godhead.

True, there are passages in the Bible that are not sufficiently clear, due to the mistakes of men; therefore, many stumble and there is controversy among the so-called Christian nations. All of that was foreshadowed by an ancient prophet in the Book of Mormon:

> . . . for behold, they have taken away from the gospel of the Lamb many parts which are plain and most precious; and also many covenants of the Lord have they taken away.
>
> . . . because of the many plain and precious things which have been taken out of the book, which were plain unto the understanding of the children of men, according to the plainness which is in the Lamb of God—because of these things which are taken away out of the gospel of the Lamb, an exceeding great many do stumble, yea, insomuch that Satan hath great power over them. (1 Nephi 13:26, 29.)

Knowing by the light of revelation of the skepticism that might attend the coming forth of this new volume of scriptures, the prophet further warned:

> Wo be unto him that shall say: We have received the word of God, and we need no more of the word of God, for we have enough!
>
> For behold, thus saith the Lord God: I will give unto the children of men line upon line, precept upon precept, here a little and there a little; and blessed are those who hearken unto my precepts, and lend an ear unto my counsel, for they shall learn wisdom; for unto him that receiveth I will give more; and from them that shall say, We have enough, from them shall be taken away even that which they have. (2 Nephi 28:29-30.)

In this day when the Bible is being downgraded by many who have mingled philosophies of the world with Bible scriptures to nullify their true meaning, how fortunate that our eternal Heavenly Father, who is always concerned about the spiritual well-being of His children, has given to us a companion book of scriptures, known as the Book of Mormon, as a defense for the truths of the Bible that were written and spoken by the prophets as the Lord directed.

Of this new witness contained in this volume of scriptures the Lord declared: "Behold, this is wisdom in me; . . . I have sent unto you . . . the Book of Mormon, containing the fulness of my everlasting gospel, . . . the record of the stick of Ephraim." (D&C 27:5.)

It has always been significant to me that, despite the greatness of the Master Teacher, Jesus the Christ (recognized now by even those who would not believe in His mission as the literal Son of God), there have been left to us no sculptured models or accurate descriptions of Him.

In this connection it should be pointed out that sculpturing was in existence among the ancient Greeks during the Master's time, as the Apostle Paul noted when he came to debate with the wise men of ancient Athens. It has seemed clearly evident to me that it was so because it was not desired that Jesus be worshiped as an idol in stone or brass, but that the profound teachings that He has left us be the center and core of that which should convince anyone of the divinity of His mission.

Just as in the wisdom of God there have been no accurate descriptions in words or in stone or parable of the Savior, so there was no elaborate explanation from the Prophet Joseph Smith, as he bore testimony of the coming forth of the gospel in this dispensation. His was only a simple, straightforward testimony of the facts with no embellishing explanations to detract from the central theme of his message and declaration of faith.

It has seemed fortunate, too, that we do not know the exact spot in the Sacred Grove where the young boy Joseph knelt in humble supplication in his search for truth and where the Father and the Son appeared. Nor do we know the exact location of the room where Joseph was visited by heavenly messengers three times as his mission began to be unfolded; no exact location where the ancient records were found in the Hill Cumorah; no exact locations where the Aaronic and Melchizedek priesthoods were

90

restored; or indeed, no exact place where the Book of Mormon translations actually took place.

From what we have seen when we have visited the Holy Land in Palestine, we can readily imagine how quickly the Lord's words, as we learn from the inspiration of His holy revelation, could in our day have led us to become worshipers of shrines rather than concentrating on the hidden things of God which can only be understood by the Spirit of God.

It has always seemed to me that the words of the Prophet Joseph Smith in counsel to the brethren, impressing the value of the Book of Mormon, have greater significance than many of us attach to them. His statement was: "I told the brethren that the Book of Mormon was the most correct of any book on earth, and the keystone of our religion, and a man would get nearer to God by abiding by its precepts, than by any other book." (*History of the Church,* vol. 4, p. 461.)

To me this means that not only in this volume of scriptures do we have portrayed the accurate truths of the gospel, but also that by this second witness we may know more certainly the meaning of the teachings of the ancient prophets and, indeed, of the Master and His disciples as they lived and taught among men. This should inspire all who would be honest seekers after truth to put these two sacred scriptures together and study them as one book, understanding, as we do, their true relationship.

As did Joseph Smith, so do we declare to the world: "We believe the Bible to be the word of God as far as it is translated correctly; we also believe the Book of Mormon to be the word of God." (Article of Faith 8.)

Truly, as has been written by the noted historian Dr. Johann Mosheim, an authority on early Christian church history: "There is no institution so pure and excellent which the corruption and folly of man will not in time alter for the worse, and load with additions foreign to its nature and original design."

# 12

# The Gospel Teacher

There are three principles that underlie the great responsibility of a teacher. The first is that it is the God-given right of every one of our Father's children to enjoy that priceless gift called free agency. If you will read Second Nephi, you will find a father's explanation to his son about how this great principle works:

And to bring about his eternal purposes in the end of man, after he had created our first parents, and the beasts of the field and the fowls of the air, and in fine, all things which are created, it must needs be that there was an opposition; even the forbidden fruit in opposition to the tree of life; the one being sweet and the other bitter.

Wherefore, the Lord God gave unto man that he should act for himself. Wherefore, man could not act for himself save it should be that he was enticed by the one or the other. (2 Nephi 2:15-16.)

But reckless spendthrifts that we are, as our Father's children, we squander that precious gift by many times choosing that which is delicious to the taste. It is desirable only to our fleshy appetites, and we throw away the greatest of our opportunities. But because of that gift, we as teachers have the opportunity and privilege of enticing all mankind to do good.

The second is another gift that our Father has given to every one of His children, which makes possible the great place of the teacher. That is spoken of in the revelations when the Lord said:

And the Spirit giveth light to every man that cometh into the world; and the Spirit enlighteneth every man through the world, that hearkeneth to the voice of the Spirit.

And every one that hearkeneth to the voice of the Spirit cometh unto God, even the Father. (D&C 84:46-47.)

That light is spoken of variously as the light of Christ, the light of truth, the Spirit of God. It is that light which our Father gives to every one of His children, no matter what color they are, or on what continent they live; every one of our Father's children has it at birth. No matter what might have been that spirit's condition before it came here, by the atonement and the blessing of the atonement, the Lord tells us that every spirit is innocent in the beginning. Each spirit comes into mortality lighted with that light.

Many of our little children begin attending Sunday School and Primary before they have been subjected to the temptations of Satan—before the age of accountability and shortly thereafter. No group of teachers in this church has a greater privilege to entice and to make an impression while that spirit is burning brightly in the souls of the children of men than do our Sunday School and Primary teachers.

The next principle related to the work of a teacher is the preparation each may have as a sower of the seeds of truth. If one who is honest, who is clean, and who is innocent comes under the influence of a teacher who is properly prepared, then it is as though a seedbed ready for the sower had been prepared; the good seed and the proper skill of a sower are needed in order for another soul to be born into the kingdom of God. We have a great privilege of planting and nourishing the most important seeds, the most potent seeds, the most vital seeds that this world knows anything about: the seeds of eternal life, the gospel of the Lord Jesus Christ.

The necessary steps in our preparation are clearly explained in the revelations of the Lord, in Doctrine and Covenants, section 42, verses 11 to 14. These are the four divine principles laid down that our teachers may be prepared to teach. We also have a great sermon on faith in chapter 32 of Alma, where we find a parable of how a teacher sows the seed and how the student receives the seed, to the mutual eternal blessing of both.

Let us look at the four rules our Father gives in section 42, a revelation that He calls "the Law," which might be said to be the law of the Lord to the teacher. First:

> Again, I say unto you, that it shall not be given to any one to go forth to preach my gospel, or to build up my church, except he be ordained by some one who has authority, and it is known to the church that he has authority and has been regularly ordained by the heads of the church. (D&C 42:11.)

That is the first requisite: One must be called of God by prophecy, through the spirit of revelation to a presiding officer, and then be set apart by him after having been sustained by the body or organization over which the person called is to preside or in which he or she is to serve.

No other teachers on earth, except those who teach in this, the church and kingdom of God, have the privilege of receiving, by the laying on of hands from authority given from the heads of the Church, the right and the authority to assist in the building up of the kingdom. One may not go forth in any church assignment until he has been so called and so set apart or ordained.

In the next verse, the Lord speaks particularly to the elders, but the law to the elders is just as much a law to the auxiliaries as to the priesthood quorums of the Church:

And again, the elders, priests and teachers of this church shall teach the principles of my gospel, which are in the Bible and the Book of Mormon, in the which is the fulness of the gospel. (D&C 42:12.)

Now you will note there is nothing said about the Doctrine and Covenants or the Pearl of Great Price, because this revelation was given in 1831, and there was no Doctrine and Covenants or Pearl of Great Price at that time. The Lord means that it is the business of those who are to teach His children to teach the principles of the gospel. We are not set apart to teach notions or guesses at truth. We are not set apart to teach philosophies or sciences of the world. We are set apart to teach the principles of the gospel as found in the four standard works—the Bible, the Book of Mormon, the Doctrine and Covenants, and the Pearl of Great Price.

As we think of that as our limitation, it is our privilege to know those truths and to have the most complete canon of scriptures known to the world. Only members of the Church have that great privilege.

The third principle states:

And they [meaning our teachers as well as the elders] shall observe the covenants and church articles to do them, and these shall be their teachings, as they shall be directed by the Spirit. (D&C 42:13.)

We are not only to teach the principles of the gospel, but also to observe these covenants and do them. A person cannot teach something that he does not himself observe. We are all expected to keep the commandments of the Lord, and it is our privilege and blessing as teachers, if we do keep the commandments, to receive thereby the qualifications of a teacher.

The fourth qualification is this:

And the Spirit shall be given unto you by the prayer of faith; and if ye receive not the Spirit ye shall not teach. (D&C 42:14.)

What is that Spirit? Every person, when he is baptized a member of this church, has hands laid upon his head and the officiating elder says: "We confirm you a member of The Church of Jesus Christ of Latter-day Saints, and say unto you, receive the Holy Ghost."

There are some, I fear, who have never lived to enjoy the companionship of that member of the Godhead and to receive His ministrations, but each one of us may have that right if we will only keep these principles that the Lord has laid down in His law to the teacher. We may have that Spirit. It was so important that Nephi, in one of the closing chapters of his testimony, makes this comment: ". . . Neither am I mighty in writing, like unto speaking; for when a man speaketh by the power of the Holy Ghost the power of the Holy Ghost carrieth it unto the hearts of the children of men." (2 Nephi 33:1.)

What a privilege it is when we gain that Spirit! And after we have done all else, then we must do one thing more in order to get that Spirit—we must invite it. The Lord says: "Behold, I stand at the door, and knock: if any man will hear my voice, and open the door, I will come in to him, and will sup with him, and he with me." (Revelation 3:20.)

We have a right to gain the Spirit by which our words and our teachings, though they may be humble, will be carried and burned into the hearts of those whom we teach so that they will feel an impression and an understanding that otherwise would not be theirs.

Have you ever gone to a meeting and listened to a speaker just arrived from another country? His language probably was tinctured with a foreign accent that indicated the country where he had lived. Perhaps it was hard for you to understand him, for he mixed the English up so that the verbs and the pronouns and the nouns and some of the rest of his words did not come just right; but somehow, as he talked, you had a warm glow come over you and found a lump in your throat and tears in your eyes as he bore his testimony.

And then you may have gone to a meeting where you heard a man who was very eloquent, who had a wonderful vocabulary and was an excellent speaker. Somehow, though, when he got through, you said to yourself, "My, he used some fine language, but somehow what he said just did not ring true."

Have you had that experience? What was the difference between those two speakers? The difference was that the one was speaking by the power of the Holy Ghost and what he said was being burned into the hearts of all who listened, while the other was devoid of the Spirit. Which kind of a teacher do you want to be, the kind who has the Spirit or one who is devoid of it?

The Lord has given us the privilege of receiving His Spirit. How many times have we heard missionaries bear testimony of how they found themselves speaking beyond their understanding? Or how many times have we been moved as those who have administered to the sick have told how they pronounced blessings that they could not withhold?

Some time ago I met a woman in Connecticut, an investigator, who was introduced to me by the missionary who had been teaching her the gospel. I said to her, "Tell me, what was it that first attracted you to this church?"

She thought for a moment and then said, "Well, I will

98

tell you, Brother Lee. I had been raised in a sectarian church, and when I started coming to this church, there was something about your missionaries that caught my attention. When they stood up to speak, their faces seemed to shine, and that is something I had never seen in the preachers of my church."

Do you know what that shining was? It was the power of the Holy Ghost, which our teachers are privileged to receive if they will only keep the law that our Heavenly Father has laid down as a requisite for their preparation.

A missionary told how he was cornered by an atheist who ridiculed many of the teachings of the scriptures. The atheist confronted our missionary before the congregation, an untrained, unschooled young man whom we had dared to send out without his having gone to a theological seminary for training and indoctrination in all the teachings of the gospel. Think what a chance we take in sending our missionaries out, unprepared except for the power of the Holy Ghost.

The atheist said, "Why, it is preposterous for you to say that you believe in a Bible that teaches about a creation when the land was together and the water was all together." Then he read to the missionary from the Book of Genesis, and continued, "Now look at the earth. Here it is divided into many parts and oceans between. How will you explain the inconsistency in this?"

Well, the missionary did not have the answer, but he bowed his head and silently prayed, "Heavenly Father, give me your Spirit to tell me what to say." Then he raised his tear-stained face, and up above the audience, at the back of the hall, he read these words: "Genesis 10:25. In the days of Peleg the earth was divided."

Never in the world had he ever read this scripture. He     99 did not know it was in the Bible, but he saw it there on the wall, and he was able to respond, under the inspiration of the Holy Ghost, to the atheist's question.

Another missionary told how he was challenged by a minister who said that Joseph Smith had never inaugurated the principle of plural marriage—that it had been inaugurated after the Prophet's death. This young man dared to stand up before a group of ministers and say to them, "We have affidavits signed by men and women testifying that what you say is not true."

When he left that room he said to himself, "My goodness, I wonder if I have told a falsehood."

He did not know there were any such affidavits in Church history, but something had told him to say it, and he dared to do so. He was so conscience-stricken that he confessed to his district president.

His supervisor said, "Well, let me give you a pamphlet. Here is the truth of the very statement that you made."

The missionary had not known of the existence of this publication. Where did he get his information from? He was speaking by the power of the Spirit.

As teachers, under the inspiration of the living God and by the power of the Holy Ghost, each of us has a right and a privilege to receive that divine gift if we will only live and prepare ourselves to receive it.

I had a testimony of how that Spirit works. I went to a hospital some years ago to administer to a girl who was to have a very critical operation that required, so the doctor said, the opening of the side of her skull and the removing of a blood clot that had formed and fastened itself to the brain. Her chances for survival were one in a hundred, he said, but that chance had to be taken because blindness and perhaps insanity would result otherwise.

The missionary group to which that girl belonged had fasted the day before the operation was to be performed. Her father and I and a young man from their neighborhood went to the hospital that night to administer to her. After we had pronounced the blessing, as we walked down the hall, the young man said to me, "Brother Lee, I had a peculiar experience today. I could have repeated the words that you said when you sealed the anointing. I knew every sentence you were going to speak before you pronounced the blessing. I could have given that same blessing that you gave."

The mother remained with the daughter and when she came out of the room, she said, "Do you know what Margaret just said? She said, 'Mother, don't be afraid, for when Brother Lee was sealing the anointing, something told me the next words that he was going to speak. I had the words given to me.' "

We have that privilege to teach by power and to receive inspiration and guidance, sometimes beyond our understanding, if we will prepare ourselves by the Spirit to receive the power of the Holy Ghost.

Is it a privilege to teach? The children in our classes have their agency, given to them by God. They can choose good or they can choose evil. We have the gospel of Jesus Christ in our volumes of scripture, the only complete truth in all the world, the only fulness. When we stand before a group who, from their birth, have the light of Christ, which makes them fit subjects to receive truth when it is taught to them, the rest is up to us.

I once talked with a young man who had been converted by some Latter-day Saint men in military service. Then he returned to his home in New York to visit his elderly Armenian mother, who had been reared in the churches of her land. When he came to Salt Lake City to

101

be baptized a few months later, I said, "What did your mother say to you when you told her you were going to join the Church?" The young man smiled and said, "Well, sir, I had a peculiar experience with Mother. She had been taught in the doctrines of her church, and I sat for several hours and explained to her the principles of this newfound gospel, principles that to my knowledge she had never heard before in all her life. When I finished, she said to me, 'My son, I have believed those principles all my life.' "

Then he added, "Brother Lee, where in the world had my mother learned those truths?"

It was the whispering of that divine voice which told her that the teachings of her son were of God.

May the Lord bless our teachers and inspire them to do their part as teachers by first receiving the blessing under the hands of their presiding officers, having been sustained and received by those whom they would teach. May they prepare themselves by studying the lessons contained in the scriptures, living the principles of the gospel that they would espouse and teach, and, finally, receiving the Spirit, which every true teacher has a right to receive.

# 13

# The Mission of the Church Schools

O ur Church school system is an auxiliary arm of the Church and kingdom of God set up by proper authority to meet the needs of the youth of the Church. Each teacher, therefore, who is employed in the Church schools is a representative of the priesthood—the presiding priesthood, the First Presidency—representing them in doing the job that is mapped out for him to do. By direction of the First Presidency, no teacher is employed in the Church schools without first having an interview with one of the General Authorities; and the prime purpose of that interview is to make certain that so far as it is possible the individual is one whose life, whose faith, and whose works are of such a character as to make him a worthy representative of this church.

Two challenges face the Church in a world that is surfeited with ideas, notions, and philosophies of various kinds. Two statements point out what those challenges may be. First, Napoleon I made this significant statement in 1817: "I would believe in a religion, if it existed ever since the beginning of time. But when I consider Socrates, Plato, Mohammed, I no longer believe. All religions have been made by man."

Any religion that cannot trace its foundation back to the beginning of time is in the category of which he speaks. The Church of Jesus Christ of Latter-day Saints is the one church that declares that the gospel was upon the earth from the days of Adam, and today it is but a restoration of that early church. I think no other church makes such a claim.

The second challenge was made by a man named Blatchford, who wrote in the book *God and My Neighbor:*

> Religions are not revealed, they are evolved. If a religion were revealed by God, that religion would be perfect in whole or in part, and would be as perfect in the first moment of its revelation, as after a thousand years of practice. There has never been a religion which fulfills those conditions.

It is a bold claim we make that this is the church of Jesus Christ, the church and kingdom of God on earth. A man who was on the same boat as President David O. McKay when he went around the world to visit the missions said, "Mr. McKay, if you claim your church to be the church of Jesus Christ, yours must be a perfect organization. Your church must be prepared to meet every need of the human soul." That is our claim, and our Church school system is but one of the arms by which that claim is realized.

What, then, is the mission of the Church schools? May I suggest five objectives or purposes, gleaned from some reading and a study of sermons by the brethren.

1. One purpose is to teach secular truth so effectively that students will be free from error, free from sin, free from darkness, free from traditions, vain philosophies, and the untried, unproven theories of science. To me that is one of the prime purposes for which we are organized.

One fast day in my own ward I listened to a young university student who declared his faith after the experiences he had been having at school. He said something to the effect that when he had announced to some of his friends that he was going to take some courses in philosophy at the university, they had said, "Oh, don't you do it. Stay out of those courses, because almost everyone who goes to those classes loses his faith."

However, he said he didn't heed their warning. He was like many other young people: if you want them to take a course, tell them not to do it. Out of curiosity he wanted to see what it was that destroyed faith, and out of his experience, he made this rather interesting observation:

I found that course in philosophy intensely interesting, but I found there was one danger—that it caused doubts, and when those doubts were aggravated by inactivity in the Church, they then resulted in loss of faith and a moving away from the gospel of Jesus Christ. My safety was in continuing to study the gospel of Jesus Christ.

I talked with a man who is prominent at our state university and who has been guilty of the same error of which this young man spoke. While a member of the Church, he had been insidiously inciting and magnifying the doubts that were intended to destroy the faith of these youngsters. He said, "I haven't been doing it this last quarter, though, Brother Lee."

When I asked, "What has changed you?" he made an interesting confession:

For twenty years I had never looked at the Book of Mormon, but I was given an assignment in the Church to do something. That assignment took me into the study of the Book of Mormon and the gospel, and I have joined the Church all over again in the last few months. Now when my students come to me, disturbed because of the teachings of philosophy, I say to them in private, "Now, don't get disturbed. You and I know that the gospel is true and the Church is right."

Every teacher who can make a statement like that—     105

to help to stabilize youth—is a valuable teacher, advancing the work of the kingdom. A scientist of renown at the University of Utah who is eminently heralded throughout the world for his work will take young students aside and declare, "I know the gospel is true," and because of what he says, these budding scientists say, "Well, if he, a great scientist, knows that the gospel is true, who am I to doubt, with my limited knowledge?" Oh, the value of such a teacher!

So I say, ours is the responsibility to teach secular truth so effectively that, as the Master said, we will know the truth, and the truth will make us free. Free from what? Free from error, sin, darkness, the traditions, the vain philosophies, and the untried, unproven theories of the scientists. That is part of our job, to stabilize youth today.

2. The second purpose of the Church schools is to educate youth not only for time, but for all eternity. At a conference in California a doctor who is in one of our stake presidencies delivered a rather interesting address. He said that of late he had become greatly concerned about his profession as a medical man. "When I get on the other side," he said, "if I read the scriptures correctly, there are going to be none of the ills and the difficulties and the physical ailments with which we are now afflicted so that I will be out of a job. I have resolved that I am going to spend some time preparing myself with the kind of a vocation that will last through eternity." Then he referred to other kinds of professions. He wondered if there would be any place for lawyers who spend all their time practicing law to help people out of difficulties, or for certified public accountants; and as he called the roll of the professions, the value of which ended with time, he pretty well woke everyone up to the realization that all of us have

the responsibility of preparing ourselves not only to live in time, but for vocations that last for the eternity.

We buried one of our brethren who had a doctor's degree, and everyone who spoke of him in the funeral service called him "doctor." One of the brethren remarked, "Have you ever stopped to think that that title of doctor ends with this service? But he had another title that nobody referred to, the title of elder—a holder of the priesthood of Almighty God. That is really the only degree that amounts to much when we leave this world." I have thought about that. That is the kind of degree that we in our Church schools should be developing and giving to those who come under our influence.

President Joseph F. Smith said the following about this:

> This knowledge of truth, combined with proper regard for it, and its faithful observance, constitutes true education. The mere stuffing of the mind with a knowledge of facts is not education. The mind must not only possess a knowledge of truth, but the soul must revere it, cherish it, love it as a priceless gem; and this human life must be guided and shaped by it in order to fulfil its destiny. The mind should not only be charged with intelligence, but the soul should be filled with admiration and desire for pure intelligence which comes of a knowledge of the truth. The truth can only make him free who hath it, and will continue in it. And the word of God is truth, and it will endure forever.
>
> Educate yourself not only for time, but also for eternity. The latter of the two is the more important. Therefore, when we shall have completed the studies of time, and enter upon the commencement ceremonies of the great hereafter, we will find our work is not finished, but just begun. (*Gospel Doctrine*, p. 269.)

Our Church schools have the responsibility of preparing people for eternity.

3. We must so teach the gospel that students will not be misled by purveyors of false doctrines and vain speculations of faulty interpretations.

107

The story is told of a man who stood one time to deliver an address and began, "Now, my brethren and sisters, I will now proceed to elucidate upon a matter on which the Lord has revealed but very little." That is not the kind of sermon for any of us to undertake. If the Lord hasn't seen fit to reveal it, then we ought not to be trying to elucidate upon doctrines that we think the Lord may have left out of his program of instructions.

When I think of the notions around the Church about the "one mighty and strong" (D&C 86:7), I think about what they are talking about—the United Order. You would be surprised how many literal descendants of Aaron present themselves and want to become the presiding bishop of the Church. There are health enthusiasts who are always trying to tie on to the Word of Wisdom to make it appear as though their ideas on nutrition were the word of the Lord. Adherents to the order of Aaron, the new polygamists or cultists, are those who are supposedly translated, who set themselves up as divine beings, and then become "translated." I heard a rather interesting story about one such person. She was supposedly "translated" just after she was excommunicated from the Church, and the next day she returned home; she had forgotten her upper dentures and had to come back to get them before she left to become "translated."

I have had a little experience reading some lessons for the various organizations. The First Presidency has a publications committee charged with the responsibility of looking over all the lessons prepared. In reading them over, I have been amazed to see how many of our writers fail to have sufficient understanding when they are making interpretations of scriptural teachings. They often fail to realize that the very interpretation that they are straining for is spelled out clearly in the Book of Mormon, the Doctrine and Covenants, the Bible, and the Pearl of Great Price. We have what no other church has: four great books, the truth of which, if we would read them all, is so clear that we need not be in error. For instance, when we want to know about the interpretation of the parable of the tares as the Lord meant it, all we have to do is read the revelation known as the 86th section of the Doctrine and Covenants and we have the Lord's interpretation. If we want to know something as contained in the teachings of the Beatitudes or the Lord's Prayer, we can read the more correct version in Third Nephi. Many concepts that otherwise would be obscure are made clear and sure in our minds. Our job, as one of our presidents said, is to see to it that these purveyors of false notions and speculations are put to flight.

The wisest statement we can make is, "I don't know," to the many questions youth may ask on matters about which the Lord has not spoken. We must never presume to elucidate upon a matter on which the Lord has revealed but little.

Two of our brethren were riding out to a conference. They were anxious about what they were going to say, and the younger man said to Elder Joseph R. Merrill, with whom he was traveling, "Brother Merrill, have you any suggestions for a sermon at the coming conference?"

Brother Merrill answered, "My dear brother, I don't know that we are under the responsibility to bring forth anything new."

It isn't the business of our teachers of religion to bring forth anything new. Their responsibility is to teach the old truths, the simple truths, the foundation teachings of the gospel of Jesus Christ, and not to be concerned about speculations that are startling and intriguing, whether true or not.

109

President Joseph F. Smith made some comment about that. He said:

> Among the Latter-day Saints, the preaching of false doctrines disguised as truths of the gospel may be expected from people of two classes, and practically from these two only; they are:
>
> First—The hopelessly ignorant, whose lack of intelligence is due to their indolence and sloth, who make but feeble effort, if indeed any at all, to better themselves by reading and study; those who are afflicted with a dread disease that may develop into an incurable malady—laziness.
>
> Second—The proud and self-vaunting ones, who read by the lamp of their own conceit; who interpret by rules of their own contriving; who have become a law unto themselves, and so pose as the sole judges of their own doings. More dangerously ignorant than the first.
>
> Beware of the lazy and the proud; their infection in each case is contagious; better for them and for all when they are compelled to display the yellow flag of warning, that the clean and uninfected may be protected. (*Gospel Doctrine,* p. 373.)

Karl G. Maeser said, "Rather I would that a child of mine be in a den of serpents than under the influence of a teacher who has no faith in God." Ours is the responsibility, then, to make certain that these speculations and these notions in the Church are not given an airing in the classes taught to the Latter-day Saint youth.

4. We must prepare students to live a well-rounded life. President David O. McKay said something that I think defines this better than I can:

> The aim of education is to develop resources in the child that will contribute to his well-being as long as life endures; to develop power of self-mastery that he may never be a slave to indulgence or other weaknesses, to develop virile manhood, beautiful womanhood that in every child and every youth may be found at least the promise of a friend, a companion, one who later may be fit for husband or wife, an exemplary father or a loving intelligent mother, one who can face life with courage, meet disaster with fortitude, and face death without fear. (*Gospel Ideals,* p. 436.)

We are living in an age of grave uncertainty for youth. There has never been a time in my lifetime when they have been so disturbed as right now. Ours must be the kind of teaching that helps to stabilize.

While I was attending a stake conference, I was to interview some of the prospective missionaries. Before one boy came to see me, the stake president said, "Now here is a boy that has just come through a serious experience. He is just out of the service. He suffered shell-shock in battle, and I think we need to talk pretty carefully to him and make certain that he is prepared to go."

So as I talked with the young man, I said, "Why do you want to go on this mission, son? Are you sure that you really want to go, after all the harrowing experiences you have had?"

He sat thoughtfully for a few moments and then said, "Brother Lee, I had never been away from home when I went into the service, and when I got out into the camps, every waking hour I heard filthy, profane language. I found myself losing a certain pure-mindedness, and I sought God in prayer to give me the strength not to fall into that terrible habit. God heard my prayer and gave me strength. Then we went through the basic training, and I asked Him to give me physical strength to continue, and He did. He heard my prayer. As we moved up toward the fighting lines and I could hear the booming of the guns and the crackling of the rifles, I was afraid. Again I prayed to God to give me the courage to do the task that I was there to do, and He heard my prayer and gave me courage.

"When I was sent up with an advance patrol to search out the enemies and to send back for the reinforcements, telling them where to attack—and sometimes the enemy would almost hedge me around until I was cut off, and it seemed that there was no escape—I thought that surely my life would be taken. I asked for the only force of power to guide me safely back, and God heard me. Time and again

111

through the most harrowing experiences He led me back. Now," he said, "I am back home. I have recovered, and I would like to give thanks to that power to which I prayed—God, our Heavenly Father. Going out on a mission, I can teach others that faith which I was taught in Sunday School, in seminary, in my priesthood class, and in my home. I want to teach others so that they will have that same strength that guided me through this difficult experience."

This is the kind of teaching that our Church schools are organized to do.

A president of the United States has said, "This is what I have found about religion. It gives you courage to make decisions when you must in a crisis, and then the confidence to leave the result to a higher power. Only by trusting God can a man carrying great responsibility find repose." That is the kind of stability we expect our teachers to help build in our youth.

5. The final objective of Church schools is to set the stage for students to acquire a testimony of the reality of God and of the divinity of His work, and to help them to gain a testimony that God lives and that this work is divine.

One of our institute teachers told me of an experience he had. While he was in the U.S. Navy, where he was a group leader, a member of his group suffered a terrible experience. The young man's father was in the U.S. Army on a mission in the Pacific, when the ship was torpedoed and the men were thrown into burning oil on the water, and the father of this boy was badly burned. Just before that, the boy's mother had died of cancer. The servicemen, knowing of his past, had tried to comfort him. They had hoped that by their teaching and through their prayers he would gain a testimony before he was transferred. He would talk in their meetings and say that he was thankful for their friendship, but never once did he say that he knew or that he believed.

Then the time came when he received his combat assignment to go overseas, and the group met for the last time with him. At the meeting he stood up and said, after thanking the men for their kindness and their friendship, "I want to tell you that as a result of my studies and my prayers with you, I know that God lives and that the gospel is true."

The next day, when the fleet sailed out and his boat disappeared over the horizon, his fellow Saints who had heard that testimony said, "Thank God he is fortified for the experiences through which he is now to pass."

The strength of this church is not in organization, not in strong authority, but in the individual testimony that burns in the breast of every member in it. And the greatest thrill that our teachers can give each of our youth is the thrill that comes when the Spirit of the Almighty comes into his soul and whispers that testimony—when he knows that God lives and that this is the church of the kingdom of God. That is the greatest of all the thrills.

May our teachers, charged with representing the Presidency of this church to meet a great and important need, rise to the full responsibility, and may theirs be the task to which they go humbly to bring out these objectives, which are the prime purposes for which the Church schools have been organized.

# 14

# Education for All

*T*he Lord has given a charge to this church and the world: "And even so I have sent mine everlasting covenant into the world, to be a light to the world, and to be a standard for my people, and for the Gentiles to seek to it, and to be a messenger before my face to prepare the way before me." (D&C 45:9.)

This revelation should be a reminder that every institution that is a part of the kingdom of God must keep in mind the purpose of the restored gospel—to be a light unto the world and a standard for this people and all men to seek. We must never forget our role in bringing to reality the ancient prophecy—to build the mountain of the Lord's house in the top of the mountains so great and so glorious that all nations may come to this place and be constrained to say, "Show us your way that we may walk therein." (See Isaiah 2:3.)

We charge our leaders to constantly remember that profound and oft-repeated admonition of the apostle James:

If any of you lack wisdom, let him ask of God, that giveth to all men liberally, and upbraideth not; and it shall be given him.

But let him ask in faith, nothing wavering. For he that wavereth is like the wave of the sea driven with the wind and tossed. (James 1:5-6.)

Obedient to that instruction, the fourteen-year-old Joseph Smith, in a quest for truth, was led to seek, in fervent prayer to Almighty God, the answer to a burning question that caused him great concern. The answer to that question, delivered in the Sacred Grove, commenced the ushering in of the dispensation of the fulness of times. This instruction is just as applicable to all of us today as it was to Joseph Smith: to find the answers to unsolved problems and seek for guidance beyond the wisdom of men. We too must many times go to our Sacred Grove in our quest for truth.

As we meet the challenging problems of today, may we see, as it were, written on the darkened walls of our sequestered chamber the words of heavenly wisdom that will give us the assurance, when we are faced with momentous decisions, that we can place our trust in God and leave the rest with Him.

When we stand at the crossroads of two alternative decisions, let us remember what the Lord said we should do: Study the whole matter out in our mind to a conclusion; before action, ask the Lord if it be right; and attune ourselves to the spiritual response—either to have our bosom burn within us to know that our conclusion is right, or to have a stupor of thought that will make us forget it if it is wrong. Then, as the Lord has promised, ". . . the Spirit shall be given unto [us] by the prayer of faith." (D&C 42:14.)

May we have before us always the ideals of scholarship in fields of secular knowledge, and never forget those lofty goals to which we have been pointed by our inspired

115

leaders and by the Lord's own revelations. I refer to two very significant inspired declarations: "It is impossible for a man to be saved in ignorance" (D&C 131:6) and "A man is saved no faster than he gets knowledge" (*DHC,* vol. 4, p. 588).

In the interpretation of these quotations, let us not make the mistake of assuming that this means that one with an advanced degree in secular learning is more assured of salvation than one with only an elementary schooling. The Prophet Joseph Smith, speaking to this subject, declared that "knowledge through our Lord and Savior Jesus Christ is the grand key that unlocks the glories and mysteries of the kingdom of heaven." (*Teachings of the Prophet Joseph Smith,* p. 298.) He also declared: "A man is saved no faster than he gets knowledge, for if he does not get knowledge, he will be brought into captivity by some evil power in the other world. . . . Hence it needs revelation to assist us, and give us knowledge of the things of God." (Ibid., p. 217.)

The limitless expanse of these truths in their fulness must ever be kept in mind as our teachers counsel the inquiring minds of their students. "We believe all that God has revealed, all that He does now reveal, and we believe that He will yet reveal many great and important things pertaining to the Kingdom of God." (Article of Faith 9.)

It was never intended that the leaders in this church be an ignorant ministry in the learning of the world. May I refer to a few verses to show the immense field that is laid before us to keep pace with scientists and scholars and the development of modern knowledge.

Teach ye . . . Of things both in heaven and in the earth, and under the earth; things which have been, things which are, things which must shortly come to pass; things which are at home, things which are abroad; the wars and the perplexities of the nations, and the judgments which are on the land; and a knowledge also of countries and of kingdoms—

That ye may be prepared in all things when I shall send you again to magnify the calling whereunto I have called you, and the mission with which I have commissioned you. (D&C 88:78-80.)

·We must never forget that which was impressed by the ancients: "Wisdom is the principal thing; therefore get wisdom: and with all thy getting get understanding." (Proverbs 4:7.)

This, then, is our instruction and guide to keep before us: to prepare ourselves and those we may teach for the work of the ministry as they go out to take their places in worldly affairs.

We should also remember the divine admonition to have those under our tutelage "study and learn, and become acquainted with all good books, and with languages, tongues, and people." (D&C 90:15.)

The educational system of the Church has been established to the end that all pure knowledge must be gained by our people, handed down to our posterity, and given to all men. We charge our teachers to give constant stimulation to budding young scientists and scholars in all fields and to urge them to push further and further into the realms of the unknown.

One of these possibilities was predicted by a great scientist, Dr. David Sarnoff. It was his expectation that within twenty years from the time that he made his prediction, we would begin to solve the riddle of communication by some electronic device by which one could speak in English and our hearers would understand, each in his own language. With our responsibility to teach the peoples of the world in fifty nations and in seventeen different languages, as we are now doing, think what it would mean to

117

our missionary and teaching efforts if some of our scholars were to contribute to this possibility.

We would hope that our students might make a significant contribution to the discovery of a cure for cancer, or that we would continue to graduate great teachers, inspired by the life and superb example of the greatest teachers of our day. We would hope that we might be instrumental in developing statesmen—men not only with unsurpassed excellence of training in the law, but also with an unwavering faith that the Constitution of the United States was divinely inspired and written by men whom God raised up for this very purpose.

Teachers, hold up before your students the prophetic statement of the Prophet Joseph Smith—that if and when our inspired Constitution should hang as by a thread, there would be prepared, well-qualified defenders of the faith of our fathers, the elders of this church, who would step forth and save the Constitution from destruction.

In education, members of our church have a great tradition. Many hold positions of distinction in the educational world, as well as in business, medicine, politics, trades, and many other fields.

Our charge is that our educators, our teachers, seek for balanced educational ideals and inspire their students with a high degree of intellectual competence, prepared to face the problems of life. In short, a balanced education should bring forth upright, honorable citizens, to whom we can point with pride as individuals who find favor not only with their fellowmen but also with God.

We indulge the hope that a method might be devised to discover the greatness of that soul who, as measured by some arbitrary set of academic measurements, may not be accepted. With the vision of eternal acceptance in the presence of God constantly before us, thereby is laid the foundation for the awakening of wellsprings of spiritual powers that will bring forth miraculous accomplishments.

To one schooled in the doctrines of salvation and the history of the restoration and with a testimony of the divine origin of this church, we would remind you that the acquiring of knowledge by faith is no easy road to learning. It demands strenuous effort and a continual striving by faith. We need only to be reminded of the means by which Daniel learned the secret of Nebuchadnezzar's vision or how Joseph Smith had to prepare himself for his prophetic calling.

David Whitmer, one of Joseph's intimate associates in the early days of the Church, gives us a glimpse as to why Joseph could obtain learning by faith: "Joseph Smith was a good man when I knew him. He had to be or he could not go on with his work."

In short, learning by faith is no task for a lazy man. Someone has said, in effect, that such a process requires the bending of the whole soul, the calling up from the depths of the human mind and linking it with God—the right connection must be formed. Then only comes "knowledge by faith."

I am reminded of that oft-repeated charge of President Brigham Young to the first principal of Brigham Young University, Karl G. Maeser. This charge summarizes, in one sentence, the spiritual admonition that has done more to guide teachers and students alike in their attitudes and their labors than has ever come from those of scholarly wisdom of the world. That profound educational formula was not to teach even the multiplication tables without the Spirit of God.

So we say, never hesitate to declare your faith, as did the Apostle Paul, that the gospel of Jesus Christ is indeed "the power of God unto salvation." (Romans 1:16.)

We charge the Saints to set a proper example in their own personal conduct; to see that their families and home life are in proper order; to be careful not to neglect their families; and to hold family home evenings.

May we keep always a deep sense of gratitude for our pioneer heritage, a love for this country, and a deep-seated reverence for the Constitution of the United States, to the end that we will never forget our civic and political obligations. Our greatest joy comes when, in the years that lie ahead, our youth become honored citizens in their communities and active participants in building up the kingdom of God.

If we seek earnestly, we can reach into that spiritual dimension for answers that will secure for us not only great blessings, but also the sublime witness in our hearts that our acts, our life, and our labors have the seal of approval of the Lord and Creator of us all.

# 15

# Seek Learning by Study and Also by Faith

Several years ago I presided over an afternoon session of the Pioneer Stake conference held in the Salt Lake Tabernacle. Our visitor was President Brigham H. Roberts of the First Council of the Seventy. Brother Roberts had just been released from the hospital, where he had undergone a severe and painful operation that resulted in the amputation of part of his foot. When I asked him if he felt up to speaking in the Tabernacle, he said after some thought, "I understand there is an official Church stenographer to take down the sermons delivered there. I have a feeling that some of our members are following the philosophies of the world and are in danger of slipping from their moorings in the fundamental doctrines as taught by our early leaders. I have felt that there are a few things I would like to speak where they can be recorded, things which might be read after I am gone."

Now you can understand how I felt about that stake conference session, to listen to this message that he was addressing to me and to all of my generation to be read after he had gone. Somehow what he said on that occasion has come back to me again and again, and the Lord willing, I should like to introduce a part of what he said and then add to it some of my own reflections.

He began with a recital of the statements of scientists that indicated a marked trend of so-called knowledge away from a belief in God and to deny the continuance of the universe; and with that, of course, would fall all hope of immortality and eternal life, promised in the revelations of God.

He spoke for about half of the session, and his strength was waning, so he turned to the Tabernacle Choir members who were there and asked if they would sing while he recovered some of his strength. After a few moments' rest he then addressed himself to the most glorious part of his whole sermon. He spoke of the restoration of the gospel of Jesus Christ as not merely sweeping away the rubbish of past ages, such as disputations as to the mode of baptism, or how one's sins are remitted, or the various forms of church government. But he impressed the fact that a new dispensation of the gospel had been ushered in, built upon a strong "foundation of the apostles and prophets, Jesus Christ himself being the chief corner stone." (Ephesians 2:2.)

Those called to the ministry received two significant instructions by revelation as to how they should be prepared for the ministry to which they were called in the restored church of Jesus Christ. The doctrines of the kingdom and the ordinances of the temple were instituted, the Lord said, that they might be "instructed more perfectly in theory, in principle, in doctrine, in the law of the gospel, in all things that pertain unto the kingdom of God, that are expedient for you. . . ." (D&C 88:78.)

122    Then President Roberts read that oft-repeated

passage that teachers of the gospel were to interest themselves in secular learning in all fields. After he had said this, he then quoted another profound statement addressed to all others who "hath not faith." Possibly this meant, in its broadest sense, those who have not yet matured in their religious convictions. This is what the Lord said: "And as all have not faith, seek ye diligently and teach one another words of wisdom; yea, seek ye out of the best books words of wisdom; seek learning, even by study and also by faith." (D&C 88:118.)

Now, with that as an introduction, I would like to address myself to that last thought, "seek learning even by study and also by faith." This call to higher wisdom has been trumpeted through all the ages by the prophets. The Apostle Paul asked this soul-searching question: "For what man knoweth the things of a man, save the spirit of man which is in him?" and then he declared that most profound statement to all those who would drink more deeply of inspired wisdom than merely the teachings of men: "But God hath revealed them unto us by his Spirit: for the Spirit searcheth all things, yea, the deep things of God."

Said he, "Eye hath not seen, nor ear heard, neither have entered into the heart of man, the things which God hath prepared for them that love him." (See 1 Corinthians 2:9-11.)

Fortunately, there are great men schooled in worldly learning who attest to the need of a kind of learning that goes beyond secular knowledge. I will illustrate a few.

A letter from Colonel Edward H. White, a national hero who eventually gave his life while engaged in an experiment designed for exploration of outer space, was printed in the local press a few years ago. In answer to an inquiry as to his beliefs in law and order in the universe, he answered in this rather unusual way:

123

I believe that law and order exist in God's creations, and that God has surely given life to others outside our earth. In our vast universe there are no fewer than billions and billions of solar systems comparable to our own—in dimension and magnitude far beyond the ability of the finite mind to comprehend. "Out there" could be places where life, similar to our own, perhaps superior or, perhaps, inferior, may be a reality. We would be rather egotistical to believe that ours is the only life among all those possible sources.

How accurately this man's learning by faith has brought him into full accord with what the Lord declared in a great revelation to His prophet Moses: "And worlds without number have I created; and I also created them for mine own purpose; and by the Son I created them, which is mine Only Begotten.

"And the first man of all men have I called Adam, which is many." (Moses 1:33-34.)

Moses was not an astronomer. He tells us that he "beheld the earth, yea, even all of it; and there was not a particle of it which he did not behold, discerning it by the spirit of God." (Moses 1:27.)

Colonel White concluded with this declaration of his own personal faith: "As to evidence of God's presence during our journey in space and during the short period that 'I walked in space,' I did not feel any nearer to Him there than here, but I do know that His sure hand guided us all the way during that four-day mission."

Presumably he is telling us that he was guided by faith in God, which transcended his scientific knowledge.

One of our own great scientists, Dr. Henry Eyring, in the field of physical chemistry, a few years ago wrote an article for one of our Church periodicals under the heading "Myriads of Worlds."

He quoted from a professor emeritus of astronomy at Harvard University, Dr. Harlow Shapley, in which the professor declared that out of the millions of suns, at least one sun in a thousand would have acquired planets, and that of those with planets, at least one in a thousand has a planet the right distance for life. And then Dr. Eyring wrote:

> Thus one concludes that there should be at the very minimum one hundred million planets in space which could support life, and the number is probably many times more. Thus, from the scientific point of view, it is hard to doubt that there are myriads of worlds suitable for human habitation. . . .
>
> The mysteries of the universe lead most men to worship the Supreme Intelligence who designed it all.

Then mark this next statement from Dr. Eyring:

> However, the great blessing of the Gospel is the additional avenues it opens up for developing this faith into a perfect knowledge. Now, as always, sure knowledge of spiritual matters can only come by faith, by prayer, and by living in such a way as to have the companionship of the Holy Ghost as is promised to all the faithful. (*Instructor,* November 1951, p. 373.)

The great volume of American history known as the Book of Mormon, we are told by the Lord, was translated by the Prophet "through the mercy of God, by the power of God" (D&C 1:29), and "the interpretation thereof by the gift of God" (title page of Book of Mormon).

The Prophet Joseph Smith tells us something of the process by which knowledge by faith may come:

> A person may profit by noticing the first intimation of the spirit of revelation; for instance, when you feel pure intelligence flowing into you, it may give you sudden strokes of ideas, so that by noticing it, you may find it fulfilled the same day or soon; (i.e.) those things that were presented unto your minds by the Spirit of God, will come to pass; and thus by learning the Spirit of God and understanding it, you may grow unto the principle of revelation, until you become perfect in Christ Jesus. (*Teachings of the Prophet Joseph Smith,* p. 151.)

A similar comment illustrates the working of the Spirit of God, or the light which lightens every person who comes into the world, as a man of science, not of the Church, would define it. Some years ago in a class of

125

seminary teachers at Brigham Young University, Dr. Edwin Starbuck, a University of Iowa professor, remarked that "every great scientific discovery came as an intuition to the mind of the discoverer." When he explained what he meant by intuition, his students said they called it inspiration.

The professor said that a careful search of the records and contacts with great living scientific discoverers made by him "explained that the scientist studies his problem, saturates his mind with it, puzzles over it, dreams about it, but seems to find progress impossible, blocked, as it were, by a black impenetrable wall. Then at last and suddenly as if 'out of the nowhere' comes a flash of light, the answer to his quest. His mind is now illumined by a great discovery." The professor was positive that no great discovery had been made by pure reasoning. Reason would lead to the borderland of the unknown, but it could not tell what was within.

Certainly learning by faith is not an easy road or a lazy means to knowledge. For instance, a prophet tells us there are times when no miracles can be found among the people: "And the reason why he ceaseth to do miracles among the children of men is because that they dwindle in unbelief, and depart from the right way, and know not the God in whom they should trust." (Mormon 9:20.)

And then concerning directly the working of miracles, which of course is an evidence of the wisdom of God working through men, the prophet Nephi declared: "And now it came to pass that according to our record, and we know our record to be true, for behold, it was a just man who did keep the record—for he truly did many miracles in the name of Jesus; and there was not any man who could do a miracle in the name of Jesus . . . save he were cleansed every whit from his iniquity." (3 Nephi 8:1.)

126

Thus, you see, such heavenly gifts of the Spirit are only to be enjoyed by those who have learned by faith and living worthily to receive the right to exercise these divine powers.

Our own Prophet who gave us the first revelations of this dispensation said:

> We would say to the brethren, seek to know God in your closets, call upon him in the fields. Follow the directions of the Book of Mormon, and pray over, and for your families, your cattle, your flocks, your herds, your corn, and all things that you possess; ask the blessings of God upon all your labors, and everything that you engage in. Be virtuous and pure; be men of integrity and truth; keep the commandments of God; and then you will be able more perfectly to understand the difference between right and wrong—between the things of God and the things of men; and your path will be like that of the just, which shineth brighter and brighter unto the perfect day. (*Teachings of the Prophet Joseph Smith*, p. 247.)

Yes, God isn't in the earthquake; he isn't in the whirlwind; he isn't in the fire; but he is in the still, small voice. We won't always have Him in sight, but if we are living as we ought to live, we can always be sure He is there. Some of the most severe taskmasters that the world can know are sometimes beating us into a shape so we can pass such tests as necessary to gain that divine privilege.

I bear you my testimony of the Master, as the Apostle Paul spoke of Him, "Though he were a Son, yet learned he obedience by the things which he suffered;

"And being made perfect, he became the author of eternal salvation unto all them that obey him." (Hebrews 5:8-9.)

I know this through the refining processes of some severity. May I not fail whatever test the Lord may have to qualify me for the place which I am now occupying. With all my soul and conviction, and knowing the seriousness and import of that testimony, I will tell you that I know that He lives. I am conscious of His presence much of the

127

time when I have needed Him most; I have known it out of the whisperings of the night, the impressions of the daytime when there were things for which I was responsible and on which I could receive guidance. So I testify to you and tell you that He is closer to the leaders of this church than you have any idea. Listen to the leaders of this church and follow their footsteps in righteousness, if you would learn not only by study, but also by faith, which testimony I bear most humbly and sincerely.

# 16

# And the Spirit Shall Be Given You by the Prayer of Faith

Some years ago at a stake conference, the late President J. Reuben Clark, Jr., made a significant statement to teachers and a promise to youth: "Youth of the Church are hungry for the words of the Lord. Teachers, be sure you are prepared to feed them the 'bread of life'—which is the teachings of Jesus Christ. If they, the youth, will live up to His teachings, they will have more happiness than they ever dreamed of."

Having in mind that many who are called to teach in the Church organizations have never had formal training to teach, nor is it required, how then are they to be prepared? The Doctrine and Covenants says: "And the Spirit shall be given unto you by the prayer of faith; and if ye receive not the Spirit ye shall not teach." (D&C 42:14.) How is the teacher to get that Spirit? "Ask, and it shall be given you; seek, and ye shall find; knock, and it shall be opened unto you: For every one that asketh receiveth; and he that seeketh findeth; and to him that knocketh it shall be opened." (Matthew 7:7-8.) Thus spoke the Master to the multitudes who came to be taught by Him.

In the years gone by, I have had the experience of being under the influence of many teachers, a few of whom made a profound impression upon me during my growing-up years, and later when I was instructing as a teacher.

One of these, Howard R. Driggs, left to those of us who were taught by him some lasting lessons, particularly as he drew from the record of Jesus, the Master Teacher, these examples and principles of good teaching:

1. The Master had a true love of God and God's children.

2. He had a burning belief in His mission to serve and save mankind.

3. He had a clear and sympathetic understanding of human beings and their vital needs.

4. He was a constant, earnest student. He knew the law and the prophets. He knew history and the social conditions of His time.

5. He could discern truth and was uncompromising in upholding it.

6. His simple language enabled Him to reach and to hold hearers of every class and condition.

7. His creative skill made the lessons He taught live for all time.

8. He led people to "hunger and thirst" after righteousness.

9. He inspired active goodness—a desire to apply the gospel in uplifting service.

10. He demonstrated His faith by living it constantly and courageously.

I have had the good fortune to have had as my eternal companions in my home two great teachers. From what I have seen demonstrated by them in their teaching and examples, and from my own experience as a teacher and a

Church leader, I will document briefly some of the lessons I have learned.

Each of the two teachers called to teach was given the gift of the Holy Ghost at baptism as a comforter and a guide. Each was called by one having authority.

Hands were laid upon the head of each of these teachers, and each was set apart for a definite work and blessed that while she held that position, she would receive direction, inspiration, revelation, and discernment, according to her need, if she was faithful and sought to be guided by the Spirit of the Lord. The following actual experiences in the lives of these two inspired teachers will illustrate how divine blessings are obtained through faithful service and how precious lives are molded by the teachings of one who teaches by the Spirit. I will illustrate with two examples from their "Books of Experience," as it were, for others to follow.

One of these, a choice daughter of a noble lineage, received as a young girl a blessing under the hands of an inspired patriarch. In this blessing she was counseled to "be diligent in applying thy mind to faithful study. Seek the Lord in earnest prayer and thy heart will be filled with joy and satisfaction with the work thou wilt accomplish. Thou wilt have much delight in teaching the little folks and in watching their development into youth and maturity. The love thou shalt win from them will be ample reward for thy labors."

Another of my lovely companions had her mission likewise foretold in her young womanhood when she was promised in a sacred blessing that "as thou art called upon for service in the Church, thou art to respond thereto in all humility. In that service, joy shall come unto thee for thou art to know and to understand the word of God and to

131

have power to teach it unto others . . . thou art to be a messenger of peace and to bring joy and appreciation unto many homes. Thou art one to bring cheer unto the sick. Thou shalt help remove the burden from the hearts of those who have sinned and thy voice shall bring comfort and hope to those who are weary and heavy laden, and thus direct them to Him, the Lord Jesus Christ."

How wonderfully well these two lived to see fulfilled these promised blessings is borne out by two true-to-life incidents to immortalize themselves into the hearts and lives of those to whom they devoted themselves in the Master's art of teaching.

The blessing pronounced upon the head of this first teacher as a young girl was later to find beautiful expression in the fulfillment of that blessing. She was young and she loved life. Many times there were temptations, but always there would come before her the faces of the little ones who trusted her. She must live to be worthy of that trust.

A young man in uniform told a close friend of that teacher, whom he characterized as the best teacher he ever had, "She trusted me." It was one of those mornings that had been trying. She had left the class discouraged, wondering if anything had been accomplished. A young boy from her class quickened his step to walk by her side and said, "I sure liked the lesson this morning." Then, looking longingly at a beautifully bound volume of the life of Christ that she was carrying, he said, "If I had a book like that, I could answer some of the questions too." "Would you like to take mine?" she asked, offering it to him. "Oh, could I? Thanks!" With almost a caress he took the book, and the look on his face said much more than thanks. She learned later that he came from a large family where there were no books, no pictures on the walls. He was hungry for the teachings contained in that book. He brought the book back to her the following Sunday, carefully wrapped. He had read it through, and it was not soiled or harmed in any way. Yes, she had trusted him.

This other great teacher extended her service far beyond the classroom as she instilled into one lovely young girl qualities that were to blossom into beautiful womanhood. The blessings given to her as a young woman, now a trained teacher, bore sweet fruit in her lifetime of teaching. Thus she turned what could have been a stark tragedy in a girl's life into a beautiful accomplishment as she guided the footsteps of a motherless and later an orphan child into beautiful girlhood, and then courtship, and into temple marriage. I once wrote of her:

"She has the key that unlocks many a child's heart. She has the ability to teach the teacher this secret. Her conversation with a child is beautiful to hear. Her skill and understanding are born of a lifetime of knowledge and application of child psychology. She is constantly reaching out to the child who is not understood."

Someone has said that not all teaching is done in the classroom. How true this is! A true teacher is always in character. Her students' eyes are always upon her. She is their teacher wherever they see her, though it is almost impossible in the brief minutes she has them in the classroom as a group for her to know them as individuals.

There is opposition everywhere in the world. ". . . even the forbidden fruit in opposition to the tree of life; the one being sweet and the other bitter. Wherefore, the Lord God gave unto man that he should act for himself. Wherefore, man could not act for himself save it should be that he was enticed by the one or the other." (2 Nephi 2:15-16.)

". . . lovest thou me? . . . Feed my sheep," were the words spoken by the resurrected Lord unto Peter. (John

133

21:16.) What a privilege is given to teachers called and set apart by those holding authority from Him: to feed His lambs! Blessed will be their lives, for, as President Clark said, "the love they win from them will be ample reward for their labors."

Yes, these teachers can bear witness to the truthfulness of that statement. Contacts begun in a small classroom may grow through the years into friendships that transcend teacher-student relationships. Rather, these friendships are nurtured through mutual love and understanding of each other and of the glorious gospel of Jesus Christ that first brought them together. Such are the ample rewards that come to those who accept the challenge: "And ye shall teach!"

In a lecture at a dinner club, a nationally known speaker concluded with three significant declarations to emphasize the work of a teacher:

> The teacher is the human sculptor whose business it is to mold the living clay.
>
> Young people are particularly malleable, and with proper teaching can be taught correct principles.
>
> If you want to change the face of the world, you must change the hearts of man. (Dr. Carl S. Winters, in *Salt Lake Tribune,* March 24, 1971.)

My prayer is for all teachers to sense the magnitude not only of the importance of their callings, but also of the great opportunities in improving the minds and the hearts of men as well.

# CHURCH HISTORY
# AND PROGRESS

# 17

# Strengthen the Stakes of Zion

In 1832, two years after the organization of the Church, the Prophet Joseph Smith received a revelation that today has even greater meaning, viewed in the light of the demands of the increasing membership in the Church. The revelation said: "For Zion must increase in beauty, and in holiness; her borders must be enlarged; her stakes must be strengthened; yea, verily I say unto you, Zion must arise and put on her beautiful garments." (D&C 82:14.)

As used here, Zion undoubtedly referred to the Church. At that time there was but a small body of members just beginning to emerge as an organization, after having experienced harsh treatment from enemies outside the Church. They had then been directed to gather together in Jackson County, Missouri, which the Lord had designated as the "land of Zion."

As though to impress upon these early struggling members their destiny in the world, the Lord in another revelation told them this: "Therefore, verily, thus saith the Lord, let Zion rejoice, for this is Zion—THE PURE IN HEART;

therefore, let Zion rejoice, while all the wicked shall mourn." (D&C 97:21.)

To be worthy of such a sacred designation as Zion, the Church must think of itself as a bride adorned for her husband, as John the Revelator recorded when he saw in vision the Holy City where the righteous dwelt, adorned as a bride for the Lamb of God. Here is portrayed the relationship the Lord desires in His people in order to be acceptable to our Lord and Master, even as a wife would adorn herself in beautiful garments for her husband.

The rule by which the people of God must live in order to be worthy of acceptance in the sight of God is indicated by the revelation found in the Doctrine and Covenants, section 82. This people must increase in beauty before the world and have an inward loveliness that may be observed by mankind as a reflection in holiness and in those inherent qualities of sanctity. The borders of Zion, where the righteous and pure in heart may dwell, must now begin to be enlarged; the stakes of Zion must be strengthened—all this so that Zion may arise and shine by becoming increasingly diligent in carrying out the plan of salvation throughout the world.

While the Church was in its infancy, the Lord pointed to a time when those earlier gathering places would not have room for all who would be gathered to unite His church. Here are His words: "For thus shall my church be called in the last days, even The Church of Jesus Christ of Latter-day Saints." And then this command: "Arise and shine forth, that thy light may be a standard for the nations." (D&C 115:4-5.)

Here is clearly inferred that the coming forth of His church in these days was the beginning of the fulfillment of the ancient prophecy when—

138

the mountain of the Lord's house shall be established in the top of the mountains and shall be exalted above the hills; and all nations shall flow unto it.

And many people shall go and say, Come ye, and let us go up to the mountain of the Lord, to the house of the God of Jacob; and he will teach us of his ways, and we will walk in his paths. (Isaiah 2:2-3.)

In these revelations the Lord speaks of organized units of the Church that are designated as stakes, each of which those not of our faith may think of as a diocese. These units so organized are gathered together for a defense against the enemies of the Lord's work, both the seen and the unseen.

The Apostle Paul said with reference to these enemies about which we should be concerned: "For we wrestle not against flesh and blood, but against principalities, against powers, against the rulers of the darkness of this world, against spiritual wickedness in high places." (Ephesians 6:12.)

In the preface to all the Lord's revelations that He gave from the beginning of this dispensation, He issued this fateful warning, which must never be absent from our minds. This prophetic warning of 1831 was given, as the Lord declared, so that "all men shall know that the day speedily cometh; the hour is not yet, but is nigh at hand, when peace shall be taken from the earth, and the devil shall have power over his own dominion." (D&C 1:35.)

Today we are witnessing the fury of this time, when Satan has power over his own dominion with such might that even the Master in His day referred to Him as the "prince of this world," the "enemy of all righteousness."

Despite these dire predictions and the evidences of their fulfillment before us, there is promised in this same revelation an even greater power to thwart Satan's plans to destroy the work of the Lord. The Lord makes this promise to the Saints of the most high God, the righteous in heart

139

to whom He has referred as "the people of Zion": "And also the Lord shall have power over his saints, and shall reign in their midst, and shall come down in judgment upon Idumea, or the world." (D&C 1:36.)

This has reference to the world in the same sense as when the Master spoke of the worldliness from which He warned His disciples, that while they would be engulfed in the world, they must keep themselves from the sins to be found therein.

I believe there has never been a time since the creation that the Lord has left the dominion of the devil to destroy His work without His power being manifest in the midst of the righteous to save the works of righteousness from being completely overthrown.

Today we are witnessing the demonstration of the Lord's hand in the midst of His saints, the members of the Church. Never in this dispensation, and perhaps never before in any single period, has there been such a feeling of urgency among the members of the Church as we find today. Her boundaries are being enlarged; her stakes are being strengthened. In the early years of the Church specific places to which the Saints were to be gathered together were given, and the Lord directed that these gathering places should not be changed, but then He gave one qualification: "Until the day cometh when there is found no more room for them; and then I have other places which I will appoint unto them, and they shall be called stakes, for the curtains or the strength of Zion." (D&C 101:21.)

At the Mexico City Area Conference in August 1972, Elder Bruce R. McConkie of the Council of the Twelve, in a thought-provoking address, made some comments pertinent to this subject, including the following:

Of this glorious day of restoration and gathering, another Nephite prophet said: "the Lord . . . has covenanted with all the house of Israel that 'the time comes that they shall be restored to the true church and fold of God'; and that 'they shall be gathered home to the lands of their inheritance, and shall be established in all their lands of promise.' " (2 Nephi 9:1-2.)

Now I call your attention to the facts set forth in these scriptures, that the gathering of Israel consists of joining the true church; of coming to a knowledge of the true God and of his saving truths; and of worshiping him in the congregations of the Saints in all nations and among all peoples. Please note that these revealed words speak of the folds of the Lord; of Israel being gathered to the lands of their inheritance; of Israel being established in all their lands of promise; and of there being congregations of the covenant people of the Lord in every nation, speaking every tongue, and among every people when the Lord comes again.

Elder McConkie then concluded with this statement, which certainly emphasizes the great need for the teaching and training of local leadership in order to build up the Church within their own native countries:

The place of gathering for the Mexican Saints is in Mexico; the place of gathering for the Guatemalan Saints is in Guatemala; the place of gathering for the Brazilian Saints is in Brazil; and so it goes throughout the length and breadth of the whole earth. Japan is for the Japanese; Korea is for the Koreans; Australia is for the Australians; every nation is the gathering place for its own people.

The most frequently asked question from inquirers is, "How do you account for the phenomenal growth of this church when so many others are on the decline?"

Among the primary and many other factors that account for the continued growth of the Church, I will mention only a few, for those who would ask this question to ponder.

No longer might this church be thought of as the "Utah church," or as an "American church," for the membership of the Church is now distributed over the earth in seventy-eight countries, teaching the gospel in seventeen different languages at the present time.

This greatly expanded church population is today our most challenging problem, and while we have cause for much rejoicing in such a widespread expansion, it does pose some great challenges to our leadership to keep pace with many problems.

Two basic principles have always guided the leaders of the Church in their planning to meet these circumstances. The first is the basic principle of the plan of salvation for the redemption of mankind, which has been revealed to the prophets of this dispensation and has not been changed from before the foundation of the world, for as the Apostle Paul declared in his day, so do we declare today:

> But though we, or an angel from heaven, preach any other gospel unto you than that which we have preached unto you, let him be accursed.
> But I certify you, brethren, that the gospel which was preached of me is not after man.
> For I neither received it of man, neither was I taught it, but by the revelation of Jesus Christ. (Galatians 1:8, 11-12.)

If we were to answer those who ask us about the steady growth, we would answer that we have held our course in teaching the fundamental doctrines of the Church. We declare in one of our Articles of Faith: "We believe [and, we might add, teach] all that God has revealed, all that He does now reveal, and we believe that He will yet reveal many great and important things pertaining to the Kingdom of God." (Article of Faith 9.)

In one of the latest of the Lord's revelations in this dispensation, He gave the reason for the confusion among the many churches then in existence: because they have, as He said,

> strayed from mine ordinances, and have broken mine everlasting covenant;
> They seek not the Lord to establish his righteousness, but every man walketh in his own way, and after the image of his own God, whose image is in the likeness of the world. (D&C 1:15-16.)

Therefore a new restoration was necessary, as He plainly declared:

Wherefore, I the Lord, knowing the calamity which should come upon the inhabitants of the earth, called upon my servant Joseph Smith, Jun., and spake unto him from heaven, and gave him commandments;

And also gave commandments to others, that they should proclaim these things unto the world; and all this that it might be fulfilled, which was written by the prophets—

But that every man might speak in the name of God the Lord, even the Savior of the world;

That the fulness of my gospel might be proclaimed by the weak and the simple unto the ends of the world, and before kings and rulers.

. . . after the manner of their language, that they might come to understanding. (D&C 1:17-18; 20, 23-24.)

There are those who speak of an ecumenical movement, in which theoretically, it is supposed, all churches would be brought together into a universal organization. In essence it probably would contemplate that they would give up their basic principles and be united in a nebulous organization that would not necessarily be founded on the principles as have traditionally been the doctrines of the church of Jesus Christ from the beginning.

When the revelations of the Lord are clearly understood, there is set forth the only basis of a united and universal church. It could not be accomplished as set forth by a man-made formula; it could only be accomplished when the fulness of the principles of the gospel of Jesus Christ are taught and practiced, as declared by the Apostle Paul to the Ephesians, who said that the church is "built upon the foundation of the apostles and prophets, Jesus Christ himself being the chief corner stone." (Ephesians 2:20.)

The mission of the Church has also been defined:

And the voice of warning shall be unto all people, by the mouths of my disciples, whom I have chosen in these last days.

143

Wherefore, the voice of the Lord is unto the ends of the earth, that all that will hear may hear. (D&C 1:4, 11.)

Obedient to that instruction, and from the beginning of the Church, we have had missionaries sent to all parts of the world. Today we have increasing numbers of missionaries, mostly younger men, most of whom have been schooled from their childhood to prepare themselves for a call to serve as missionaries.

From a handful of missionaries in the early days of the Church, this number has been increased to many thousands serving today, each at his own expense, or at the expense of his immediate family, for a period usually of two years, and each with a conviction in his heart that one so called has the divinity of his calling in his mind as he may go forth into any part of the world to which he may be called.

Another reason that might be given for the increase in the Lord's work: perhaps as never before have there been so many people of the world searching for answers to many perplexing problems.

While the principles of the gospel of Jesus Christ have not changed, the methods in meeting these challenges of the needs of today's world must respond to the demands of our time. Fortunately the Lord has given, in the revelations to this church, the guidelines by which we should respond to the demands of the times.

The plan of salvation has defined the way by which He would have us deal with the temporal needs of the people. Our welfare plan seeks out those in distress. Where the newly found members are located, the plan of temporal salvation is primarily intended to teach individuals how to take care of themselves. The Lord has provided a hedge against the terrifying impact upon the sanctity of the home and marriage by strengthening the home and by providing guidelines to parents to teach their children the basic principles of honesty, virtue, integrity, thrift, and industry.

There is concern in the Church for the individual members, from childhood to youth, and from youth into, adulthood.

In answer to questions as to whether or not there may have been any dropouts or members who have fallen away, our answer has always been to recall the Master's parable of the sower. When the sower went out to sow, some of the seeds fell on fertile ground, but among the seeds that fell on fertile ground, some produced thirtyfold, some sixtyfold, and some ninetyfold. So today, in about that same ratio, we have some who are partially active, some who are more so, and some who are thoroughly active in the Church; but we are always reaching out to the ones who have strayed away, and we are constantly trying to bring them back into full activity.

But perhaps the most important reason of all for the growth of the Church is the individual testimonies of the divinity of this work, as multiplied in the hearts of the individual members of the Church. Our strength is not in numbers nor in the magnitude of chapels and temple buildings, but because in the hearts of faithful members is found conviction that this is indeed the church and kingdom of God on the earth. Without that conviction, as one of my eminent business associates remarked, "The welfare plan of the Church would be but a shambles"; missionary work would not flourish; and members would not be faithful in making generous contributions to the Church to finance its many operations. The secret of the strength of this church may be found in the statement of the president of the student body at one of our state-    145 operated universities, whose identity, of course, is confidential. This is a quotation from his personal letter addressed to me:

> With the rule of the radical ideas which are sweeping the country, there has come a breakdown of family ties which is despised in many intellectual circles. The country is seemingly plied with sex education, abortion, planned parenthood, pornography, women's liberation, communal living, premarital sex, and postmarital permissiveness. . . .

And then this young college student leader concludes with this heartwarming declaration, which I know came from the depths of his soul:

> President Lee, I want you to know that the Latter-day Saint students on campus who keep the commandments are 100 percent behind you. Thank God we have leaders who stand firm against the subtle battle of the adversary who is striking at the home, the most vital unit of the world. Thank you for being the kind of person that we, as young people growing up in this mixed-up world, can understand and can follow.

By that same token, and in the language of that brilliant college student, I am convinced that the greatest of all the underlying reasons for the strength of the Church is that those who keep the commandments of God are 100 percent behind the leadership of the Church. Without that united support it would be readily understood that we could not go forward to meet the challenges of the day. Our call is for the total membership to keep the commandments of God, for therein lies the safety of the world. As one keeps the commandments of God, he is not only persuaded as to the righteousness of the course that is being followed under the leadership of the Church, but he also will have the Spirit of the Lord to guide him in his individual activities. The reason for this is that each baptized member has been given a sacred endowment when he was baptized, an endowment that is committed to every baptized member of the Church by the authority of the priesthood: the gift of the Holy Ghost, which, as the

146

Master declared, would teach all things, would bring all things to their remembrance, and would even show things to come. (See John 14:36.)

It will be clearly understood, then, that the great responsibility that the leaders and teachers in the Church have is to persuade, to teach, and to direct aright, that the commandments of Almighty God will be so lived as to prevent the individual from falling into the trap of the evil one who would persuade him not to believe in God and not to follow the leadership of the Church.

I bear my sacred witness that because I know of the divinity of this work, I know that it will prevail; and that though there may be enemies within and without the Church who would seek to find fault and try to undermine the influence of the Church in the world, the Church will stand through the test of time, when all the man-made efforts and weapons forged against the Lord's word will fall by the wayside. I know that our Lord and Master Jesus Christ is the head of the Church; that He has daily communion through agencies known to Him, not only with the leaders in high positions, but also with individual members as they keep the commandments of God.

# 18

# The Church
# in the Orient

W hen John the Baptist sent his disciples to Jesus, after he had received reports about the work of the Master, they came asking him, "Art thou he that should come? or look we for another?" Jesus told them to carry back to John the Baptist this answer: "Go your way, and tell John what things ye have seen and heard; how that the blind see, the lame walk, the lepers are cleansed, the deaf hear, the dead are raised, to the poor the gospel is preached." (Luke 7:20, 22.)

Today I testify, as the Master told the disciples to testify to John, that the miraculous power of divine intervention is among us, which is one of the signs of the divinity of the work of the Lord.

In recent weeks we have seen one "nigh unto death" raised miraculously; we have seen the hand of the Almighty stay the storms and the winds; and we have overcome obstacles that might have made impossible the fulfillment

Note: This chapter is adapted from a talk given by President Lee in general conference in October 1954 following a tour of the Far East.

of our mission. We have passed through danger-ridden areas only a few hundred miles from where war is brewing [in Korea]. We have seen the humble and the poor having the gospel preached to them. The signs of divinity are found in many areas of the world. The work of the Almighty is increasing with a tremendous surge.

Some years ago I read a statement in Parley P. Pratt's book *Key to the Science of Theology*. I wondered then at the meaning of this statement, and now I can humbly testify that it was a prophecy that is today being fulfilled:

Physically speaking, there seems to need but the consummation of two great enterprises more, in order to complete the preparations necessary for the fulfilment of Isaiah and other Prophets, in regard to the restoration of Israel to Palestine, from the four quarters of the earth . . . under the auspices of that great, universal and permanent theocracy which is to succeed the long reign of mystery.

Then he named two great enterprises: the Europe-to-Asia railroad, which was then in the process of being consummated, and the Great Western Railway from the Atlantic to the Pacific in the United States; and he said that "politically speaking, some barriers yet remain to be removed, and some conquests to be achieved, and the triumph of constitutional liberty among certain nations where mind, and thought, and religion are still prescribed by law." (Deseret Book Co., 1965.)

Sister Lee and I, with President and Sister Hilton A. Robertson, visited our native Saints and servicemen in Japan from Hokkaido on the north to Kyushu on the south. We then went to Korea, Okinawa, Hong Kong, the Philippines, and Guam. We met a total of 1563 Latter-day Saint boys in military service. They had arranged district conferences that simulated our stake conferences, and it was like holding a stake conference every other day all     149 through this trip, because of the thoroughness with which they had organized their work.

I have never listened to better sermons than I heard preached by our Latter-day Saint chaplains and group leaders there. They are studying the gospel. The excellence of their organization and the orderliness of their procedures is worthy of note. In every camp where we went, under military orders, we were accorded every privilege that could be accorded us. The first procedure was invariably an introduction to the commanding general of the camp and a brief interview, during which he extended to us all the courtesies of the camp, bade us welcome, and, in a number of instances, came to our meeting.

They know of our servicemen. They know of the work of the Latter-day Saints, and perhaps their attitude toward our men is best summed up in what General Richard S. Whitcomb said to us at Pusan, Korea:

> I have always known the members of your church to be a substantial people.
>
> Here in the Pusan area I have the largest court-martial responsibility of any command in the United States Army, but I have never had one of your faith brought before me for a court martial or disciplinary action, in this command. Wherever I have been, I have never known of a Latter-day Saint ever to be brought up for any disciplinary action.

On Guam, I was furnished with a little paper from the camp that indicated that for the month of August one of our boys there, Brother Douglas K. Eager, had been designated as the "Airman of the Month," and the citation read: "He won the award on the basis of his devotion to duty, character, appearance, industry, and military bearing."

One of the supervising chaplains at Clark Field in the Philippines said to me, as we walked out of a meeting with the Protestant chaplains on the base, "I have never known any group of men in my military experience who have greater devotion to their country, and to their God, and to their church—no finer characters than are to be found among the boys of the Latter-day Saints."

All through our visits, our men had arranged their own programs, and they sang three songs almost everywhere we went. They sang "We Thank Thee, O God, for a Prophet," and in every district conference they sustained the General Authorities of the Church. They also sang "Come, come, ye Saints, no toil nor labor fear/But with joy, wend your way. . . ." And finally, they sang about the hills of home, "O ye mountains high, where the clear blue sky/Arches over the vales of the free."

I think my appraisal of what I saw among the boys there might be expressed in what Ralph Waldo Emerson is quoted as having said: "It is easy in the world to live after the world's opinion. It is easy in solitude to live after one's own, but the great man is he, who in the midst of the crowd, keeps with perfect sweetness the independence of solitude." Such is the way I found our servicemen, with the marks of true greatness upon their brows, keeping "with perfect sweetness the independence of solitude."

From the contributions of our military men in the Far East, sufficient money is being raised each month to sustain many full-time missionaries from Japan who otherwise could not fill missions.

Directly as a result of the work of the Latter-day Saint servicemen, there have been dozens of converts. One Sunday at 6:30 in the morning, just at the break of day, in Seoul, Korea, we baptized a native Korean student and a young serviceman. At Clark Field another Sunday morning we baptized four persons, including a young native Filipino mother, who later bore her testimony in the conference session.

What this means to servicemen as they come into the Church is perhaps best expressed in a humble testimony from a young seaman who came to Tokyo from the aircraft carrier *Hornet,* which had docked at Yokohama. He came to us at the close of the meeting in Tokyo, his arm in a sling, and explained that he had a badly infected arm. As he shook hands with me, he said, "I am getting ready to be baptized a member of the Church, and if we are down at Manila when I meet you there, I hope to tell you that I have been baptized."

At Manila he came, his arm now perfectly healed, and said, "I was baptized on August 27. Something happened to me after I left that conference in Tokyo. My arm was swollen and was painful all through the meeting, but after I had shaken hands with you, I got on the train going back to the boat. Suddenly the pain ceased, my arm was healed, and now I am going back to that lovely wife who has been praying that I would straighten my life. I smoked, and I drank, and I did a lot of things to cause her sorrow, and I am going back to that sweetheart of mine, and I am going to spend the rest of my life trying to prove myself worthy of her love." His faith had brought healing to his body and his soul. That is what the gospel meant to this seaman who became a convert to the gospel of Jesus Christ.

We met young men who are homesick for home. How they are thinking about their mothers and their wives and sweethearts is suggested by the fact that when Sister Lee spoke, they would ofttimes come up at the close of services and say, "We really appreciated Sister Lee's talk," and they gathered around her because she was a touch of mother. They would tell her how she reminded them of their mothers. She was the symbol of the home to which they hoped to return.

152         Perhaps what our men are doing in the Orient can

best be illustrated in what Elder Aki, a young Japanese missionary at beautiful Nikko, a recipient of the missionary contributions of our servicemen, said as he bore his testimony in English: "As terrible as was war in Japan, it proved a great blessing, because as a result, it brought the Latter-day Saint servicemen back to Japan and paved the way for the reopening of the Japanese Mission."

One of the things that was startling to me—and significant—pertains to the languages there. The Lord is seemingly helping us even to solve that problem. Since American troops came in, every school in Japan and in Korea is teaching English, and most of those young students who are being attracted by the gospel can speak some English. They are helping to break down language barriers and making easier the work of the missionaries.

At Osaka where we had 179 in attendance, I looked over that audience and tried to estimate the ages of those in attendance; I would say that there were fewer than 16 who were over 30 years of age. What these young people will do in aiding in that conversion is best illustrated by two incidents.

Some time ago while I was in the Hawaiian Islands I interviewed and set apart, under instructions from the First Presidency, six lovely young girls to go to Japan as missionaries. One of them, a young Japanese sister, was a bit hesitant to go because she came from a Buddhist family. Her mother had opposed her going, and her brother had beaten her rather cruelly because of her insistence on Church activity. She was almost a nervous wreck, but she had the faith that somehow the Lord would help her through her problems, and we sent her on her way.

I met her at one of these conferences, and she whispered to me her story. She said: "Twenty-three people, 153

Brother Lee, are being attracted to the gospel partly by my efforts," and then she introduced me to an elderly grandmother whose husband is an Episcopal minister. The young granddaughter of this elderly grandmother was the one who played for our singing during the conference. She came home after she had joined the Church and said to her grandmother, "Grandma, your church is not true because you do not understand God, and you do not understand about the Godhead," and she then proceeded to teach her the missionary lesson about the Godhead. This elderly grandmother said, "Any church that can teach a child like that must have something."

Our young Japanese missionary sister from the Hawaiian Islands then reported that the grandmother was preparing to become baptized a member of the Church through the missionary efforts of her little granddaughter, who is perhaps not more than eleven or twelve years of age.

There is another evidence of an awakening in Japan. Representatives of some of the leading newspapers in Japan, many of them, interviewed us and wrote articles both in English and in Japanese. Our Japanese Saints were a bit amused about one of these articles, in which the heading was "Mormon Polygamist Visits Japan." Fortunately the misleading statement was corrected in the body of the article. Following that announcement we received an invitation from a group who styled themselves "The League of New Japan's Religious Organizations," who claim to have a following of ten million people. For the first time Japan is enjoying religious freedom. They asked that I meet the fifteen leaders of the fifteen religious organizations that comprise the league, and talk with them about Mormonism and then submit to a discussion.

Their invitation is a bit interesting. It reads:

Invitation to the friendly talk meeting with one of the leaders of the "Mormon" Church. As Rev. Harold B. Lee who is one of the highest leaders of "Mormon Church" (The Church of Jesus Christ of Latter-day Saints) which is one of the most influential churches in America, is visiting Japan on his journey to fulfil his mission in the Pacific Ocean area. In order to promote good will we would like to hold a friendly talk meeting. . . . Also, paying respect to the laws of Mormonism no refreshment of tea or cake will be served at that meeting.

For that hour, with Brother Tatsui Sato from the mission office translating my words, they listened. None of these men claimed to be Christians, and yet in the discussion that followed I learned that they were in truth more Christian than many of the so-called Christians who accept neither the divinity of the mission of Jesus nor his reality as the Son of the living God.

They recorded my talk, and when the half hour for discussion was over, they were still asking questions, so our interview extended into two and a half hours. I told them that if they were interested and would send me their names and addresses, I would see that each got a copy of the Book of Mormon for them to study.

A few days later I received a letter in Japanese, which Brother Sato translated; in the letter the president of the group gave me a list of names and addresses. His letter read:

We have no words to express our thanks for your very instructive address, which you gave us the other day. Although you were very busy and must have been tired on your way to preach the gospel in the Oriental area, yet you shared your very precious time for us, for which we have to be very grateful.

May we take advantage of your words that you would present us the Book of Mormon that we may understand better? We send you the list of names who attended the meeting.

Copies of the Book of Mormon have been sent to these people.

At Pusan, where we had only three members on record, we found to our astonishment that we had in attendance at our meeting not just three members in addition to more than 100 LDS servicemen, but we also had 103 Koreans, mostly young people of about high school age. As a part of the proceedings they presented to me a scroll, written and presented by a group composed primarily of nonmembers:

> We sincerely welcome Apostle Harold B. Lee who come to Korea. The mission of his visiting Korea is very important and we are thankful to our Father in heaven from our heart deeply for the great support you have given us for the people of Korea.
>
> Here we would like to express our gratitude to the soldiers who stayed in Korea, and preached the true gospel to us, and also the chance we have had of gathering together with them under the name of our Heavenly Father; therefore we are under a vow to repay their kindness. With thanks with all of our eulogy to you for your distinguished service of the faithfulness which will perform your important mission to come our Korea. And visiting our Korea in spite of it is long distance. We humbly pray in the name of Jesus Christ, A Men. From: Korean Group in Pusan of the Church of Jesus Christ of Latter-day Saints.

In Hong Kong we had no meeting place, but in our hotel room overlooking the harbor from Kowloon to Hong Kong, we held a sacrament meeting. We bore testimony to those in attendance. We had gone up to that high point overlooking Hong Kong where Elder Matthew Cowley and a group of Saints had dedicated that land to the preaching of the gospel, on July 14, 1949. There we too bowed our heads and thanked the Lord for the degree of Brother Cowley's blessing that had been received, and asked the Lord for a further outpouring of his blessing.

Afterwards we visited briefly with some young Chinese students, one of whom was a young girl, Yook Sin Yuen—they call her Nora—a beautiful little girl who speaks good English, taught to her by the missionaries. As our bus was leaving the hotel the next day to take us to the airport, she reached up her hand through the window and said to me, "Apostle Lee, tell President McKay to please send the Church back to China." And I said to her, as tears welled up in my eyes, "My dear sweet girl, as long as we have a faithful, devoted band like you who, without a shepherd, are remaining true, the Church is in China."

We have seen how the gospel has been preached to these wonderful people as an evidence of its divinity. God grant that the time shall not be far distant until the death grip of Communism shall be unloosed, and those peoples shall be free to receive in fulness the gospel of Jesus Christ, for I am convinced that there are hundreds of thousands of souls there who are longing for the truth.

# 19

# The Work in Great Britain

Some of the most soul-stirring incidents and experiences in the history of missionary work in this dispensation occurred in the midlands of Great Britain, in Preston. The first missionaries there were submitted to one of the greatest demonstrations of the power of evil spirits perhaps ever experienced by anyone. Brother Heber C. Kimball, Elder Willard Richards, Elder Orson Hyde, and Elder Isaac Russell had, for an hour and a half, as they timed the experience, an awful demonstration of that power.

President Heber C. Kimball, in writing about it afterward, said: "I cannot even look back on the scene without feelings of horror; yet by it I learned the power of the adversary, his enmity against the servants of God, and got some understanding of the invisible world." (Orson F. Whitney, *Life of Heber C. Kimball,* Deseret Book Co., second ed., 1945, pp. 130-31.)

When he returned home, he asked the Prophet Joseph what was the matter with them that they had to be subjected to such an experience, and the Prophet surprised them when he said something to this effect: "When I heard of [your experience], it gave me joy, for I then knew that the work of God had taken root in that land." Then he related some of his own experiences and made this significant statement: "The nearer a person approaches the Lord, a greater power will be manifested by the adversary to prevent the accomplishment of His purposes." (Ibid., p. 132.)

I have no doubt that the Prophet had in mind the terrifying experience he had in the grove when he prayed for light and was seized upon by this power until he was released therefrom by the coming of the Father and the Son. He no doubt had in mind the experiences when he first went to see the plates, when, as he sought to receive them, he again saw a demonstration of the evil powers.

We were permitted, as we traveled in that same vicinity in England, to follow the course that Wilford Woodruff was directed under inspiration to go, from the potteries near Hanley down to Froomes Hill, probably some fifty or sixty miles to the south, where, directed by the Spirit, he found a people ready to receive the coming of the servants of the Lord. Within two days after his arrival there, after having met John Benbow and his wife and those who were affiliated with a sect called the United Brethren, he baptized six members; and in thirty days he had baptized forty-five preachers of the United Brethren and 160 members, and had obtained the possession of one chapel and forty-five houses for use as meeting places. In eight months he had baptized over 1800—including all but one of the 600 members of the United Brethren—and 200 ministers of various denominations in the area.

As a true missionary would do, without boasting he wrote this simple summary: "The power of God rested upon us and upon the mission in our field of labor. . . . The

159

sick were healed, devils were cast out, and the lame made to walk."

The work of these first missionaries was not without opposition, and later in an article in the *Times and Seasons* they related the following about the work around Liverpool: "They [the ministers] were so good in general and so pure that they had no room for the gospel. They were too holy to be righteous, too good to be pure, and had too much religion to enter into the Kingdom of Heaven." And then they added, "It seemed that it almost required a horn to be blown from the highest heavens, in order to awaken the attention of the people." (*Times and Seasons,* vol. 2, p. 404.)

I thought of that experience when, after elaborate arrangements had been made by President T. Bowring Woodbury of the British Mission for all the publicity possible, through the great news-gathering wire services throughout the world, to get a full coverage of the organization of a stake in Manchester, to find the next day, in an obscure place in one of the two Manchester papers, this brief reference to our missionary conference at which we created this stake and organized a new mission:

> British Mormons formed their first diocese in Europe yesterday at a mass meeting of more than 2000 members of the Church of the Latter-day Saints in Manchester, the new center to be built without delay at Wythenshawe, Manchester, at a cost of about 100,000 pounds. The diocese, or stake, covers Manchester, Halifax, Huddersfield, Dewsbury, and Leeds. (Manchester *Guardian.*)

In one year, 1840 to 1841—one year and fourteen days, to be exact—nine members of the Twelve were called to labor in the British Mission. At home, those years marked the period of some of the severest persecution that the Church was to undergo in this dispensation. In that one year and fourteen days the nine members of the

Twelve, with their associates, established churches in every important town and city in the kingdom of Great Britain. They baptized between 7,000 and 8,000 converts. They printed 5,000 copies of the Book of Mormon, 3,000 hymnbooks, and 50,000 tracts, and they published 2,500 volumes of the *Millennial Star* and directed the emigration of 1,000 souls to America.

These figures of the missionary work in Great Britain might give you something of an idea of what has happened in the past century and a quarter in that great country. Between 1849 and 1851 over 8,000 baptisms were performed in each year, or approximately 1,000 converts for each missionary for each of those years. The total number of converts from 1837, when the work was first started, until the end of 1959 totaled 136,026. The recorded number of emigrants during that same period was 57,159, and we have reason to believe that thousands of others emigrated without any record being made.

Twelve of our General Authorities have been British-born. It was the estimate of Elder Richard L. Evans, who wrote an excellent history of the Church in Great Britain during the first one hundred years, that a large percent of the total membership of the Church today trace their genealogy to Great Britain.

By assignment of the First Presidency, on Sunday, March 27, 1960, we organized the Manchester Stake with a total membership of 2400 members—the first stake in Great Britain.

It was interesting to discover that the leadership of the stake and wards and the branches was largely composed of brethren who were baptized converts to the Church of less than five years. This stake has become a training ground for leaders of organizations yet to come.

This stake [and other stakes organized in the British  161

Isles since] brings the full Church program into action, as a demonstration to the world to "shine forth" as a "standard for the nations," showing the work of the Church at full flower. Zion, which the Lord declared is "the pure in heart" in Great Britain now, will "increase in beauty, and in holiness." Zion is beginning to "arise and put on her beautiful garments." (See D&C 115:5; 82:14; 97:21.)

In truth, then, it now begins to build "a defense, . . . a refuge from the storm, and from wrath when it [is] poured out without mixture upon the whole earth" (D&C 115:6), which, as the Lord declared, was the purpose of a stake being organized. The power of God is resting again in the missions of Europe today, as in the century that has passed.

# 20

# The Spirit of Gathering

Some time ago there appeared in a local newspaper an account of an interview with an elderly statesman who wielded great influence in American politics. This elderly statesman, in explaining the reason for his determination and zeal, told of a statement his own father—now long since dead—had made to his four sons just before he died. This is what the father said: "America, with its government and constitution, is the greatest insitution invented by the mind of man. If you let them touch a stick or stone of it, I will come back and haunt you."

As I thought of that statement, my mind went back to our ancestors who pioneered in this dispensation an even greater constitution than that of the American nation, even the constitution of the kingdom of God, which might be said to be another definition of the gospel of Jesus Christ. As I thought of our pioneers, I was reminded of their virtues and their accomplishments and of the underlying principles that made them willing to leave all that they possessed and even willing to sacrifice their lives, if need be, to uphold and to maintain their beliefs. As I remembered that and thought of the statement of this aged American patriot, I wondered if we might not say: "The Lord help us to keep in memory our ancestors that we might be willing to uphold and sustain, by our lives and all that we possess, that for which they gave so much."

In every gospel dispensation the Lord has invoked, by command, the great principle of gathering. The first reference we have in the revelations to gatherings of the Lord's faithful people was that spoken of when Adam gathered together his seven righteous sons, from Seth to Methuselah, and all of their posterity in the valley of Adam-ondi-Ahman, and there he gave them his last blessing and prepared them for the appearance of the Lord, which they received at that time.

I have thought it more than mere coincidence that one of the first martyrs in this dispensation, David W. Patten, a member of the Council of the Twelve Apostles, lost his life near the valley of Adam-ondi-Ahman, that same valley in which Adam had gathered his posterity. The Lord had revealed to the Prophet Joseph Smith that this valley was near Wight's Ferry, at a place called Spring Hill, Daviess County, Missouri. To me it has also been significant that this martyrdom resulted directly from the obedience of the Latter-day Saints to the commands that had been given to them to gather in certain places as members of the newly restored church.

The Master lamented, just before His crucifixion, "O Jerusalem, Jerusalem, thou that killest the prophets, and stonest them which are sent unto thee, how often would I have gathered thy children together, even as a hen gathereth her chickens under her wings, and ye would not." (Matthew 23:37.)

Apparently the Master was referring to the repeated

revelations He had given to the prophets from Adam down to His time, in which He had told of not only the scattering of the children of Israel, but also of a subsequent gathering. To Jeremiah He had promised, "I will take you one of a city, and two of a family, and I will bring you unto Zion: And I will give you pastors according to mine heart, which shall feed you with knowledge and understanding." (Jeremiah 3:14-15.)

To Ezekiel He said: "And I will bring you out from the people, and will gather you out of the countries wherein ye are scattered, with a mighty hand, and with a stretched out arm, and with fury poured out. And I will bring you into the wilderness of the people, and there will I plead with you face to face." (Ezekiel 20:34-35.)

An apt description of those who would be gathered thus, by command of the Lord, is given in the parable of the Master, when He said that "the kingdom of heaven is like unto a net, that was cast into the sea, and gathered of every kind: Which, when it was full, they drew to shore, and sat down, and gathered the good into vessels, but cast the bad away." (Matthew 13:47-48.)

In this dispensation, the first command to gather was within six months after the Church was organized. The Prophet Joseph Smith, in announcing this revelation, made this significant declaration as recorded in the *History of the Church:* "We soon found that Satan had been lying in wait to deceive, and seeking whom he might devour." (*DHC,* vol. 1, p. 109.)

The meaning of that revelation and the purpose of it all was explained in these words:

And ye are called to bring to pass the gathering of mine elect; for mine elect hear my voice and harden not their hearts;

Wherefore the decree hath gone forth from the Father that they shall be gathered in unto one place upon the face of this land, to prepare their hearts and to be prepared in all things against the day when tribulation and desolation are sent forth upon the wicked.

For the hour is nigh and the day soon at hand when the earth is ripe; and all the proud and they that do wickedly shall be as stubble; and I will burn them up, saith the Lord of Hosts, that wickedness shall not be upon the earth. (D&C 29:7-9.)

Three years later the Lord again spoke upon this subject: "Behold, it is my will, that all they who call on my name, and worship me according to mine everlasting gospel, should gather together, and stand in holy places." (D&C 101:22.)

Thus, the Lord has said plainly to His saints that the gathering was to prepare their hearts "according to the everlasting gospel," and to be prepared in all things by standing in holy places.

Six years after the Church was organized, the keys of gathering were committed to Joseph Smith and Oliver Cowdery in the Kirtland Temple. The record of that marvelous restoration is given in these words: "After this vision closed, the heavens were again opened unto us; and Moses appeared before us, and committed unto us the keys of the gathering of Israel from the four parts of the earth, and the leading of the ten tribes from the land of the north." (D&C 110:11.)

The spirit of gathering has been with the Church from the days of that restoration. Those who are of the blood of Israel have a righteous desire, after they are baptized, to gather together with the body of the Saints at the designated place. This, we have come to recognize, is but the breath of God upon those who are converted, turning them to the promises made to their fathers.

The designation of gathering places is qualified in another revelation by the Lord. After designating certain places in that day where the Saints were to gather, the Lord said: "Until the day cometh when there is found no more room for them; and then I have other places which I will appoint unto them. . . ." (D&C 101:21.)

Thus, the Lord has clearly placed the responsibility for directing the work of gathering in the hands of the leaders of the Church, to whom He will reveal His will where and when such gatherings would take place in the future. It would be well, before the frightening events concerning the fulfillment of all God's promises and predictions are upon us, that the Saints in every land prepare themselves and look forward to the instruction that shall come to them from the First Presidency of this church as to where they shall be gathered. They should not be disturbed in their feelings until such instruction is given to them as it is revealed by the Lord to the proper authority.

Again, in 1838, the Lord gave a further reason for the gathering: "Verily I say unto you all: Arise and shine forth, that thy light may be a standard for the nations; And that the gathering together upon the land of Zion, and upon her stakes, may be for a defense, and for a refuge from the storm, and from wrath when it shall be poured out without mixture upon the whole earth." (D&C 115:5-6.)

Why was this to be called a "place of refuge" and a "place of safety"? Said the Lord in another revelation: "And the glory of the Lord shall be there, and the terror of the Lord also shall be there, insomuch that the wicked will not come unto it, and it shall be called Zion." (D&C 45:67.)

The time when these events shall occur would be, as the Lord said, when "the wicked shall slay the wicked, and fear shall come upon every man; And the saints also shall hardly escape; nevertheless, I, the Lord, am with them, and

167

will come down in heaven from the presence of my Father and consume the wicked with unquenchable fire." (D&C 63:33-34.)

Another and further reason for the gathering is given us with this revelation:

> Wherefore, seeing that I, the Lord, have decreed all these things upon the face of the earth, I will that my saints should be assembled upon the land of Zion;
>
> And that every man should take righteousness in his hands and faithfulness upon his loins, and lift a warning voice unto the inhabitants of the earth; and declare both by word and by flight that desolation shall come upon the wicked. (D&C 63:36-37.)

Today we should be mindful of the fact that we are those of whom these revelations have spoken. We are those who have been gathered from out of spiritual Babylon, or perhaps we represent the second or third or even the fourth or fifth generation of those who heeded the call and felt the spirit of gathering. Just as was the case in the days of the Prophet Joseph Smith, so in our day the leaders of the Church have told us that "Satan has been lying in wait to deceive, and seeking whom he might devour."

As I have thought about these scriptures, I have been sobered by the realization that during my lifetime three presidents of the Church have spoken upon those dangers within the Church that are seeking to destroy us and to defeat the purpose of our gathering.

It was President Joseph F. Smith who said:

> There are at least three dangers that threaten the Church within, and the authorities need to awaken to the fact that the people should be warned unceasingly against them. As I see these, they are flattery of prominent men in the world, false educational ideas, and sexual impurity.
>
> But the third subject mentioned—personal purity, is perhaps of greater importance than either of the other two. We believe in one standard of morality for men and women. If purity of life is neglected, all other dangers set in upon us like the rivers of waters when the flood gates are opened. (*Gospel Doctrine,* Deseret Book Co., 1959, pp. 312-13.)

It was President Grant who, during his declining years, repeatedly urged the Latter-day Saints to keep God's commandments, time and again impressing upon us that there was no greater mission for him to perform, as the President of the Church, than to so warn the Latter-day Saints. By divine inspiration, he directed a movement to build brotherhood in this day, designed to foster the greatest security possible in this material world, the Church welfare program.

President George Albert Smith repeatedly counseled the authorities of the Church and the membership of the Church of the dangers that are confronting the homes of our people: the carelessness of marriage out of the Church and out of the temple; the lack of the sanctity of marriage; the lack of an understanding of the sanctity of the marriage covenant; the increase of divorce among us; the failure to hold sacred the covenants we have made in the house of the Lord. Well might we remember the warning of the Lord to John the Revelator when he said: "Behold, I come as a thief. Blessed is he that watcheth, and keepeth his garments, lest he walk naked, and they see his shame." (Revelation 16:15.)

As I think of the counsel of these leaders, I am reminded of a story told of the president of one of the great universities in Nova Scotia who called his representatives to him and sent them out to teach a great principle to the humble fishermen of that land. His parting counsel to them was: "If you want to educate a man, you have to let him see a ghost."

May the Latter-day Saints be haunted, if it need be, by the memory of those who pioneered the work of gathering in this dispensation, and be haunted by the memory of the teachings and work of Adam and Moses; of Joseph Smith and Brigham Young and others of the prophets. And may the Saints be haunted too by the purposes for which the gospel has been restored, which the Lord told us in His preface to the revelations was because He knew the calamities which were about to come forth upon the children of men.

May we, as a people, see the "ghost" of our possibilities and that which we might be able to accomplish by our own strength and ability to stir us up to deeds of righteousness and to build a greater brotherhood to provide that defense against the evils which threaten to destroy our homes today.

May we do all this in preparation for the coming of the Son of Man, which, I pray God, may not be long delayed. God speed us in that preparation while it is yet day, and increase within us the testimony of the divinity of the work in which we are engaged. And as we may live in the day when the terrors and trials and struggles, all foretold by the prophets, come to pass when "fear shall come upon every man" (D&C 63:33), and when it shall seem that there is no place safe upon the earth, may the Latter-day Saints who are living the commandments of God be comforted again by those words with which the Master has comforted those who have lived before us in similar times: Be humble, and the Lord will take you by the hand, as it were, and give you answer to your prayers. (See D&C 112:10.) "Be still, and know that I am God." (Proverbs 46:10.) I bear solemn witness that I know these teachings by the prophets are true. I know that those who have counseled us in our day of the dangers that are before us have spoken as the prophets of the living God.

*Section Five*

# DUTY TO
# COUNTRY

# 21

# True Patriotism—An Expression of Faith

On July 4 the American people celebrate the anniversary of the signing of the immortal documents that declared to the world the independence of this nation and the inalienable right of all men to enjoy life, liberty, and the pursuit of happiness; and to preserve these rights, "governments are instituted among men, deriving their just powers from the consent of the governed. . . ." (Declaration of Independence, July 4, 1776.)

Also during this month, on July 24, the citizens of the State of Utah and all members of The Church of Jesus Christ of Latter-day Saints celebrate the anniversary of the entrance of the pioneers into Salt Lake Valley in 1847.

These anniversaries have particular significance to the pioneers and their descendants. These pioneers had faith in the future of America. They had an understanding of the sacred obligations and responsibilities God has imposed upon those who enjoy the blessings of this great land. To their children who form the membership of the Church, they have transmitted the sacred writings that foretold the destiny of America. What is more important, they bequeathed the testimony of their lives as an example of true patriotism, which was an expression of the faith they possessed.

A pronouncement of the faith and understanding of the Latter-day Saints concerning the destiny of this land of America comes at a time when it may not be easy for those without this understanding to have full faith and confidence in the future of our democracy. We in America have viewed great depressions; we remember the armies of the unemployed and restless who have frequently raised strange flags of sedition above fearful masses of people. Our anxiety has been increased when we have listened to the attempts of men in high stations to stir up class hatreds that contradict the age-old constitutional guarantee of free enterprise. We have looked over our broad land at clouds of dust from drought-stricken areas, at abandoned mines and factories, and have pondered the effects of public relief and doles that have resulted therefrom. We have observed ominous and frightening defense against the ugly monster of dictatorship that threatens to engulf the world.

These and other similar conditions indicate to the thinking person a day of reckoning that may result in near-chaotic conditions that God in His mercy may not turn aside from us. Indeed, it has been said by a prophet in our generation that the time would come when the destiny of this nation would hang as by a single thread, but that it would be saved by the people who possessed faith in America and in her destiny.

And what is to be that destiny? It is the patriotism possessed by this people and an expression of their faith in the promises of the Lord concerning the place that this great country and its people may occupy in the moving drama of God's dealings with men and nations. We Latter-day Saints believe that we have come to a time when we need to do more to demonstrate our patriotism than merely wave the flag and doff our hats at its passing and join lustily in singing the strains of patriotic songs. We believe that the American people must subscribe to a patriotism born of an understanding of the ultimate destiny of this land. Let us inquire briefly into some of these teachings and promises upon which our faith and patriotism were founded.

To the pioneers of 1847, this land of America was to be a choice land above all other lands as an inheritance to the faithful of the Lord. It was to be a land of liberty upon which no king should ever rule. It would be so fortified against all other nations that whosoever would raise up a king or would fight against this nation should perish, because the Lord, the king of heaven, was to be their king. (See 2 Nephi 10:10-14.)

To them, this was the land of Zion, a land of peace, a city of refuge, a place of safety.

There would come a time when every man who would not "take his sword against his neighbor must needs flee" (D&C 45:68) to this country for safety. To this promised land men were to be gathered out of every nation under heaven. In a time when war would be waged abroad, this, the American people, would be the only people that would not be at war one with another. So strongly fortified should this land be that among the wicked it would be said, "Let us not go up to battle against Zion, for the inhabitants of Zion are terrible; wherefore we cannot stand." (See D&C 45:66-70.)

It was also here on this, the American continent, that the New Jerusalem spoken of in the holy scriptures was to be built, and a holy temple would be reared where the Savior of the world was to appear to usher in His millen-

175

nial reign. In the tops of these everlasting hills, the mountain of the Lord's house would be established, to which many would come to learn of His ways and to walk in His paths. From here, the land of Zion, the law was to go forth to the world. (See Isaiah 2:2-3.)

To the membership of The Church of Jesus Christ of Latter-day Saints, the Constitution of the United States is as a tree of liberty under whose cooling branches one might find a haven from the scorching sun of turmoil and oppression and have his rights protected according to just and holy principles. To them, the Constitution was established by the hands of wise men whom God raised up for this very purpose, and they devoutly believe that if it should be in danger of being overthrown, their lives, if need be, are to be offered in defense of its principles. (See D&C 101:77-80.)

What wonder, then, that with this sublime faith in America and this understanding of her future destiny, the intrepid, reverent band that entered the Salt Lake Valley in 1847 should have first hoisted on a topmost peak of the valley the flag of the United States, and that written into their basic doctrines was the declaration that "we believe in being subject to kings, presidents, rulers, and magistrates, in obeying, honoring, and sustaining the law" (Article of Faith 12), to attest to their faith in the divine decrees of God concerning this nation. Indeed, they believed and taught that "no man [should] break the laws of the land, for he that keepeth the laws of God hath no need to break the laws of the land" (D&C 58:21); that "governments were instituted of God for the benefit of man; and that he holds men accountable for their acts in relation to them, both in making laws and administering them, for the good and safety of society" (D&C 134:1), and that thus should men rule "until [the Master] reigns whose

176

right it is to reign, and subdues all enemies under his feet" (D&C 58:22).

It is not surprising that as a result of such teachings there should have been developed in the communities fostered by the pioneers a sincerity of purpose and a patriotic loyalty to government that was to stand as a pattern for generations yet unborn to follow.

Let us analyze a typical community built by these people where this practical patriotism was demonstrated so clearly. We will take for our example the first settlement in southern Idaho; the time, 1860. Thirteen families comprising this new settlement faced the usual privations and obstacles of those western frontier days. One historian records three kinds of pests with which they were afflicted—Indians, grasshoppers, and hypocrites. In this pioneer history is recorded in detail, and sometimes humorously, how they successfully overcame these obstacles, human and otherwise. Nine years after the beginning of this community a pioneer newspaper editor named five main characteristics, and his description might well have been used as a fitting epitaph to have been inscribed on a future monument in memory of those early builders.

First, every family in the community had available for its study the official publication printed and circulated under the direction of the pioneer leaders. This publication served both as a newspaper and as a medium through which they obtained the counsel and instructions from their leaders whose utterances they considered inspired and of unquestioned wisdom. From its pages they were able to satisfy in part their desire for knowledge and learning.

Second, they had the reputation for paying their debts promptly.

Third, they were public-spirited, as evidenced by the fact that in the nine years since their settlement they had

177

built a fort as a protection, a school, a church, a cooperative store, a post office with pony express routes to other communities, a sawmill, a telegraph, and a brass band.

Fourth, the man who had been named as their leader, or bishop, as he was called, had so distinguished himself as to be given the title "a working bishop." Of him it was said he worked until he was tired, then rested by changing jobs.

Fifth, they did not forget their poor.

There you have a formula and an incontestable index of a progressive, patriotic people. They were courageously in search of truth; they had honor and integrity; they were industrious and thrifty; they were led by men of good example; and they were charitable.

Indeed, in their teachings and by their example they had fathered a new concept of religion and patriotism. For them a place in the celestial world could be won not merely by *being* good, but by *doing* good. Every man was to exercise his agency in choosing his own course and was "free to choose liberty and eternal life, through the great mediation of all men, or to choose captivity and death, according to the captivity . . . of the devil." (2 Nephi 2:27.)

Likewise, true patriotism was not merely refraining from breaking the law, but was to be evidenced by a constant and courageous effort on the part of each to render service to his community and to his fellowmen. No man was to construe freedom as his right "to exercise control or dominion or compulsion upon the souls of the children of men, in any degree of unrighteousness. . . ." (D&C 121:37.)

I fear we have traveled a long way from that pioneer day when it was considered a patriotic duty to be self-sustaining; when it was considered a Christian responsibility to help others to be likewise able to live by their own efforts and not be dependent upon some public agency for

178

sustenance. We have come to a time when some seem to feel that because they have paid taxes in the past, now the government is obligated to care for them in idleness. We are also aware today that many of those with means have the feeling that they have discharged their full duty toward the unfortunate when their annual taxes are paid.

It is indeed a sad commentary on the loyalty and devotion of the citizens of the United States to those early American ideals if we have come to a time when it is thought that the distressed should look to a paternalistic agency rather than to their own for help in time of need; when it is expected that the cost of calamities must be compensated by the government or by some other agency. I fail to find in such attitudes of dependence on the government, which means an increasing burden of taxation, any show of patriotism and loyalty to this nation that characterized those who pioneered this great country. The first real step toward self-sufficiency and true patriotism is taken when a man resolves in his heart not only to be self-sustaining and independent, but also to aid others to be likewise.

In commenting on the results of a survey made a few years ago that revealed the present-day trends of the thinking of many, a nationally known writer declared, "The escape from a personal and moral obligation which this trend represents could only occur in a society which lacked religious convictions and principles. . . . Like the disciples who wanted to send the hungry multitude elsewhere, the voters hope to escape responsibility for the unemployed."

The descendants of the early Utah pioneers are sincere in their convictions that the economic problems of this great democracy, or of any other nation, for that matter, will not be solved by some "cure-all" or patented panacea or by wild schemes of a socialistic nature, but only by the

179

application of the same principles and practices that have made this a "land of the free, and the home of the brave."

Oh, that all men who are citizens of this favored land could learn the lessons taught by their noble ancestors and could understand that our inheritance in this land of liberty is not merely liberty and freedom that are bequeathed to us without effort on our part, even as the air we breathe. The only true inheritance we have from our pioneer heritage is the knowledge and understanding that the basic principles of courage, honesty, integrity, virtue, and charity are the verities that have made men free. In our veins runs the blood of a virile ancestry, and in our sinews their strength that gives to us, as their descendants, the will to do and the capacity to achieve, even as they have achieved.

We believe that no American citizen who has the same faith as those early pioneers can be true to the teachings handed down to them without having a love for this country and its institutions. In this land, we, together with all those who form the citizenship of this country, are dwelling "in the secret place of the most High" and in "the shadow of the Almighty." (Psalm 91:1.)

But the fulfillment of all these promises of the Lord concerning this land and its people was to be predicated upon just one condition, namely, that those who dwell upon this land should worship the God of the land, even Jesus Christ, our Lord. In this event, the nation possessing it should be free from bondage and captivity. Failing in their obedience to God's divine command, they would be swept off when the fulness of his wrath would come upon them because of their repeated iniquities.

Through the prophet Isaiah the time was foretold when God would "judge among the nations, and . . . rebuke many people." (Isaiah 2:4.)

180

No one who reads current history will doubt that the judgment of the Almighty has been declared among the nations of the world and that His rebuke is now being administered.

It was perhaps this day of terrible slaughter and devastation now raging that the Master had in mind when He declared, "And except those days should be shortened, there should no flesh be saved." (Matthew 24:22.)

You may well ask, But what of this United States and the land of America? Shall we suffer the terror of God's judgment because of wickedness among us?

To Cain, the unrighteous son of Adam, God, in part, answered this question. Said He, "If thou doest well, shalt thou not be accepted? and if thou doest not well, sin lieth at the door." (Genesis 4:7.)

Reaffirmed in the language of a prophet in this generation, the Lord declared, "There is a law, irrevocably decreed in heaven before the foundations of this world, upon which all blessings are predicated—And when we obtain any blessing from God, it is by obedience to that law upon which it is predicated." (D&C 130:20-21.)

Again the words of a prophet: "Say ye to the righteous, that it shall be well with him: for they shall eat the fruit of their doings." (Isaiah 3:10.)

To serve the God of this land requires keeping His commandments and yielding obedience to His law, which men who inhabit this land must do or suffer the chastening of His wrath.

May I voice a plea for all Americans to love this country with a fervor that will inspire each to so live as to merit the favor of the Almighty during this time of grave uncertainties, as well as in times to come. I would that all men could believe in the destiny of America as did the early pioneers: that it is the land of Zion; that the founders of this nation were men of inspired vision; that the Constitution as written by the inspiration of heaven must be preserved at all costs.

I make a further plea that the citizens of this favored land live righteously that they might enjoy the fruits of their righteousness in this land of promise.

Love the Lord thy God with all thy heart, with all thy might, mind, and strength, and in the name of Jesus Christ, serve him.

Love thy neighbor as thyself.

Do not steal, nor commit adultery, nor kill, nor do anything like unto it.

Thank the Lord thy God in all things.

Be willing to sacrifice for the good of others.

Avoid the temptation to get something for nothing.

Take time to be holy.

May you comprehend that to be truly patriotic in this land made sacred by Almighty God, who has consecrated this to be a land of promise, you must live according to just and holy principles. You must in very deed live the good life.

And now I invoke the blessings of the Lord upon this nation and its people in the words of King Solomon's prayer at the consecration of the temple:

> Then hear thou from heaven thy dwelling place, and forgive, and render unto every man according unto all his ways, whose heart thou knowest; (for thou only knowest the hearts of the children of men:)
>
> That they may fear thee, to walk in thy ways, so long as they live in the land which thou gavest unto our fathers. (2 Chronicles 6:30-31.)

May this desire be in the hearts of all, I humbly pray, as I give you my witness that these principles are true and that the promises of the Lord will not fail those who keep His commandments.

# 22

# A Time of Decision

Some have said that this is the most critical period in the history of this nation and of the world. I believe it is an illusion to say that this is *the* most critical, decisive time. Write it upon the hearts of all of us that every dispensation has been just as decisive, and likewise that every year has been the most decisive year and time for ourselves, for this nation, and for the world. This is our day and time when honorable men must be brought forward to meet the tremendous challenges before us.

We are in an era of intense political activity, when men of every persuasion in the political arena are clamoring for attention and acceptance by the electorates. There is controversy, debate, conflict, and contention, which seem to be the order of political campaigns.

In its loftiest sense, controversy may mean disputations because of honest differences of opinion. In its most degrading sense it may mean quarreling, strife, and name-calling. An example of that which degrades is the bitter personal abuse that so frequently is heaped upon an opposing candidate. Name-calling is continued until listeners are left with doubt and mistrust that honor and integrity are to be found in any of those who may eventually be elected. The obvious hazard is that when elected leaders have been maligned and downgraded, the seeds of disrespect to authority and law and order are sown in the minds of youth, instead of respectful obedience to counsel and to the laws enacted by those whose integrity and honesty have been thus impugned.

The old story, presumably authentic, is told that during the Civil War when the fortunes of the Union armies, under the command of General Ulysses S. Grant, were going badly, some concerned ministers called on President Abraham Lincoln at the White House and forcefully urged the dismissal of Grant. To these men Lincoln is alleged to have said: "Gentlemen, General Grant has under his command all that we hold dear in this nation. Instead of criticism, you too should get down on your knees and pray God that He would see this nation through to victory."

We related this story to a president of the United States some years ago and assured him that no matter what his name or his political party, we too were frequently on our knees, praying God that He and the leaders of this nation and of the world would bring us through the crises of the present.

We were heartened by his reply when he said, "I think that every president of this country during his term of office has been frequently on his knees praying to Almighty God."

We have recorded the angelic refrain at the time of the Savior's birth as given to us by Luke: ". . . on earth peace, good will toward men." (Luke 2:14.)

184    In seeming contradiction to that message are the

recorded words of the Master: "Think not that I am come to send peace on earth: I came not to send peace, but a sword.

"For I am come to set a man at variance against his father. . . . And a man's foes shall be they of his own household." (Matthew 10:34-36.)

How can these seemingly contradictory quotations be reconciled?

The earliest revelations of this dispensation speak of two so-called conflicting dominions on the earth today. One is spoken of as the dominion of the devil, "when peace shall be taken from the earth." (D&C 1:35.)

In the book of Revelation, as well as in other scriptures, we read that before the earth was peopled, "there was war in heaven." (Revelation 12:7.)

One of the ambitious sons of God's spiritual creations in the premortal world promised salvation for all mankind without effort on their part, provided he would be given almighty power even to the dethroning of God Himself, whose divine right it is to reign over the earth. Intense bitterness ensued between that son, who became Satan, and those who followed after him, and the beloved Son of God and those who followed after Him, whose plan of salvation, by contrast, would give to every soul the right of choice, with glory to the Father. He even offered himself as "the Lamb slain from the foundation of the world" (Revelation 13:8), that by the redemption of His atoning sacrifice "all mankind may be saved, by obedience to the laws and ordinances of the Gospel" (Article of Faith 3)

Satan and his hosts were cast out because he set about to destroy the agency of man, and he became the author of falsehood to deceive and to blind men and to lead captive all who would not hearken to the words and teachings of God's eternal plan.

185

The other dominion in the earth today of which the scriptures speak is the Lord's dominion, when He "shall have power over his saints, and shall reign in their midst." (D&C 1:36.)

Today we are constantly hearing from the unenlightened and misguided who demand what they call free agency, by which they apparently mean, as evidenced by their conduct, that they have agency to do as they please or to exercise their own self-will to determine what is law and order, what is right and wrong, or what is honor and virtue.

These are frightening expressions. A moment's reflection helps us to see that when one sets himself up to make his own rules and presumes to know no law but his own, he is but echoing the plan of Satan, who sought to ascend to God's throne, as it were, in being the judge of all that rules mankind and the world. There has ever been, and ever will be, a conflict between the forces of truth and error; between the forces of righteousness and the forces of evil; between the dominion of Satan and the dominion under the banner of our Lord and Master, Jesus Christ.

What would it be like if we were to live in a vacuum, with everything coming our way without any effort or struggle on our part to overcome these obstacles?

One of my esteemed colleagues told me of his efforts to aid a young college student who was feeling sorry for himself and who was lacking motivation and had no sense of responsibility. My friend made an attractive proposal to this young man. In a conversation that went something like this, he said, "Son, I'm going to take over full responsibility of your affairs from now on and relieve you of your worries. I'll pay your tuition at college, buy your clothes, furnish you an automobile and a credit card for gasoline. When you get ready to marry, don't worry about it; I'll look for a wife for you, and I will supply you with a house that is furnished. I'll support you and your family thereafter without any effort on your part. What do you think of my offer?"

After a moment of sobered thinking the young man replied, "Well, if you did that, what would there be for me to live for?"

Then my friend replied, "That is what I'm trying to make you see, my boy. That is the purpose of life—there is no joy without struggle and the exercise of one's own natural abilities."

In the exercise of the God-given right of free agency, or freedom of choice, how may one distinguish between what is truth and what is error?

A noted columnist, Frank Crane, wrote: "Truth is the logic of the universe. It is the reasoning of destiny; it is the mind of God. And nothing that man can devise can take its place."

Another man of wisdom, Hamilton Wright Mabie, wrote: "There is no progress in fundamental truth. We may grow in knowledge of its meaning and in the modes of its application, but its great principles will forever be the same."

At the time of Christ's arraignment before Pilate, the Master declared that His whole mission was to bear witness of the truth. Pilate then asked, "What is truth?"

Whether or not the Savior answered that question on that occasion, we have no record: but in our day the Lord Himself *has* answered, as He might have answered Pilate at that time, and I quote His words: "And truth is knowledge of things as they are, and as they were, and as they are to come; And whatsoever is more or less than this is the spirit of that wicked one who was a liar from the beginning." (D&C 93:24-25.)

Now I mention certainties upon which one may depend in his search for truth.

The first is that which is variously referred to in the scriptures as the light of Christ, the spirit of truth, or Spirit of God, which in essence means the influence of Deity that proceeds forth from the presence of God, that which quickens the understanding of man. (See D&C 88:49.) The apostle John spoke of it as "the true light, which lighteth every man that cometh into the world." (John 1:9.)

A President of the Church makes this further explanation: "There is not a man [or person] born into the world, but has a portion of the Spirit of God, and it is that Spirit of God which gives to his spirit understanding." ". . . each in accordance with his capacity to receive light . . . [which] will never cease to strive with man, until man is brought to the possession of the higher intelligence. . . ." (Joseph F. Smith, *Gospel Doctrine,* pp. 63, 62.)

To those not acquainted with the language of the scriptures, it might be explained that the Light of Christ could be described as one's conscience, or the voice of the divine within one's own soul.

As a public official in my young manhood, I was given some wise counsel by a Church leader. He said: "The only action we will ever ask you to take is to vote for that which in your heart you feel is right. We would rather many times over that you would make a mistake doing that which you felt was right, than to vote for a policy sake."

I pass these wise words of counsel to others in public office for what they are worth and strongly urge that those having heavy responsibilities in public office or elsewhere should meditate prayerfully and give the Lord a chance to aid them in solving the problems of life.

"Expedients are for an hour," Henry Ward Beecher said, "but principles are for the ages."

188

Now another certainty of which I would make note:

The Constitution of the United States is the basis of wise decisions in fundamental principles as applied to all matters pertaining to law and order, because it was framed by men whom God raised up for this very purpose. In addition to that inspired document, we must always keep in mind that the greatest weapons that can be forged against any false philosophy are the positive teachings of the gospel of Jesus Christ.

We constantly impress upon all who go out as true ambassadors of the kingdom of God to follow the wise counsel of the Apostle Paul, one of the ablest defenders of the faith of all time. In his declaration to the Corinthians, he has given us his counsel if we would be as powerful as he in our ministry. This was his secret in combating evil:

> And I, brethren, when I came to you, came not with excellency of speech or of wisdom, declaring unto you the testimony of God.
>
> For I am determined not to know any thing among you, save Jesus Christ, and him crucified.
>
> That your faith should not stand in the wisdom of men, but in the power of God. (1 Corinthians 2:1-2, 5.)

It has been well said that one does not teach honesty by telling a man how to burglarize a safe, nor do we teach chastity by telling a youth all about sexual activities.

So, likewise, it is inspired wisdom that our efforts must be spent in teaching truth by the power of Almighty God, and thus we can forge the most powerful of all weapons against the vicious doctrines of Satan.

The Prophet Joseph Smith was asked how he governed the Church members in his day. His answer in one sentence was, "I teach them correct principles, and they will govern themselves."

If we overemphasize the philosophies of the enemies of righteousness instead of teaching forcefully the principles    189 of the gospel of Jesus Christ, such overemphasis can only serve to stir up controversy and strife and thus defeat the very purpose of our missionary work in all the nations of the world.

Those who have served as public officials soon learn that there is always the imperative necessity of deciding whether or not demands on a controversial issue are being made by a well-organized loud minority or by a greater majority of those who might be less vocal but whose cause is just and in accordance with righteous principles. Always we would do well to reflect upon the counsel of a wise king of ancient times:

> Now it is not common that the voice of the people desireth anything contrary to that which is right; but it is common for the lesser part of the people to desire that which is not right; therefore . . . do your business by the voice of the people. (Mosiah 29:26.)

Let this counsel be our counsel to our church members and the honorable of the earth everywhere. Be alert and active in your business and political interests. The great danger in any society is apathy and a failure to be alert to the issues of the day, when applied to principles or to the election of public officials.

The fourth certainty to keep in mind in our civic responsibility is to choose those to govern us as "civil officers and magistrates [who will] enforce the laws . . . and . . . *administer the law in equity and justice*" (D&C 134:3; italics added), as we are admonished by inspired men of God.

In a word, we must seek for statesmanlike men who will ask, "Is it right and is it good for the country or the community?" instead of those who may merely ask, "Is it politically expedient?"

Wherever we are, wherever we live, we should pray for the leaders of our country, for they hold in their hands all that we hold dear. "Wherefore be subject to the powers

190

that be, until he reigns whose right it is to reign, and subdues all enemies under his feet." (D&C 58:22.)

And now, finally, the supreme of all certainties is God's eternal plan as given in the gospel of Jesus Christ. Here we may find the never-failing principles that will keep our feet firmly planted on the path of safety. By these eternal principles we can readily detect truth from error.

By the light of gospel truths we can be shown that "everything which inviteth to do good, and to persuade to believe in Christ, . . . ye may know with a perfect knowledge it is of God." (Moroni 7:16.) But also we may know that "whatsoever thing persuadeth men to do evil, and believe not in Christ, and deny him, and serve not God, then ye may know with a perfect knowledge it is of the devil" (Moroni 7:17), whether it be labeled religion, philosophy, science, or political dogma.

What a wonderful feeling of security can come in a crisis to one who has learned to pray and has cultivated listening ears so that he can "call, and the Lord shall answer"; when he can cry and the Lord shall say, "Here I am." (Isaiah 58:9.)

The supreme commander of the Allied Forces during World War II, General Dwight D. Eisenhower, when faced with some of the most momentous military decisions that were to change the course of the world, made this humble acknowledgment: "This is what I found about religion: It gives you courage to make the decisions you must make in a crisis and then the confidence to leave the result to a Higher Power. Only by trust in God can a man carrying responsibilities find repose."

There we have it: the constant reminder that God is in His heaven and all can be right with the world, if we seek for Him and find Him, ". . . though he be not far from every one of us: For in him we live, and move, and have

191

our being; . . . For we are also his offspring." (Acts 17:27-28.)

In all humility I bear my own witness to the power of these guidelines in my life. I have learned by my own experience that the heavier the responsibilities, the greater is my dependence on the Lord. In some measure I begin to understand the import of the declaration of Moses, who, after his great spiritual experience, said, "Now . . . I know that man is nothing, which thing I never had supposed." (Moses 1:10.)

Through the lights and shadows of my life, I also have the assurance that aided by God's holy power, doubts can be resolved into certainties, burdens can be lightened, and a literal rebirth can be realized as the nearness to my Lord and Master becomes more certain.

# 23

# *Remaining Steadfast*

What is it that, *having*, we are strong in overcoming temptations and personal difficulties, and *having not*, we are afraid, weak, and an easy prey to the temptations of the world?

Often I have asked myself that question as I have had opportunity to visit many of our young Latter-day Saint men in military camps. There I have observed many of our young men who were meeting the problems of their strange environment with great fortitude, and who were optimistic and hopeful. They were maintaining the highest Church standards. They were applying themselves diligently to the business of military training and were steadily advancing in rank. They were seeing in this experience a great opportunity for missionary work among their fellow soldiers. They were seeking out other Latter-day Saints to enjoy with them, whenever possible, the sweet communion of a sacred hour spent in sacrament meeting or in a study of the gospel. During their leisure hours, they were finding social relaxation in wholesome associations and seemed to be little affected by the tawdry and cheap entertainment that beckons in the vicinity of nearly every armed camp.

The thought has often been expressed that not sending young men into the mission field during time of war would result in great spiritual loss to the Church, but after seeing the splendid young men in the military—many of them returned missionaries—and the work they have done in military camps, I am convinced that upon their return home the Church receives a great spiritual uplift as these young men bear testimony to the guiding hand of the Lord in their preservation and of the good that they have been able to do.

Others have been melancholy and discouraged and have seemingly yielded to the deadly fatalism all too often found among soldiers. These have adopted a sort of indifference and an "Oh, what's the use" attitude. These are the ones who frequently yield to the enticing invitations that lead to harmful practices and vices and are encouraged in their indulgences by the "eat, drink, and be merry, for tomorrow we die" philosophy frequently expressed by men in the armed services.

In one of the U.S. Army camps I visited, I met with some of our men to consider what the Church might do to provide materials for use in religious services and to aid them in making proper social contacts with organized branches of the Church adjacent to the camp. After a prolonged discussion of these matters, a young captain in the group made this remark: "To my mind it's a question of spirituality. If a man lacks that, then there is little gained by anything you try to do for him; if he has spirituality, then he will be all right whether you do little or much."

What is meant by spirituality? The dictionary defines it as "the faculty that gives a feeling of confidence; sense of the spiritual; belief in divine things; an inclination to interpret prospects of promise in one's own favor."

I found out later what spirituality meant to that young army captain when I met him on the street in Salt Lake City and learned that during a short furlough prior to his leaving for overseas duty he had brought his wife and family with him to the temple where, by the authority of the holy priesthood, they were sealed together in the everlasting covenant for time and all eternity. He was living with "an eye single to the glory of God" to lead him through a trying period.

I once visited with a young man returning from a mission. When I asked him what he thought had been the most important lesson he had learned from his mission experience, he replied, "I expect shortly to be drafted for military service. I have gained a testimony that if I live a clean life I will be entitled to the companionship of the Holy Ghost, which will warn me of needless danger and keep me safe until my work here on earth is completed. Also I have gained a testimony that life on this earth is but a preparation for eternity, and that if I live worthily, after this life I will have important work there. I have overcome the fear of death and am better prepared to go into the service than I would have been without my missionary experience."

In my heart I said, "Thank God for the seeds of the teachings of the gospel planted in the hearts of the youth of Israel that build faith to fortify them in times of danger, adversity, and temptation."

Sometime in his youth, and through the experiences of his mission, there had been burned into the heart of that young man the truth that if he was purified and cleansed from sin, he could ask whatsoever he would in the name of Jesus and it would be done (D&C 50:29-30); that the     195

Spirit of the Lord would not always strive with man; and that when the Spirit ceased to strive with man, there came speedy destruction (2 Nephi 26:11). He had learned that if he were wise and had received the truth and had taken the Holy Spirit for his guide, he should not be hewn down and cast into the fire, but should abide the day (D&C 45:57). The scriptures had taught him that his body was the temple of the Holy Ghost which was in him, which he had of God (1 Corinthians 6:19), and that "whatsoever temple is defiled, God shall destroy that temple" (D&C 93:35).

One who has a testimony of the purpose of life sees the obstacles and trials of life as opportunities for gaining the experience necessary for the work of eternity; he sees death as one of the greatest experiences of life. One of the saddest conditions I see as I travel throughout the stakes and wards of the Church is a person who, because of a little worldly learning or wealth, has come to think he has outgrown the Church and the faith of his fathers.

To one who has high spirituality, faith in the gospel and in the doctrines of the Church supersedes scientific theories and the philosophies of men; priesthood quorum activities supplant service clubs and lodges; and Church social and recreational responsibilities come before fraternities and sororities.

Security that comes from the brotherhood of a priesthood quorum with church membership and the living of church standards is valued above a fancied security that is purchased with wealth or political prestige.

The spiritually minded person seeks the respect of the high-minded who obey the law, who revere womanhood and virtue and encourage purity of thought and action rather than cater to the applause of those who secretly despise the man who thinks and acts below the standards he professes.

When prospering in a material way, a person with great spirituality shows appreciation to God, to whom he is indebted for all that he has, by a thrifty, frugal husbanding of his substance and by extending generosity to the unfortunate according to the laws of the Church, rather than indulging in reckless, riotous living as a prodigal in defiance of the laws of both God and man. In adversity he does not despair; when his bank fails he does not commit suicide; he lives above his world, and all that he does is with his eye ever fixed upon the goal of eternity.

If face to face with death, such a one will not fear if his feet have been "shod with the preparation of the gospel of peace" (D&C 27:16); and those who lose their loved ones will have the faith of Moroni, the captain of the army, who declared, "For the Lord suffereth the righteous to be slain that his justice and judgment may come upon the wicked; therefore ye need not suppose that the righteous are lost because they are slain; but behold, they do enter into the rest of the Lord their God." (Alma 60:13.)

It is my conviction that the devastating scourge of war in which so many are slain, many of whom are no more responsible for the causes of the war than are our own boys, is making necessary an increase of missionary activity in the spirit world and that many of our boys who bear the holy priesthood and are worthy to do so will be called to that missionary service after they have departed this life.

The Lord, ever mindful of the welfare of his children, has, through his prophets, given wise counsel as to the rock upon which men should anchor their lives.

And now, my sons, remember, remember that it is upon the rock of our Redeemer, who is Christ, the Son of God, that ye must build your foundation; that when the devil shall send forth his mighty winds, yea, his shafts in the whirlwind, yea, when all his hail and his mighty storm shall beat upon you, it shall have no power over you to drag you down to the gulf of misery and endless wo, because of the rock upon which ye are built, which is a sure foundation, a foundation whereon if men build they cannot fall. (Helaman 5:12.)

### And again in another place we are counseled:

O, remember, my son, and learn wisdom in thy youth; yea, learn in thy youth to keep the commandments of God.

Counsel with the Lord in all thy doings, and he will direct thee for good; yea, when thou liest down at night lie down unto the Lord, that he may watch over you in your sleep; and when thou risest in the morning let thy heart be full of thanks unto God; and if ye do these things, ye shall be lifted up at the last day. (Alma 37:35, 37.)

### The time is here when we would do well to sing again the song that comforted the pioneers of a former day:

Think not when you gather to Zion,
Your troubles and trials are through,
That nothing but comfort and pleasure
Are waiting in Zion for you:
No, no, 'tis designed as a furnace,
All substance, all textures to try,
To burn all the "wood, hay, and stubble,"
The gold from the dross purify.
—*Hymns*, no. 21

### May we survive the fiery furnace of God's judgment and prove true to whatever test shall be made of us and abide the day of the second coming of the Son of Man.

# LIFE, DEATH, RESURRECTION

# 24

# Salvation for the Dead

The question most often asked by visitors who become acquainted with the broad scope of genealogical research, family histories, books of remembrance, family organizations, the worldwide microfilming of vital statistics, and the work of temples throughout the Church raises the question, "What is the purpose of this tremendous activity that is going on within the Church today?"

To students of the scriptures, I call attention to one or two significant incidents in the life of the Master. As recorded by the apostle John, there came to Jesus by night one Nicodemus who was a ruler among the Jews. He said to the Master, declaring his faith, "Rabbi, we know that thou art a teacher come from God." The Master answered, "Verily, . . . I say unto thee, Except a man be born again, he cannot see the kingdom of God." Nicodemus, not understanding, asked, "How can a man be born when he is old?" Jesus answered, "Except a man be born of water and of the Spirit, he cannot enter into the kingdom of God." (John 3:2-5.)

There is abundant evidence from that which followed in the ministry of the Master's disciples that this meant baptism by immersion, followed by the conferring of the gift of the Holy Ghost. Both ordinances were to be performed by men who had authority given by the Master to His disciples and then by them to others properly ordained. We read that John was baptizing in Aenon near Salim by those having authority because "there was much water there." (John 3:23.) We read about the baptism of Cornelius and his gentile household by direction of Peter. (Acts 10:44-48.) The Apostle Paul at Ephesus baptized a man in water and conferred the Holy Ghost by the laying on of hands. This interesting history is recorded in the Book of Acts:

And it came to pass, that, while Apollos was at Corinth, Paul having passed through the upper coasts came to Ephesus: and finding certain disciples,

He said unto them, Have ye received the Holy Ghost since ye believed? And they said unto him, We have not so much as heard whether there be any Holy Ghost.

And he said unto them, Unto what then were ye baptized? And they said, Unto John's baptism.

Then said Paul, John verily baptized with the baptism of repentance, saying unto the people, that they should believe on him which should come after him, that is, on Christ Jesus.

When they heard this, they were baptized in the name of the Lord Jesus.

And when Paul had laid his hands upon them, the Holy Ghost came on them; and they spake with tongues, and prophesied. (Acts 19:1-6.)

From this scripture we can make three observations: (1) these ordinances must be performed only by those having proper authority; (2) baptism is to be performed in water; and (3) conferring of the Holy Ghost must be by the laying on of hands.

The authority necessary to the performance of these sacred ordinances was explained to Peter and the disciples

202

at the time when they withdrew to Caesarea Philippi for a rest. Apparently the Master asked for a sort of a report meeting. "Whom do men say that I the Son of man am?" Some answered in various ways, and then He asked, directly, "But whom say ye that I am?" Peter gave a great testimony that the Lord told him had been revealed to him by God, that Jesus was the Christ. (Matthew 16:13-16.) Then the Master conferred a divine power on Peter in these words: "And I will give unto thee the keys of the kingdom of heaven:and whatsoever thou shalt bind on earth shall be bound in heaven: and whatsoever thou shalt loose on earth shall be loosed in heaven." (Matthew 16:19.)

In many other scriptures, the Apostle Paul spoke of this divine power as the Melchizedek Priesthood; Peter spoke of it as the Royal Priesthood, and in other scriptures as "after the order of the Son of God."

With baptism by immersion in water and the conferring of the Holy Ghost by the laying on of hands thus made so essential to the salvation of mankind, the believing Christian must find the answer to the obvious—but to many churches a disturbing—question.

What, then, is to become of millions of those who have lived upon the earth during periods when there has been no dispensation of the gospel and when there has been no authority upon the earth authorized to perform these ordinances of salvation? Are these to be condemned without the opportunity to be baptized by water and of the Spirit as Jesus had told Nicodemus was essential in order to "see" or to "enter" the kingdom of God. (See John 3:3, 5.) Were this the case, the gates of hell would have prevailed against the church of Christ, which the Master declared to Peter it would not. Some churches have sought to bridge this gap by prayers for the dead and by various other methods, but the Lord had provided in His plan of salvation for those who, through no fault of their own, have not received the essential ordinances of salvation in their mortal lives.

The Lord's plan was foreshadowed by a statement of the Master that has aroused much discussion among students of scriptures. He declared, as recorded by John, "Verily, verily, I say unto you, The hour is coming, and now is, when the dead shall hear the voice of the Son of God: and they that hear shall live." (John 5:25.) Then, as though He wanted to make it so plain that He could not be misunderstood with reference to the word *dead,* He further declared:

> Marvel not at this: for the hour is coming, in the which *all that are in the graves shall hear his voice.*
>
> And shall come forth; they that have done good, unto the resurrection of life; and they that have done evil, unto the resurrection of damnation. (John 5:28-29. Italics added.)

The fact that those who were in their graves did hear the voice of the Son of God is attested to by no less a competent witness than the apostle Peter—the chief one of the Twelve unto whom the Master gave the keys to the kingdom of God.

Following his crucifixion, the Master appeared to Mary at the Garden Tomb, presumably as a resurrected being. Jesus said to her: "Touch me not; for I am not yet ascended to my Father: but go to my brethren, and say unto them, I ascend unto my Father, and your Father; and to my God, and your God." (John 20:17.)

He appeared on the third day following His crucifixion. As recorded again by John: ". . . when the doors were shut where the disciples were assembled for fear of the Jews, came Jesus and stood in the midst." (John 20:19.) Upon this occasion He showed the marks inflicted upon Him on the cross, as though to demonstrate the reality of His resurrection. He then declared, ". . . a spirit hath not flesh and bones as ye see me have." (Luke 24:39.)

A marvelous work was performed by the Master during the three days intervening His death and His subsequent resurrection, and before His final ascension, for we find Peter testifying:

> For Christ also hath once suffered for sins, the just for the unjust, that he might bring us to God, being put to death in the flesh, but quickened by the Spirit:
>
> By which also he went and preached unto the spirits in prison;
>
> Which sometime were disobedient, when once the longsuffering of God waited in the days of Noah, while the ark was a preparing, wherein few, that is, eight souls were saved by water. (1 Peter 3:18-20.)

The purpose of the Master's preaching to those who had died without a knowledge of the gospel is also explained by Peter: "For, for this cause was the gospel preached also to them that are dead, that they might be judged according to men in the flesh, but live according to God in the spirit." (1 Peter 4:6.)

How were these who had not the privileges of the saving ordinances of the gospel to be judged as though they were men in the flesh, in order that they might live according to God in the spirit?

The Apostle Paul, in his great sermon to the Corinthians, among whom were many nonbelievers of the Savior's power of vicariously redeeming the dead from the graves, referred to an ordinance vicariously performed that was obviously known unto the Corinthians.

He asked, "Else what shall they do which are baptized for the dead, if the dead rise not at all? why are they then baptized for the dead?" (1 Corinthians 15:29.) Doing work for the dead vicariously is not out of harmony with the teachings and mission of the Savior. His atonement was and is a vicarious service for all mankind, that we might live eternally with Him. Historians also record these ordinances having been performed vicariously for the dead,

205

even as the Master's vicarious redemption for all mankind.

Epiphanius, a writer of the fourth century, in speaking of a sect of Christians to whom he was opposed, said:

> In this country—I mean in Asia—and even in Galatia, their school flourished eminently; and a traditional fact concerning them has reached us, that when any of them had died without baptism, they used to baptize others in their name, lest in the resurrection they should suffer punishment as unbaptized. (B. H. Roberts, *The Gospel*, p. 247.)

In an article on baptism in the early Christian churches, Dr. Kersopp Lake, professor of ecclesiastical history at Harvard University, wrote:

> It would also seem from 1 Co[rinthians] 15:29 that St. Paul recognized the practice of vicarious baptism for the dead. It is impossible that "Else what shall they do who are baptized for the dead? If the dead are not raised at all, why then are they baptized for them?" can refer to anything except vicarious baptism. (Quoted by J. Reuben Clark, Jr., in *On the Way to Immortality and Eternal Life*, pp. 185-86.)
>
> Dr. Lake doubts that Tertullian "was acquainted with any contemporary Christian custom of baptism for the dead." If this be true then . . . Tertullian's words would suggest that by the end of the second century they were offering prayers for the dead in lieu of baptism for the dead, a great corruption . . . which still maintains in certain great churches. (Ibid., p. 187.)

The greatest of obligations placed upon The Church of Jesus Christ of Latter-day Saints was expressed by a prophet in this day; he said: "Our greatest responsibility in this world that God has laid upon us is to seek after our dead." (*Teachings of the Prophet Joseph Smith*, p. 356.) The Lord has spoken this to a modern prophet, as recorded in the Doctrine and Covenants:

> Now the great and grand secret of the whole matter, and the *summum bonum* of the whole subject that is lying before us, consists in obtaining the powers of the Holy Priesthood. For him to whom these keys are given there is no difficulty in obtaining a knowledge of facts in relation to the salvation of the children of men, both as well for the dead as for the living." (D&C 128:11.)

The prophet Malachi made a great statement:

Behold, I will send you Elijah the prophet before the coming of the
great and dreadful day of the Lord:

And he shall turn the heart of the fathers to the children, and the heart
of the children to their fathers, lest I come and smite the earth with a curse.
(Malachi 4:5-6.)

The keys of Elijah have been again committed to men
as a part of the restoration of the gospel in this dispensation. With the bestowal of these keys of work for the dead,
it was made plain that the children here upon the earth
can be baptized for their loved ones who have passed away
without having enjoyed this privilege. The knowledge of
this great truth has caused the hearts of the children to
turn to their fathers, and the children to seek out their
genealogy so they can be baptized for their kindred dead.

The application of this principle accounts for the
great work that must be performed by the priesthood authority restored by the prophet Elijah and for the tremendous genealogical research being carried out among
members of the Church in this dispensation of the fulness
of times. Thus it might be said of all who engage in this
great work of salvation that they are "saviors on Mount
Zion" (see Obadiah 21)—building temples, erecting bap-
tismal fonts, and receiving all the ordinances in behalf of
their progenitors who are dead, redeeming them that they
might come forth in the morning of the first resurrection.

May we all, by engaging in this work, be as saviors on
Mount Zion. To all of this I add my own personal witness
that the gospel of Jesus Christ is, as declared by the Apostle
Paul, "the power of God unto salvation to everyone that
believeth. . . ." (Romans 1:16.) To this I add salvation of
the dead as well as the living. All of this is made possible
through the great atonement of our Lord and Savior Jesus

207

Christ, to whose mission I bear solemn witness; today His work is going forward as was foreordained, and the gates of hell shall not prevail against it.

# 25

# The Temple Endowment

In the writings of world philosophers in the centuries that followed the apostolic period are found flashes of inspiration that approach the true concept as to man's relationship to God and the eternal quest of man to reach his ultimate goal in the presence of God.

The Greek philosopher Epictetus taught that because all men are sons of God and have a spark of divinity within them, humanity forms a universal brotherhood. The Italian poet Dante, in his poetic composition *Divine Comedy*, narrates a story about a journey down through hell, up the mountain of purgatory, and thence through the revolving heavens into the presence of God. In this unique way, he summarizes the literature, the science, the philosophy, and the religion of the Middle Ages.

Whatever fragments of truth concerning man's salvation were preserved through these earlier writers, it remained for the revelations from God, which came with the restoration of the gospel at the beginning of this dispensation, to give us the fulness of truth concerning these vital questions. In a profound, prayerful declaration with which the Master closed His divine mission, He clearly set forth that essential knowledge which saves: "And this is life eternal, that they might know thee the only true God, and Jesus Christ, whom thou hast sent." (John 17:3.)

It was of this subject that the Prophet Joseph Smith spoke when he said: "The principle of salvation is given us through the knowledge of Jesus Christ" (*Teachings of the Prophet Joseph Smith*, p. 297), and that "knowledge through our Lord and Savior Jesus Christ is the grand key that unlocks the glories and mysteries of the kingdom of heaven." (Ibid., p. 298.) The Prophet also warned that

a man is saved no faster than he gets knowledge, for if he does not get knowledge, he will be brought into captivity by some evil power in the other world, as evil spirits will have more knowledge, and consequently more power than many men who are on the earth. Hence it needs revelation to assist us, and give us knowledge of the things of God. (Ibid., p. 217.)

As early as 1841, the Lord revealed to Joseph Smith that

there is not a place found on earth that he may come to and restore again that which was lost unto you, or which he hath taken away, even the fulness of the priesthood.

For I deign to reveal unto my church things which have been kept hid from before the foundation of the world, things that pertain to the dispensation of the fulness of times. (D&C 124:28, 41.)

These revelations, which are reserved for and taught only to the faithful Church members in sacred temples, constitute what are called the "mysteries of Godliness." The Lord said He had given to Joseph "the keys of the mysteries, and the revelations which are sealed. . . ." (D&C 28:7.) As a reward to the faithful, the Lord promised: "And to them will I reveal all mysteries, yea, all the hidden mysteries of my kingdom from days of old. . . ." (D&C

76:7.) In this sense, then, a mystery may be defined as a truth which cannot be known except by revelation.

In the writings of the Prophet Joseph Smith there is found an explanation of these so-called mysteries that are embodied in what the Prophet speaks of as the holy endowment. He said in part:

> I spent the day in the upper part of the store, that is in my private office . . . in council with [then he names several of the early leaders], instructing them in the principles and order of the Priesthood, attending to washings, anointings, endowments and the communication of keys pertaining to the Aaronic Priesthood, and so on to the highest order of the Melchizedek Priesthood, setting forth the order pertaining to the Ancient of Days, and all those plans and principles by which any one is enabled to secure the fullness of those blessings which have been prepared for the Church of the Firstborn, and come up and abide in the presence of the Eloheim in the eternal worlds. (*Teachings of the Prophet Joseph Smith*, p. 237.)

President Brigham Young, at the laying of the cornerstone for the Salt Lake Temple, added this further enlightenment as to the meaning of the endowment and the purpose of temple building with relation thereto:

> . . . be assured, brethren, there are but few, very few of the Elders of Israel, now on earth, who know the meaning of the word endowment. To know, they must experience; and to experience, a temple must be built.
> . . . Your endowment is, to receive all those ordinances in the house of the Lord, which are necessary for you, after you have departed this life, to enable you to walk back to the presence of the Father, passing the angels who stand as sentinels, . . . and gain your eternal exaltation in spite of earth and hell. (*Discourses of Brigham Young*, pp. 415-16.)

When the first revelations came relative to the building of a temple, the Lord made significant statements to indicate the exclusive and sacred nature of temples as contrasted with other buildings for public worship meetings.

> I will show unto my servant Joseph all things pertaining to this house,

and the priesthood thereof, and the place whereon it shall be built. (D&C 124:42.)

. . . Like unto the pattern which I have given you.

. . . And inasmuch as my people build a house unto me in the name of the Lord, and do not suffer any unclean thing to come into it, that it be not defiled, my glory shall rest upon it;

Yea, and my presence shall be there, for I will come into it, and all the pure in heart that shall come into it shall see God.

But if it be defiled I will not come into it, and my glory shall not be there; for I will not come into unholy temples. (D&C 97:10, 15-17.)

It was the lament of the Master in His day: "The foxes have holes, and the birds of the air have nests; but the Son of Man hath not where to lay his head." (Matthew 8:20.) President Brigham Young explained the reason for this statement of the Savior:

Because the house which the Father had commanded to be built for his reception, although completed, had become polluted, and hence the saying: "My house is the house of prayer; but ye have made it a den of thieves." . . . Although he drove out the money-changers, . . . that did not purify the house, so that he could not sleep in it, for an holy thing dwelleth not in an unholy temple. (*Discourses of Brigham Young*, p. 414.)

Dr. Hugh Nibley of Brigham Young University, writing under the heading "Christian Envy of the Temple," comments on this subject:

A favorite symbol of the transition from crass Jewish materialism to the Christian Temple of the Spirit has always been the New Testament episode of the driving out of the money-changers. Yet how much this "obvious transfer" (as St. Leo calls it) left to be desired is apparent from many a bitter comment that the Church itself was as much "a den of thieves" as ever the Temple was, with the obvious difference, already voiced by Origen, that "today Jesus comes no more to drive out the money-changers and save the rest"! Furthermore, it has often been pointed out that the purging of the Temple, far from being its death-sentence, was rather "a demonstration by the Lord that he would not tolerate the slightest disrespect for his Father's House."

Students today are more inclined than they have been in the past to concede to the temple a high place in the estimation of Jesus, of the prophets before him, and of the Apostles and the Church after him . . . not only as a "basic component of Israel's religion," but of early Christianity as well. For both the way to heaven led through the Temple and if that was but an inter-mediate step in the salvation of the race, it was nonetheless an indispensable one. . . . The Christian still needed the Temple, and always remained a pil-grim to Jerusalem in a very literal sense. (*Jewish Quarterly Review,* October 1959.)

This recognition of the building of temples by the Lord's people is one of the marks of the divinity of the true church and is found today in the true church of Jesus Christ, as it has been found in the true church of previous dispensations.

Thus, it would seem that just as in the days of animal sacrifice, in prototype of the vicarious atonement of the Savior, the animal sacrificed must be without blemish even as the Master was without blemish, so we who enter these sacred places to perform ordinances for ourselves and vicariously for those who are dead must be without blemish so far as human limitations permit.

Within these temples, we may be as near heaven on earth as is possible. To enter therein, we should prepare to enter into the sacred presences abiding there, even as the Lord taught the people of Nephi to prepare to enter into the presence of God:

And no unclean thing can enter into his kingdom; therefore nothing en-tereth into his rest save it be those who have washed their garments in my blood, because of their faith, and the repentance of all their sins, and their faithfulness unto the end. (3 Nephi 27:19.)

Outside the walls of the Alberta Temple in Cardston is this inscription, which summarizes the preparation all must make who would be worthy of "the greatest blessing of life—the holy endowment":

> Hearts must be pure to come within these walls,
>> Where spreads a feast unknown to festive halls.
> Freely partake, for freely God hath given,
>> And taste the holy joys that tell of heaven.

213

Here learn of Him who triumphed o'er the grave,
And unto men the keys, the kingdom gave:
Joined here by power that past and present bind,
The living and the dead perfection find.
—Orson F. Whitney

# 26

# God's Kingdom: A Kingdom of Order

The great historian Will Durrant once said, "In my youth I wanted freedom. In my mature years I want order." There is nothing so important in the kingdom of God as order; yet the tendency today is to resist law and order, which must be maintained in the kingdom of God if we are to be pleasing in the sight of the Lord. "Be one," the Lord said; "and if ye are not one ye are not mine." (D&C 38:27.) The only way we can be one is by following the leadership of the Church as the Lord has directed.

Even in the matter of temple ordinances, there is sometimes resistance to order. We have many requests from young couples who, for one reason or another, want to have a civil marriage first—perhaps someone in one of the families is not a member of the Church—and then they want to have a temple marriage immediately thereafter. When we deny the request and explain that a sealing following a civil marriage is not a temple marriage but a sealing after marriage, they frequently ask, "Why isn't such a subsequent sealing just as valid as a temple marriage in the first place?" The simple answer has to be, "Because a temple marriage is the Lord's way by His command." Any other way than that lacks some of the blessings that could have been enjoyed if the Lord's way had been chosen.

There are sometimes requests from sealers in one temple who want to perform sealings in another temple. When we tell them that their work must be confined to the temple for which they have been set apart, they ask why, and we tell them that there must be order in the kingdom of God. Sometimes a former temple president asks years after his release if he can have permission to go back into the temple to perform another sealing, perhaps for a grandchild. His request is denied because that isn't God's way. When a member releases the keys that he formerly held, the keys do not belong to him anymore. They belong to somebody else, and he doesn't have the authority he once had because there is order in the Church.

The request for persons other than bishops and stake presidents to perform civil marriages is a frequent one. Some ask, "Why not by permission?" And again we answer, "Because there is order, and stake presidents and bishops are ordained ministers and are so certified to civil authorities."

The requirements for entry into the temple are that a newly baptized member should not be given a temple recommend for even his own temple ordinances until he has been a member of the Church at least one year. Any flexibility in this requirement would be out of order in the Lord's church. It is analogous to making sure that before one is ready to eat meat, he is taught to drink milk; and one year is the length of time prescribed for this learning process.

There was a convert to the Church who had a Ph.D. in psychology, and after eight months in the Church

216

someone suggested to him that he have his temple endowments. When his request was not granted, it was explained to him that it was contrary to the rule. It was implied that because this man was a professor in a university his case should be handled differently. I answered, "Yes, he may have a Ph.D. in science or philosophy, but he is only an eight-month-old child in the Church. Until he has been schooled in the fundamentals of the Church, he will never understand and enjoy to the fullest the temple ordinances." We say that until he is prepared, it would be folly to have him go to the temple for instructions that would be beyond his understanding.

The simple answer to all these exceptions mentioned could be given by the single phrase, "Trust in the Lord's way."

I sat by the editor of the *Reader's Digest* at a luncheon some time ago, and he asked if the lack of modern revelation and a dwindling trust in the Lord were our biggest problems today. I said that they weren't problems with us. We know that the Lord gives revelation today. We are waiting for Him to reveal His mind and will. The only people who find it a problem are those who don't believe in revelation. Therein lies one of the greatest problems among those who are criticizing and finding fault and wanting exceptions. They don't trust the Lord. They are not willing to listen to the admonition of the Lord as He prefaces His revelations in this dispensation. These are His words:

"And the arm of the Lord shall be revealed; and the day cometh that they who will not hear the voice of the Lord, neither the voice of his servants, neither give heed to the words of the prophets and apostles, shall be cut off from among the people." (D&C 1:14.)

One day a brother who was critical of the Church asked a rather interesting and even presumptuous question: "In the early days, the Prophet Joseph Smith, when faced with a difficult ecclesiastical problem in the establishment of the Church, went before the Lord and sought a revelation for the direction and guidance of the Church. Are you brethren so living today that you might receive similar guidance?"

My reply was a quotation from the words of Moroni after he had been compiling the teachings of the Jaredites. Having read the great experience of the brother of Jared, I suppose, Moroni closed with this thought: "And now, I, Moroni, would speak somewhat concerning these things; I would show unto the world that faith is things which are hoped for and not seen."

And then, quoting from Moroni again, I said to this professor, ". . . wherefore, dispute not because ye see not, for ye receive no witness until after the trial of your faith." (Ether 12:6.) Then I asked this brother, "Have you ever thought that you're the one who ought to be doing some praying and getting close enough to the Lord to know whether or not what the brethren are saying today is the mind and will of the Lord?"

This is excellent advice for each of us. May we all support the brethren and ask the Lord, in faith, for confirmation of His will.

# 27

# Spiritual Rebirth and Death

Shortly after World War II I had an interview with a young man who was just making a remarkable recovery from very serious wounds that he received on the European battlefield. In an explosion of a land mine this young man suffered a severe spinal injury that had almost completely paralyzed him, and when the rescue squad came and was carrying him off the field, the enemy turned loose a burst of machine-gun fire from which he suffered six bullet wounds in his chest. He was taken to the hospital in what was thought to be a dying condition. As he lay there on his cot after having been treated by the surgeons, a chaplain came to him wearing an insignia of a sectarian church. He asked this young man what his religion was. On being told that he was a Latter-day Saint, the chaplain said: "Well, then, perhaps you would rather I would not pray for you."

"Oh, yes," said the young man, "I would like to have you pray for me if you feel so inclined."

Then the chaplain with great deference said, "Well, I will remove the insignia of my church and kneel down here at your cot. The two of us will then just pray together as two men of God."

The young man said the chaplain prayed for about twenty minutes. The burden of his prayer and the main idea that he could remember of what the chaplain said, which sustained him and put into him the feeling that he wanted to live, was this: "O God, help us that in our living we are not afraid to die, and that in our dying we are not afraid to live."

I have thought about that prayer many times since, and I have asked myself, How many thousands are there among us today who are living such lives that would make them, unless they repent, afraid to die, and that in their dying they might be afraid to live hereafter?

The purpose of the gospel of Jesus Christ is to teach men to live so that when they die, in the words of the immortal "Thanatopsis,"

> Thou go not, like the quarry-slave at night,
> Scourged to his dungeon, but, sustained and soothed
> By an unfaltering trust. . . .
> —William Cullen Bryant

Baptism by immersion symbolizes the death and burial of the man of sin; and the coming forth out of the water, the resurrection to a newness of spiritual life. After baptism, hands are laid upon the head of the baptized believer, and he is blessed to receive the Holy Ghost. Thus does the one baptized receive the promise or gift of the Holy Ghost, or the privilege of being brought back into the presence of one of the Godhead; by obedience and through his faithfulness, one so blessed might receive the guidance and direction of the Holy Ghost in his daily walks and talks, even as Adam walked and talked in the Garden of

Eden with God, his Heavenly Father. To receive such guidance and such direction from the Holy Ghost is to be spiritually reborn.

Unfortunately, there are many of those who are blessed to receive the Holy Ghost and that companionship of one of the Godhead in their mortal lives who fail of their blessings. This was taught plainly by the Master in the parable of the sower, who was represented as a teacher of the gospel. He classified those to whom the gospel is taught into four different groups. Of one group he said, in effect: "These are they who receive the seed by the wayside, and the birds come quickly and catch it up and steal it away," suggesting those who hear the word but lack understanding, and thus the devil is quick to take the word away from their hearts lest they would receive it and would believe to their salvation.

Another class he compared to those who receive the seed on stony ground and it begins to take root, but when the sun comes out, it is scorched and withers away because it hás not had much root, suggesting those who receive the seed and for a time have joy in that understanding, but then when persecution and affliction come because of the word, they become offended and dwindle in their belief.

Another group of those who hear the gospel are the ones who receive it as among thorns, and the thorns after a time choke out the seed. These, he said, were like those who let the cares of the world, the deceitfulness of riches, and the pleasures and the lusts of the world destroy their activity in the Church, which might have brought them safely into eternal life.

Fortunately, there are some who receive the gospel in good ground, and these bring forth some a hundredfold, some sixtyfold, and some thirtyfold. And that is just about

221

the way the active membership of the Church seems to be grouped among us today, some giving full hundred percent service and some, unfortunately, only thirtyfold.

Again, in this day the Lord has given us a revelation that suggests clearly the reasons why some men fail of their blessings. He said:

> Because their hearts are set so much upon the things of this world, and aspire to the honors of men, that they do not learn this one lesson—
>
> That the rights of the priesthood are inseparably connected with the powers of heaven, and that the powers of heaven cannot be controlled nor handled only upon the principles of righteousness.
>
> That they may be conferred upon us, it is true; but when we undertake to cover our sins, or to gratify our pride, our vain ambition, or to exercise control or dominion or compulsion upon the souls of the children of men, in any degree of unrighteousness, behold, the heavens withdraw themselves; the Spirit of the Lord is grieved; and when it is withdrawn, Amen to the priesthood or the authority of that man.
>
> Behold, ere he is aware, he is left unto himself, to kick against the pricks, to persecute the saints, and to fight against God. (D&C 121:35-38.)

That, it seems to me, is about the progressive way that men begin to fall away. They first begin to "kick against the pricks." I have wondered what that means. These no doubt are the pricks of the gospel. I wonder, perhaps, if they are not those things referred to by President J. Reuben Clark, Jr., as "restraints"—the restraints of the Word of Wisdom, the restraints imposed in keeping the Sabbath day holy, injunctions against card playing, the restraints imposed by following the welfare program, and so on. These are the restraints against which some people seem to rebel and are kicking constantly against—the "pricks" of the gospel.

I remember in this connection what somebody said in classifying humankind. He said there were only three kinds of people in the world—"Saints, Ain'ts, and Complaints," and perhaps the "Complaints" would represent those who seem to be kicking against the pricks. These are the ones

222

who "persecute the Saints" and, finally, "fight against God."

Speaking of those who would persecute the Saints, I am reminded of what the Prophet Joseph said:

> From apostates the faithful have received the severest persecutions. Judas was rebuked and immediately betrayed his Lord into the hands of His enemies, because Satan entered into him. There is a superior intelligence bestowed upon such as obey the Gospel with full purpose of heart, which, if sinned against, the apostate is left naked and destitute of the Spirit of God, and he is, in truth, nigh unto cursing, and his end is to be burned. When once that light which was in them is taken from them, they become as much darkened as they were previously enlightened, and then, no marvel, if all their powers should be enlisted against the truth, and they, Judas like, seek the destruction of those who were their greatest benefactors. (*Teachings of the Prophet Joseph Smith*, p. 67.)

Yes, persecution seems to be the part of those who would teach the truth. You remember what the Master said: "Blessed are ye, when men shall revile you, and persecute you, and shall say all manner of evil against you falsely, . . . for so persecuted they the prophets which were before you." (Matthew 5:11-12.)

I remember a few years ago, upon assignment from the Presidency and the Council of the Twelve, I interviewed a man who, because of his sinning, had fallen away and had been excommunicated from the Church. He said to me, "I want to bear you this testimony that the last few years have been a pretty rugged road. When I received the pronouncement of the court that excommunicated me from the Church, it was just as though someone had turned off the light to my soul. I was left in complete darkness from that time forward."

The Master, in His Sermon on the Mount, made another very expressive declaration when He said, "Blessed are the pure in heart: for they shall see God." (Matthew 5:8.)

223

You will remember that in His lifetime there were some who saw Him only as the son of the carpenter. There were some who said that because of His words He was drunken with strong wine—that He was a winebibber. There were some who even thought Him to be possessed of devils. Only those who were pure in heart saw Him as the Son of God.

There are some who look upon the leaders of this church and God's anointed as men who are possessed of selfish motives. The words of our leaders are always twisted by them to try to bring a snare to the work of the Lord. Mark well those who speak evil of the Lord's anointed, for they speak from impure hearts. Only the pure in heart see the divine in man and accept our leaders as prophets of the living God.

I bear you my testimony that the experiences I have had have taught me that those who criticize the leaders of this church are showing signs of a spiritual sickness which, unless curbed, will bring about eventual spiritual death. I bear testimony as well that those who in public seek, by their criticism, to belittle our leaders or bring them into disrepute bring more hurt upon themselves than upon those whom they seek thus to malign. I have watched over the years, and I have read of the history of many of those who fell away from this church, and I bear testimony that no apostate who ever left this church ever prospered as an influence in his community thereafter.

# 28

# *If a Man Die, Shall He Live Again?*

*A*s we speak of a national day of mourning, we must have the concept that this is but a segmented part of a funeral service being held for our illustrious leader, who has been extolled and eulogized so beautifully and appropriately . . . in this service today.* I shall take from the holy scriptures a text to introduce a few thoughts to sober us, to cause us reflection, and to do proper worship, as we have been requested by our new President and as a memorial to the passing of the President of the United States.

It was the lament of a man of God who, in difficulty, said:

Man that is born of a woman is of few days, and full of trouble.

He cometh forth like a flower, and is cut down: he fleeth also as a shadow, and continueth not.

Seeing his days are determined, the number of his months are with thee, thou hast appointed his bounds that he cannot pass;

But man dieth, and wasteth away: yea, man giveth up the ghost, and where is he?

*Address delivered at a memorial service for President John F. Kennedy, in the Salt Lake Tabernacle, November 25, 1963.

> So man lieth down, and riseth not: till the heavens be no more, they shall not awake, nor be raised out of their sleep.
>
> O that thou wouldest hide me in the grave, that thou wouldest keep me secret, until thy wrath be past, that thou wouldest appoint me a set time, and remember me! (Job 14:1-2, 5, 10, 12-13.)

And then he asks the questions that is the question of the ages, and that has been asked again today by the millions who mourn the passing of President John F. Kennedy: "If a man die, shall he live again? all the days of my appointed time will I wait, till my change come." (Job 14:14.)

The man of faith answers that question when he says:

> For thou, Lord, hast made me glad through thy work: I will triumph in the work of thy hands.
>
> O Lord, how great are thy works! and thy thoughts are very deep.
>
> But thou, Lord, art most high for evermore.
>
> The righteous shall flourish like the palm tree; he shall grow like a cedar in Lebanon.
>
> That that be planted in the house of the Lord shall flourish in the courts of our God.
>
> They shall still bring forth fruit in old age; they shall be fat and flourishing;
>
> To shew that the Lord is upright: he is my rock, and there is no unrighteousness in him. (Psalm 92:4-5, 8, 12-15.)

A nation in mourning is something for us to consider, and we of all faiths, all creeds, are a part of it. We meet today in this historic place on common ground. Throughout this nation today, and indeed throughout the whole world of free nations, we are of one mind, and that is indeed heavy and sad. The great leveler of mankind, the great reaper of death, has made us all kin, particularly all those of us who are not strangers to sorrow and suffering because of the loss of loved ones.

We mourn as a national family for the loss of a promising and dynamic young leader, cut down in the prime of his manhood. Those who have known him best have eulogized him and have extolled his virtues and accomplishments and have been kind to political, philosophical, or ideological differences of the past.

Today we mourn President John F. Kennedy as the leader of this great nation, who has held its destiny in his hands. We have remembered him frequently in our supplications, as we have sensed somewhat the heavy burdens of responsibility of his great office. There are no party lines in the country today. There are no divisions because of creed, of race, of wealth, or of position. All decent-thinking people unashamedly, with his sorrowing family, mourn as though we had part with them in this shattering tragedy—this death of our leader, cut down by the murderous hand of a foul assassin.

But perhaps our hearts should go out equally and for a different reason to the family of him who, in the commission of a cowardly act, has sinned against himself, sinned against the mother who bore him, against the family name, and against heaven and God.

In our mourning today we must turn to that never-failing source of comfort and peace, to gain the strength to live out our day and strengthen the hands and the hearts of those who must now carry on the "unfinished business," which is now the responsibility of the new President of the United States. It is to that theme and to that purpose that I shall address my brief remarks, seeking most humbly for the spirit of this occasion.

The comfort of the children of the Lord from the beginning was spoken of and recorded in the writings of Isaiah. When suffering Israel was in danger of perishing in the wilderness, there came this promise to quiet their fears. Said the Lord through His prophet:

227

Thy dead men shall live, together with my dead body shall they arise. Awake and sing, ye that dwell in dust: for thy dew is as the dew of herbs, and the earth shall cast out the dead. (Isaiah 26:19.)

And the sobering wisdom of experience of that man of God says:

Seek ye the Lord while he may be found, call ye upon him while he is near:

Let the wicked forsake his way, and the unrighteous man his thoughts: and let him return unto the Lord, and he will have mercy upon him; and to our God, for he will abundantly pardon.

For my thoughts are not your thoughts, neither are your ways my ways, saith the Lord.

For as the heavens are higher than the earth, so are my ways higher than your ways, and my thoughts than your thoughts.

Instead of the thorn shall come up the fir tree, and instead of the brier shall come up the myrtle tree. (Isaiah 55:6-9, 13.)

The pioneer people who built this historic building [the Salt Lake Tabernacle] sang as they trudged footsore and weary across a seemingly never-ending and dreary waste of prairie:

And should we die before our journey's through,
Happy day! all is well!
We then are free from toil and sorrow, too;
With the just we shall dwell!
But if our lives are spared again
To see the Saints their rest obtain,
O how we'll make this chorus swell—
All is well! all is well!
—"Come, Come, Ye Saints"
*Hymns,* no. 13

The answer, then, to the question of the man of grief—"Shall a man live again?"—has been given, and the heavens have been opened to the man of faith to ease the intensity of his suffering in times of deep sorrow.

228      Nearly 800 years had to pass before the promise to Is-

rael of resurrection of those who had died and would die thereafter was to be realized. Telling of the time of the crucifixion of the Lord, Matthew records:

> And, behold, the veil of the temple was rent in twain from the top to the bottom; and the earth did quake, and the rocks rent;
> And the graves were opened; and many bodies of the saints which slept arose,
> And came out of the graves after his resurrection, and went into the holy city, and appeared unto many. (Matthew 27:51-53.)

As it was in the days following His resurrection, so shall it be at His second coming. The graves shall be opened, and the righteous dead shall be caught up in the clouds of heaven to meet Him; and those who are living upon the earth shall likewise be caught up to dwell eternally with their Redeemer.

This is the answer of the prophets to the scoffer who ridicules the plan of the Lord. The Apostle Paul explained this plan in simple language:

> If in this life only we have hope in Christ, we are of all men most miserable.
> But now is Christ risen from the dead, and become the firstfruits of them that slept.
> For since by man came death, by man came also the resurrection of the dead.
> For as in Adam all die, even so in Christ shall all be made alive.
> But every man in his own order: Christ the firstfruits; afterward they that are Christ's at his coming.
> The last enemy that shall be destroyed is death.
> So when this corruptible shall have put on incorruption, and this mortal shall have put on immortality, then shall be brought to pass the saying that is written, Death is swallowed up in victory.
> O death, where is thy sting? O grave, where is thy victory?
> The sting of death is sin; and the strength of sin is the law.
> But thanks be to God, which giveth us the victory through our Lord Jesus Christ. (1 Corinthians 15:19-23, 26, 54-57.)

The shocking events of the past week have brought us    229

serious reflection, some of which I would voice in this solemn service today. You may have read that simply worded bit of wisdom that came out of our Mother Country:

> Isn't it strange that princes and kings,
> And clowns that caper in sawdust rings
> And common folks like you and me
> Are builders for eternity?
> To each is given a bag of tools,
> A shapeless mass, and a book of rules;
> And each must make, ere life is flown,
> A stumbling-block or a stepping stone.
> —*London Tidbits*

Freedom of choice, free agency, next to life itself, is the greatest endowment of God to His children. A prophet pointed up the real crux of the eternal warfare that has been waged since the beginning of time when he said:

For the kingdom of the devil must shake, and they which belong to it must needs be stirred up unto repentance, or the devil will grasp them with his everlasting chains, and they be stirred up to anger, and perish;

For behold, at that day shall he rage in the hearts of the children of men, and stir them up to anger against that which is good.

And others will he pacify, and lull them away into carnal security, that they will say: All is well in Zion: yea, Zion prospereth, all is well—and thus the devil cheateth their souls, and leadeth them away carefully down to hell. (2 Nephi 28:19-21.)

The two systems that are in constant conflict are pointed out in that statement. The Lord Himself clearly set forth this principle when He said: "And fear not them which kill the body, but are not able to kill the soul: but rather fear him which is able to destroy both soul and body in hell." (Matthew 10:28.)

He was talking of the devil, the power of darkness, that could destroy body and soul. After all is said about the

230

various forms of human government, it has always seemed to me that there are only two systems, with some slight shades between them. The one contemplates the domination of human souls into a system where personal aggrandizement by rulers of nations is accomplished as a reward for human slavery. The philosophy for such a system may be found in the boastful claim of the master of darkness, well known to students of the scriptures: ". . . I will redeem all mankind, that one soul shall not be lost, and surely I will do it; wherefore give me thine honor." (Moses 4:1.)

Its application can be found in governments ever since the beginning of time as one person, or a few at the top, tell the rest what they can do; whether they can or cannot build a home; what prices they can receive for their produce; what they may eat; what and how they may worship; and so on.

I hear some say, "But that couldn't happen to us in the United States of America." In a warning of dangers which could confront such a nation as ours, Abraham Lincoln once said:

Many great and good men, sufficiently qualified for any task they should undertake, may ever be found, whose ambition would aspire to nothing beyond a seat in Congress, a gubernatorial, or a presidential chair. But such belong not to the family of the lion or the brood of the eagles. What? Think you these places would satisfy an Alexander, a Caesar or a Napoleon? Never. Towering genius disdains a beaten path. It seeks regions heretofore unexplored. It sees no distinction in adding story to story upon the monuments of fame directed to the memory of others. It denies that it is glory enough to serve under a chief. It scorns to tread in the footsteps of any predecessor, however illustrious. It thirsts and burns for distinction, and if possible, it will have it, whether at the expense of emancipating slaves or enslaving freemen.

It is unreasonable, then, to expect that some men, possessed of the loftiest genius, coupled with ambition sufficient to push it to its utmost stretch, will at some time spring up amongst us, and when such an one does, it will require the people to be united with each other, attached to the

231

government and the laws, and generally intelligent, successfully to frustrate his design.

Distinction will be his paramount object, and although he would as willingly, perhaps more so, acquire it by doing good as harm, yet that opportunity being passed and nothing left to be done in the way of building up, he would sit down boldly to the task of pulling down.

Here, then, is a probable case, highly dangerous, and such a case could not have well existed heretofore.

The second system is the one proposed by the Master of Light even before this world was created wherein each soul was to have the opportunity to work out his own destiny. That plan involved sacrifice, toil and sweat, trial and error and tears, but always individual freedom was assured through the right of individual choice. Such a system is to be found in a nation or country where there is a completely unrestricted representative government such as was contemplated by our forefathers in this country and introduced in the declaration of 1776. It was fostered years before and developed later under a broad, sweeping concept expressed in these words: "We hold these truths to be self-evident: that all men are created equal; that they are endowed by their Creator with certain inalienable rights; that among these are life, liberty, and the pursuit of happiness."

In such a system, the individual is told in effect, "You are free to make your life what you will, and we will try to see that you are rewarded for worthwhile service." These lofty concepts did not spring from governments, but from the Creator Himself, penned into tenets for a stabilized government by men whom God raised up for this very purpose. The basic principles underlying these concepts of human government are contained in that great state paper, the Constitution of the United States of America. Written into the Constitution as we have it today are three prime safeguards:

232

1. There are unique restraints on power that governmental authority may exercise upon citizens, embodied in what is known as the Bill of Rights.

2. There is outlined a division of power between the federal and state governments.

3. There is defined a distinct separation of power among three branches of government—the executive, the legislative, and the judicial—in such a way as to provide checks and balances to control the exercise of governmental power.

In the wisdom of the Almighty, this ensign of liberty was raised to the nations to fulfill an ancient prophecy that "out of Zion [should] go forth the law, and the word of the Lord from Jerusalem." (Isaiah 2:3.) How could this be? The answer is clear: through the Constitution, kings and rulers and the peoples of all nations under heaven may be informed of the blessings enjoyed by the people of this land of Zion by reason of their freedom under Divine guidance, and be constrained to adopt similar governmental systems and thus fulfill the ancient law to which I have already referred.

My visits to underprivileged countries and among subjugated peoples who have placed their trust in governments of dominating men, rather than in governments of constitutional law, have shown me the importance and the great blessed privilege that is ours to live in this country where the basic law of the Constitution safeguards us in our God-given rights.

It was President Theodore Roosevelt who said, "The things that will destroy America are prosperity at any price, peace at any price, safety first instead of duty first, and love of soft living and the get-rich-quick theory of life."

May we soberly reflect upon the danger of following

233

any such course. This is the time for us to remember what Moses said, following his face-to-face revelation with God: ". . . Now, for this cause I know that man is nothing, which thing I never had supposed." (Moses 1:10.)

This is the time for us to reflect upon the priceless heritage which is ours, born out of the travail and sacrifices of those who have gone on before. As James Russell Lowell has beautifully phrased it:

> Careless seems the great Avenger; history's pages but
> record
> One death-grapple in the darkness 'twixt old systems
> and the Word;
> Truth forever on the scaffold, Wrong forever on the
> throne,—
> Yet that scaffold sways the future, and, behind the
> dim unknown,
> Standeth God within the shadow, keeping watch
> above his own.
>
> By the light of burning heretics Christ's bleeding feet I
> track,
> Toiling up new Calvaries ever with the cross that
> turns not back,
> And these mounts of anguish number how each
> generation learned
> One new word of that grand *Credo* which in prophet-
> hearts hath burned
> Since the first man stood God-conquered with his face
> to heaven upturned.
>
> For humanity sweeps onward: where today the martyr
> stands,
> On the morrow crouches Judas with the silver in his
> hands;
> Far in front the cross stands ready and the crackling
> fagots burn,
> While the hooting mob of yesterday in silent awe
> return
> To glean up the scattered ashes into History's golden
> urn.

—"The Present Crisis"

It is time to say to ourselves and to those who mourn deeply: "Search diligently, pray always, and be believing, and all things shall work together for your good, if ye walk uprightly and remember the covenant wherewith ye have covenanted one with another." (D&C 90:24.)

God lives, and because He so loved the world, He sent his Only Begotten Son as an atonement for our sins and to unlock the gates of the prison house of death. Because of His great merciful plan of salvation, our loved ones who have passed on still live in realms beyond our sight.

So, too, President John F. Kennedy likewise shall live again.

Yes, the question of every man is: "If a man die, shall he live again?" And it is answered by the certainty of the word of God: "Thy dead men shall live, together with my dead body shall they arise." (Isaiah 26:19.)

Let us bow our heads in gratitude to our merciful Creator for His redeeming Son, for the freedom of our land, and join with the prophet in His inspired utterance:

> May the gates of hell be shut continually before me, because that my heart is broken and my spirit is contrite! O Lord, wilt thou not shut the gates of thy righteousness before me, that I may walk in the path of the low valley, that I may be strict in the plain road!
>
> O Lord, wilt thou encircle me around in the robe of thy righteousness! O Lord, wilt thou make a way for mine escape before mine enemies! Wilt thou make my path straight before me! Wilt thou not place a stumbling block in my way—but that thou wouldst clear my way before me, and hedge not up my way, but the ways of mine enemy.
>
> O Lord, I have trusted in thee, and I will trust in thee forever. I will not put my trust in the arm of flesh; for I know that cursed is he that putteth his trust in the arm of flesh. Yea, cursed is he that putteth his trust in man or maketh flesh his arm.
>
> Yea, I know that God will give liberally to him that asketh. Yea, my God will give me, if I ask not amiss; therefore I will lift up my voice unto thee; yea, I will cry unto thee, my God, the rock of my righteousness. Behold, my voice shall forever ascend up unto thee, my rock and mine everlasting God. Amen. (2 Nephi 4:32-35.)

And so we say, with millions of others in America, to Mrs. Kennedy and her little ones, to the brothers and sisters, the family, the intimate friends, and all who mourn today, as the Master said to His disciples: "Peace I leave with you, my peace I give unto you: not as the world giveth, give I unto you." (John 14:27.)

Then showing us the way to peace, He said: "These things I have spoken unto you, that in me ye might have peace. In the world ye shall have tribulation: but be of good cheer; I have overcome the world." (John 16:33.)

Peace be to the souls of you who mourn. May you be comforted by that eternal assurance that God is in his heavens, and all is right with the world, to which I bear solemn testimony and witness as a disciple of the Lord Jesus Christ, and leave my blessing and add my prayers to those which have been spoken and have welled up in the hearts of the millions who have prayed to assuage the grief of the mourning family of this, our leader, who has been so tragically snatched from mortal life.

And I do it all humbly and bear my witness in the name of the Lord Jesus Christ.

# 29

# Easter Morning—A Newness of Life

*A*s Easter Day dawns, in Christian churches everywhere happy throngs gather together for the purpose, let us reverently hope, of listening in sermon and in song to the story of life as it is understood by men of various sects and creeds.

Many in these congregations add freshness and color to the scene by a display of spring finery that may often, we suspect, provide the main motive for attendance at such gatherings. But even so, such thoughtless ones, however unwittingly, by "putting off the old and taking on the new" are but typifying the deeper significance of the day.

It is springtime. "Every clod feels a stir of might, an instinct within it that reaches and towers; and groping blindly above it for light, climbs to a soul in grass and in flowers." ("The Vision of Sir Launfal.")

In autumn, we watch the leaves turn from living green to the yellow of age and drop from seemingly lifeless boughs from the chill winds and the killing frosts, warning all nature of an approaching winter. As the banks of falling snow and Mother Earth absorb these symbols of yesterday's living, a grave has been provided, and death apparently comes.

But in the spring, a beautiful spectacle meets our gaze. Watered by the dews and rains from heaven and warmed by a genial sun, the grass becomes green again, buds begin to burst from trees that before seemed dead, and flowers spring forth as though in protest against him who had thought of winter as the end.

Beautifully and dramatically, Easter morning in the springtime proclaims that divine truth that "death is not the end—it is but a beginning!"

It was to Israel in her days of travail in the wilderness that the Lord gave, through His prophet, a comforting thought that must have been understood to be both a promise as well as a prophecy: "Thy dead men shall live, together with my dead body shall they arise. Awake and sing, ye that dwell in dust; for thy dew is as the dew of herbs, and the earth shall cast out the dead." (Isaiah 26:19.)

Nearly 800 years passed before that promise was to be realized when "the earth shall cast out the dead." This event of such importance to the unnumbered dead occurred at the conclusion of the work and ministry of our Lord and Master and is recorded in these words:

> And, behold, the veil of the temple was rent in twain from the top to the bottom; and the earth did quake, and the rocks rent;
> And the graves were opened; and many bodies of the saints which slept arose,
> And came out of the graves after his resurrection, and went into the holy city, and appeared unto many. (Matthew 27:51-53.)

By whom had this mighty miracle been wrought, and what power had thus been manifested? True, the prophets had foretold a day when the Lord would "bring out the

238

prisoners from the prison, and them that sit in darkness out of the prison house" (Isaiah 42:7), and that He was to bear the sins of many and make intercession for the transgressors (Isaiah 53:12), but until the Master himself declared the purpose of His mission on earth, it is doubtful that the saints of former days comprehended its full significance. Said the Savior:

> For God so loved the world, that he gave his only begotten Son, that whosoever believeth in him should not perish, but have everlasting life.
> For God sent not his Son into the world to condemn the world; but that the world through him might be saved. (John 3:16-17.)

Thus it became clear that the coming of the Lord to earth was only a part of a divine plan conceived in the heavens before the foundation of the earth was laid "when the morning stars sang together, and all the sons of God shouted for joy." (Job 38:7.) "For as in Adam all die, even so in Christ shall all be made alive." (1 Corinthians 15:22.) "In my father's house are many mansions: if it were not so, I would have told you. I go to prepare a place for you. . . . that where I am, there ye may be also." (John 14:2-3.)

As a result of the mortal life, the death, and the resurrection of the Christ, the way was opened by which immortality and eternal life could be gained by all mankind, for, as the Apostle Paul declared, "Though he were a Son, yet learned he obedience by the things which he suffered; And being made perfect, he became the author of eternal salvation unto all them that obey him." (Hebrews 5:8-9.)

The beautiful story of the glorious resurrection of the Christ is told simply by the writers of the gospels.

> And when Joseph had taken the body, he wrapped it in a clean linen cloth,
> And laid it in his own new tomb, which he had hewn out in the rock: and he rolled a great stone to the door of the sepulchre, and departed.

239

Now the next day, that followed the day of preparation, the chief priests and Pharisees came together unto Pilate,

Saying, Sir, we remember that that deceiver said, while he was yet alive, After three days I will rise again.

Command therefore that the sepulchre be made sure until the third day, lest his disciples come by night, and steal him away, and say unto the people, He is risen from the dead: so the last error shall be worse than the first.

Pilate said unto them, Ye have a watch: go your way, make it as sure as ye can.

So they went, and made the sepulchre sure, sealing the stone, and setting a watch.

In the end of the sabbath, as it began to dawn toward the first day of the week, came Mary Magdalene and the other Mary to see the sepulchre.

And, behold, there was a great earthquake: for the angel of the Lord descended from heaven, and came and rolled back the stone from the door, and sat upon it.

His countenance was like lightning, and his raiment white as snow:

And for fear of him the keepers did shake, and became as dead men. (Matthew 27:59-60, 62-66; 28:1-4.)

Now upon the first day of the week, very early in the morning, they [meaning Mary Magdalene, the other Mary, and others] came unto the sepulchre, bringing the spices which they had prepared, and certain others with them.

And they found the stone rolled away from the sepulchre.

And they entered in, and found not the body of the Lord Jesus.

And it came to pass, as they were much perplexed thereabout, behold, two men stood by them in shining garments:

And as they were afraid, and bowed down their faces to the earth, they said unto them, Why seek ye the living among the dead?

He is not here, but is risen: remember how he spake unto you when he was yet in Galilee,

Saying, The Son of man must be delivered into the hands of sinful men, and be crucified, and the third day rise again.

And they remembered his words,

And returned from the sepulchre, and told all these things unto the eleven, and to all the rest. (Luke 24:1-9.)

But Mary stood without at the sepulchre weeping: and as she wept, she stooped down, and looked into the sepulchre,

And seeth two angels in white sitting, the one at the head, and the other at the feet, where the body of Jesus had lain.

And they say unto her, Woman, why weepest thou? She saith unto them, Because they have taken away my Lord, and I know not where they have laid him.

And when she had thus said, she turned herself back, and saw Jesus standing, and knew not that it was Jesus.

Jesus saith unto her, Mary. She turned herself, and saith unto him, Rabboni; which is to say, Master.

Jesus saith unto her, Touch me not; for I am not yet ascended to my Father: but go to my brethren, and say unto them, I ascend unto my Father, and your Father; and to my God, and your God.

Mary Magdalene came and told the disciples that she had seen the Lord, and that he had spoken these things unto her. (John 20:11-14, 16-18.)

To the membership of The Church of Jesus Christ of Latter-day Saints, Easter Day commemorates the resurrection of the Christ, but more than that, it signals the privileges and opportunities given to mankind thereby to be likewise raised from the grave either to a resurrection of the just or to a resurrection of the unjust, determined solely by the willingness of all souls "to do all things whatsoever [they are] commanded." (D&C 97:25.)

As to the resurrection of mankind taking place in an orderly manner, there can be no doubt, because of the revelations that have been given in this day. Those who are the more righteous will come forth in the morning of the first resurrection, coincident with the second coming of the Savior to this earth, and those less faithful at a time merited by the life each lived here in mortality.

Easter dawns upon a troubled world. Selfishness and lust for power on the part of rulers of nations have transformed the world into a seething cauldron of fears and hates and destruction of the innocent. Never before in the history of the world has life been valued so cheaply, when hundreds of thousands who are guiltless of the evil now rampant in the world have been sent to their death.

Fortunate indeed is that soul who has in his heart a testimony of the divine mission of the Savior of the world, who unlocked the doors of the prison house and became the first fruits of resurrection from the grave. Such a one,

241

even in the face of impending death, may sing with the righteous, "O death, where is thy sting? O grave, where is thy victory?

"But thanks be to God, which giveth us the victory through our Lord Jesus Christ." (1 Corinthians 15:55, 57.)

"If in this life only we have hope in Christ, we are of all men most miserable." (1 Corinthians 15:19.)

In our generation, the Prophet Joseph Smith with the Saints was driven from his home by his enemies, saw his friends and loved ones tormented, persecuted, and put to death, and finally met his own death at the hands of foul assassins. The Lord, as though to prepare the Prophet for these ordeals after listening to his impassioned crying and pleadings while he lay as a prisoner in Liberty Jail, gave him the comfort of a beautiful revelation:

My son, peace be unto thy soul; thine adversity and thine afflictions shall be but a small moment;

And then, if thou endure it well, God shall exalt thee on high; thou shalt triumph over all thy foes. (D&C 121:7-8.)

At the same time he voiced his wrath against those who oppressed the innocent and his anointed:

Wo unto them; because they have offended my little ones they shall be severed from the ordinances of mine house.

Their basket shall not be full, their houses and their barns shall perish, and they themselves shall be despised by those that flattered them.

They shall not have right to the priesthood, nor their posterity after them from generation to generation.

It had been better for them that a millstone had been hanged about their necks, and they drowned in the depth of the sea.

Wo unto all those that discomfort my people, and drive, and murder, and testify against them, saith the Lord of Hosts; a generation of vipers shall not escape the damnation of hell.

Behold, mine eyes see and know all their works, and I have in reserve a swift judgment in the season thereof, for them all. (D&C 121:19-24.)

242    To all the Saints abroad and to the righteous every-

where, who at this moment are undergoing the terrible ordeals of cruel war, may we offer them the hope and the comfort of the revealed words from a living Father in which he promises, through the Savior, a glorious resurrection and eternal life. And to the high and mighty who stand accused because of their wickedness, may we point out their condemnation and ultimate damnation, except they repent and turn from their evil ways.

To lead men to gain a "knowledge of the Son of God, unto a perfect man" (Ephesians 4:13), God has set up his kingdom on the earth with the holy priesthood for the perfecting of the saints and the work of the ministry. (Ephesians 4:12.)

During his advent in mortality, the Master called to service twelve apostles whom He charged with the responsibility of being special witnesses of His life, mission, and resurrection, even as He commissioned the Apostle Paul, "For thou shalt be his witness unto all men of what thou hast seen and heard." (Acts 22:15.)

In this dispensation of God's kingdom on the earth, He has likewise called men to be special witnesses of the name of Christ in all the world.

By the power of the Holy Ghost and in deep humility I solemnly bear testimony to the world that God lives and that His Son, Jesus Christ, was born in the flesh; that He was crucified and was raised from the dead with a body of flesh and bones, and sits today on the right hand of the Father as our judge and advocate; and that all those who will accept and live according to His teachings will not perish but will have everlasting life.

Thus also by the power of the Holy Ghost, all baptized members of the body of the Church may know the teachings to be true that Christ is risen, as He has said. (Matthew 28:6.)

243

# 30

# Faith to Surmount Life's Inevitables

> *N*ow upon the first day of the week, very early in the morning, they came unto the sepulchre, bringing the spices which they had prepared, and certain others with them.
>
> And they found the stone rolled away from the sepulchre.
>
> And they entered in, and found not the body of the Lord Jesus.
>
> And it came to pass, as they were much perplexed thereabout, behold, two men stood by them in shining garments:
>
> And as they were afraid, and bowed down their faces to the earth, they said unto them, Why seek ye the living among the dead?
>
> He is not here, but is risen; remember how he spake unto you when he was yet in Galilee,
>
> Saying, The Son of man must be delivered into the hands of sinful men, and be crucified, and the third day rise again.
>
> And they remembered his words. (Luke 1:1-8.)

Thus is recorded the greatest event in the history of the world, the literal resurrection of the Lord Jesus Christ, the Savior of mankind. The greatest of all the divine powers of an incarnated Son of God had been dramatically demonstrated.

Following swiftly his own resurrection, there came an evidence of a second transcendent power to raise from the grave not only Himself, but others who, though dead, had believed in Him. Matthew makes this simple, forthright record of the miraculous resurrection of the faithful from mortal death: "And the graves were opened; and many bodies of the saints which slept arose, And came out of the graves after his resurrection, and went into the holy city, and appeared unto many." (Matthew 27:52-53.)

Nor was this to be the end of the redemptive powers of this illustrious Son of God. Down through the ages, in every dispensation, has come the cheering promise: "For as in Adam all die, even so in Christ shall all be made alive" (1 Corinthians 15:22), ". . . they that have done good, unto the resurrection of life; and they that have done evil, unto the resurrection of damnation" (John 5:29). Time is rapidly moving on to a complete consummation of His divine mission.

If the full significance of these thrilling events were understood in this day when, as the prophets foretold, the wicked are preparing to slay the wicked and "fear shall come upon every man" (D&C 63:33), this understanding would put to flight many of the fears and anxieties that beset men and nations. Indeed, if we "fear God" and "honour the king" (1 Peter 2:17), we can then lay claim to the glorious promise of the Master: ". . . if you strip yourselves from jealousies and fears, . . . you shall see me . . ." (D&C 67:10).

I should like to cite a few of the "inevitables" that all may one day face and to draw some parallels from sacred writings in the hope of vitalizing the mission of the Redeemer. This evidence demonstrates, to some extent, how an unshakable faith in the reality of the resurrected Lord and in the certainty of the resurrection of all mankind would provide the essential courage to accept "insecurity with equanimity" in a material world. Thus may all

245

successfully combat the apprehensions and tensions that are so destructive among us today.

Consider as one of life's inevitables, if you will, the condition of one suffering from an incurable malady, or faced with the heart-breaking prospect of impending death of a loved one. Have you ever felt yourself spiritually devastated by inconsolable grief?

May I take you to a sacred scene portraying one whose entire strength seemed to be slipping from her grasp and let you feel her courage in a fateful hour. Huddled at the foot of the cross was the silent figure of a beautiful middle-aged mother with shawl drawn tightly about her head and shoulders. Cruelly tormented on the cross above her was her firstborn son. One can but feebly understand the intensity of the suffering of Mary's mother-heart. She now faced in reality the import of old Simeon's doleful prediction as he had blessed this son as a tiny infant: "Behold, this child is set . . . for a sign which shall be spoken against; (Yea, a sword shall pierce through thy own soul also.)" (Luke 2:34-35.)

What was it that sustained her during her tragic ordeal? She knew the reality of an existence beyond this mortal life. Had she not conversed with an angel, a messenger of God? She undoubtedly had heard of her son's last recorded prayer before His betrayal, as it has been written by John: "And now, O Father, glorify thou me with thine own self with the glory which I had with thee before the world was." (John 17:5.) This sainted mother with bowed head heard His last prayer murmured from the cross through tortured lips: "Father, into thy hands I commend my spirit" (Luke 23:46), thus inspiring her with resignation and a testimony of reassurance of a reunion shortly with Him and with God, her Heavenly Father.

246 Heaven is not far removed from him who, in deep sorrow,

looks confidently forward to a glorious day of resurrection.

Now to mention another of the inevitables:

As the press, radio, and television bring to us daily the frightening prospect of devastating war with atomic or hydrogen bombs and guided missiles, are we filled with forebodings of impending doom? What is there to set our souls free from such terrifying anxieties?

Let us look at the example of Peter, whose loyalty to the Master seemed to have exceeded his courage when, in the face of physical hazard, he denied the Master thrice on the night of the betrayal. Compare this fear-torn Peter with the boldness he manifested shortly thereafter before those same religious bigots who had so recently demanded the death of Jesus. He denounced them as murderers and called them to repentance, suffered imprisonment, and later went fearlessly to his own martyrdom.

What was it that had changed him? He had been a personal witness to the change that came to the broken, pain-racked body taken from the cross, to a glorified resurrected body. The plain and simple answer is that Peter was a changed man because he knew the power of the risen Lord. No more would he be alone on the shores of Galilee, or in prison, or in death. His Lord would be near him.

And now still another of the inevitables among us:

In the writings of Luke, just an inference is made as to what may have been thought to be the reason for mental and spiritual turmoil, and which may have been as much in evidence then as it is among us today in those who have advanced degrees in their higher learning in secular fields but who have neglected spiritual nourishment. Such a one, no doubt, was Saul of Tarsus—Paul, the Apostle to the Gentiles. During his interview and defense before King Agrippa, Festus, who was present, "said with a loud voice, Paul, thou art beside thyself; much learning doth make

247

thee mad." (Acts 26:24.) Indeed, it may have seemed so to those who had known of his zealous persecution of the followers of the Master, in contrast to his now declared allegiance to that Jesus he had before so loudly denounced.

The insinuation of Festus suggests what higher education could do to a frustrated man with but a smattering of unrelated bits of information but no unifying philosophy.

Years later, Paul explained to his beloved Timothy the simple formula that makes for a contented soul: ". . . godliness with contentment is great gain" (1 Timothy 6:6), and then explained the source from which that essential godliness comes: ". . . but godliness is profitable unto all things, having promise of the life that now is, and of that which is to come" (1 Timothy 4:8).

That promise of eternal life had given meaning and purpose to the life of Paul as it does to all of us who so believe. He had heard the Master's voice at the time of his conversion, declaring the reality of the resurrected Lord, whose teachings by His authorized servants, Paul now knew, were the "power of God unto salvation." (Romans 1:16.)

As the challenge of dictator nations is before us, with their advances in destructive military science, it is a challenge, of course, for us to be strong in military science. We must beware, however, lest our much learning in these worldly matters likewise makes us mad. It is also a challenge for us to be bold through faith in that Divine Redeemer by whom all who obediently serve Him might be saved. Atomic power and guided missiles are dangers only when they are in the hands of evil men.

And now, finally, may I make one further reference to an inevitable with which many are confronted:

248  Have you never stood seemingly defeated after years

of grueling struggle and faced the prospect of programs, principles, or policies that are dear to your heart being ruthlessly condemned to failure? Why do some men commit suicide when their bank fails or their earthly possessions are swept away? Why do some rise above the heartbreak of disaster and calamity while others go down in inglorious and pitiful despondency and bitterness as though the struggle of life had all been wasted? These and others are sobering questions.

A leading educator, after noting the great interest in industrial, governmental, and university circles in clinical psychology or in what he called behavioral science, summarized the thinking of eminent authorities with this significant statement: "This interest derives not only from the trend cited . . . but because of the tremendous social conflicts, such as war, which demonstrate behavior breakdown." (Dr. G. Homer Durham, Utah Commissioner of Higher Education.)

A final illustration may suggest a solution to these and other similar frustrating problems:

The Prophet Joseph Smith in this modern day was facing martyrdom at the hands of his enemies for saying that he had seen visions in which God the Father and His Son and others who had lived upon the earth had appeared to him as living, resurrected, glorified beings. Like the Apostle Paul, he dared not deny having had these heavenly manifestations, lest by so doing he would offend God and come under condemnation.

In the midst of bitter persecution, with his coming doom already foreshadowed, the word of the Lord came to him:

> . . . if the very jaws of hell shall gape open the mouth wide after thee, know thou, my son, that all these things shall give thee experience, and shall be for thy good.

The Son of Man hath descended below them all. Art thou greater than he?

Therefore, hold on thy way . . . for [the] bounds [of your enemies] are set, they cannot pass. . . . fear not what men can do, for God shall be with you forever and ever. (D&C 122:7-9.)

. . . let virtue garnish thy thoughts unceasingly; then shall thy confidence wax strong in the presence of God. . . .

And thy dominion shall be an everlasting dominion. . . . (D&C 121:45-46.)

There we have our answer. Better, as Paul said, "godliness with contentment" than an empty compromise for the sake of expedience or the plaudits of men. Each of us can know that our Redeemer lives, as did Job in the midst of his temptation to "curse God, and die" (Job 2:9), and we can know also that we too can open the door and invite Him in to sup with us. We can see ourselves one day as resurrected beings claiming kinship to Him who gave His life that the rewards to mortal men for earthly struggle and experience will be the fruits of eternal life even though, as measured by human standards, one's life's labors seemed to have been defeated. This is what a voice of wisdom has said: "The best thoughts, affections, and aspirations of a great soul are fixed upon the infinitude of eternity. Destined as such a soul is for immortality, it finds all that is not eternal too short, all that is not infinite too small." (Inscription on Stanford University Memorial Chapel.)

I invite the honest in heart everywhere to rise above their human fears and frustrations and to rejoice as did the Apostle to the Gentiles: ". . . thanks be to God, which giveth us the victory through our Lord Jesus Christ." (1 Corinthians 15:57.)

# 31

# From the Valley of Despair to the Mountain Peaks of Hope

This is to me a most significant occasion* and a most difficult assignment about which I have prayed most earnestly that I might have the proper spirit and inspiration. The purpose of this service is not to glorify war, but, from the Lord's own declaration, to set forth clearly the position of the Church with regard to war. We do not wish to enter into a controversy as to the rightness or wrongness of war, but to set at rest the torments of those who have loved ones engaged in the ugly conflicts of war. We are not here to open old wounds in hearts that have been torn with the devastation which comes with the sense of loneliness because of the loss of loved ones.

We are here to help lift the eyes of those who mourn from the valley of despair to the light upon the mountain peaks of hope, to endeavor to answer questions about war, to bring peace to troubled souls, not as the world giveth, but only that which comes from the Prince of Peace. We

*Note: This address was delivered at a special Memorial Day service, May 30, 1971.

are here to lift all of us out of the shadows into life and light.

In our generation the true Christian's position on war is clearly set forth by a declaration in which the Lord says, "Therefore, renounce war and proclaim peace. . . ." (D&C 98:16.)

What is the position of the Church with respect to war? A declaration of the First Presidency given during World War II is still applicable in our time. The statement said: ". . . the Church is and must be against war. The Church itself cannot wage war unless and until the Lord shall issue new commands. It cannot regard war as a righteous means of settling international disputes; these should and could be settled—the nations agreeing—by peaceful negotiations and adjustments."

There is a scripture that has direct bearing here:

> And now, verily I say unto you concerning the laws of the land, it is my will that my people should observe to do all things whatsoever I command them.
>
> And that law of the land which is constitutional, supporting that principle of freedom in maintaining rights and privileges, belongs to all mankind, and is justifiable before me.
>
> Therefore, I, the Lord, justify you, and your brethren of my church, in befriending that law which is the constitutional law of the land;
>
> And as pertaining to the law of man, whatsoever is more or less than this, cometh of evil. (D&C 98:4-7.)

Note particularly that the revelation is directed to members of the Church. Therefore, it is applicable to persons of all nations, not only those in the land we call America.

There are many who are troubled and their souls harrowed by the haunting question of the position of the soldier who in combat kills the enemy. Again, the First Presidency has commented:

When, therefore, constitutional law, obedient to those principles, calls the manhood of the Church into the armed service of any country to which they owe allegiance, their highest civic duty requires that they meet that call. If, hearkening to that call and obeying those in command over them, they shall take the lives of those who fight against them, that will not make of them murderers, nor subject them to the penalty that God has prescribed for those who kill, beyond the principles to be mentioned shortly: for it would be a cruel God that would punish his children as moral sinners for acts done by them as the innocent instrumentalities of a sovereign whom he had told them to obey and whose will they were powerless to resist.

God is at the helm.

I will paraphrase the next statement from the message of the First Presidency in order to make these words more applicable today. The whole world seems presently to be in commotion. As the Lord foretold, we are in a time when men's hearts fail them. There are many persons who are engaged in wars who are devout Christians. They are innocent instrumentalities—war instrumentalities, for the most part—of their warring sovereignties. On each side, people believe that they are fighting for a just cause, for defense of home and country and freedom. On each side they pray to the same God, in the same name, for victory. Both sides cannot be wholly right; perhaps neither is without wrong. God will work out in his own due time and in his own sovereign way the justice and right of the conflict. But he will not hold the innocent instrumentalities of the war—our brethren in arms—responsible for the conflict.

Another question often asked is, Why was not my son or brother or husband or fiance protected on the fields of battle as were others who testify that they were miraculously spared? People who have lost their loved ones are ofttimes troubled by faith-promoting incidents of those who have been miraculously spared. They may say, "Why

253

did it have to happen to my boy (or my husband or my brother or my fiance)?"

While this question may never be fully answered in this life, we are given some illuminating observations from sacred writings. Eternal law does apply to war and those who engage in it. This law was declared by the Master Himself when Peter struck off the ear of Malchus, who was a servant of the Jewish high priest. Jesus reproved Peter, saying, "Put up again thy sword into his place: for all they that take the sword shall perish with the sword." (Matthew 26:52.)

In other words, those who are the perpetrators of war shall perish by the destructive forces that they have unloosed.

The sin, as Moroni of old said, is upon those who sit in their places of power and "in a state of thoughtless stupor" (Alma 60:7), in a frenzy of hate; who lust for unrighteous power and dominion over their fellowmen, and who have put into motion eternal forces that they do not comprehend or cannot control. In His own due time God will pass sentence upon such leaders.

Therefore, let us endeavor to banish all bitterness from our hearts and to rest judgment with God, as did the Apostle Paul when he wrote, ". . . Vengeance is mine; I will repay, saith the Lord." (Romans 12:19.)

There is another question that is often asked: Why did he or she have to die? What is the purpose of life if it is to be so ruthlessly destroyed?

To the prophet Moses, the Lord answered this question in one sentence: "For behold, this is my work and my glory . . . to bring to pass the immortality and eternal life of man." (Moses 1:39.)

Immortality is a free gift to all mankind, but eternal life must be won by deeds done in the flesh.

Recently I received a letter from parents in California whose son had written home just before last Christmas and then shortly thereafter his life was taken in the war in Vietnam. This is part of what he wrote: "War is an ugly thing, a vicious thing. It makes men do things they would not normally do. It breaks up families, causes immorality, cheating, and much hatred. It is not the glorious John Wayne type thing you see in the movies. It is going a month without a shower and a change of clothing. It is fear creeping up your spine when you hear a mortar tube in the jungle. It is not being able to get close enough to the ground when coming under enemy fire; hearing your buddy cry out because of being ripped with a hot piece of shrapnel. You men be proud of your American citizenship, because many brave and valiant men are here preserving your freedom. [This letter was written to his priesthood quorum back home.] God has given you the gift of a free nation, and it is the duty of each of you to help in whatever way you can to preserve it. America is the protector of our church, which is dearer to me than life itself." And then this young man said this very significant thing: "I realize now that I have already received the greatest gift of all, and that is the opportunity to gain exaltation and eternal life. If you have this gift, nothing else really matters."

It is that hope and that faith that has sustained our Latter-day Saints in the military, both the living and the dead. This hope is declared in the scriptures: ". . . therefore this life became a probationary state; a time to prepare to meet God; a time to prepare for that endless state which has been spoken of by us, which is after the resurrection of the dead." (Alma 12:24.)

President Joseph F. Smith made an enlightening comment on this subject. He said, "Many things occur in the world in which it seems very difficult for most of us to find

255

a solid reason for the acknowledgment of the hand of the Lord. I have come to the belief that the only reason I have been able to discover by which we should acknowledge the hand of God in some occurrences is the fact that the thing which has occurred has been permitted of the Lord." (*Gospel Doctrine,* p. 56.) It was not the will of the Lord, but it occurred by permission of the Lord.

George Washington is quoted as having said at one time, "This liberty will look easy by and by when nobody has to die to get it."

No doubt many of you fathers have said in your hearts, as did King David when the sad news of his son Absalom's death was brought to him, "O my son Absalom, my son, my son Absalom! would God I had died for thee, O Absalom, my son, my son!" (2 Samuel 18:33.)

And you mothers may have reacted as did that sainted mother of the young Royal Air Force pilot who was lost in an ill-fated flight over the North Sea. Here are the words of Sister Zina C. Brown when her young son Hugh C. was killed. This lovely wife of Elder Hugh B. Brown, our beloved associate, wrote this perhaps as she remembered the words of the Master in Gethsemane:

> Forgive the clouding doubt that one instant
>     hid Thy face from mine
> With my face toward the light I shall walk
>     by faith until my summons come.
> Dear Father, through Thy Son I pray and
>     praise Thy Holy name.
> And with full heart, made glad by Thy re-
>     deeming love,
> I humbly say, "Thy Will Be Done."

"If in this life only we have hope in Christ, we are of all men most miserable," said the Apostle Paul. (1 Corinthians 15:19.) If we fail to understand this great truth, we will be miserable in time of need, and then sometimes our faith may be challenged. But if we have a faith that looks beyond the grave and trusts in divine Providence to bring all things in their proper perspective in due time, then we have hope, and our fears are calmed. Life does not end with mortal death. Through temple ordinances which bind on earth and in heaven, every promised blessing predicated upon faithfulness will be realized.

One of our friends said to me recently, "I can't make my wife believe that the Lord always answers prayers; even when He says 'no,' He's answered our prayers."

"Let not your heart be troubled" were the first of the parting words of the Master when He said, "In my Father's house are many mansions: if it were not so, I would have told you. I go to prepare a place for you.

"And if I go and prepare a place for you, I will come again, and receive you unto myself; that where I am, there ye may be also." (John 14:1-3.)

And then he said: "Peace I leave with you, my peace I give unto you: not as the world giveth, give I unto you. Let not your heart be troubled, neither let it be afraid." (John 14:27.)

Having gone through some similar experiences in losing loved ones in death, I speak from personal experience when I say to you who mourn, do not try to live too many days ahead. The all-important thing is not that tragedies and sorrows come into our lives, but what we do with them. Death of a loved one is the most severe test that you will ever face, and if you can rise above your griefs and if you will trust in God, then you will be able to surmount any other difficulty with which you may be faced.

One of America's most gifted writers, Henry Wadsworth Longfellow, wrote of this three years after his wife had died, as he longed for her still. Time had not

257

softened his grief nor eased the torment of his memories. He had no heart for poetry. He had no heart for anything, it seemed. Life had become an empty dream. But this could not go on, he told himself. He was letting the days slip by, nursing his despondency. Life was not an empty dream. He must be up and doing. Let the past bury its dead. Suddenly Longfellow was writing in a surge of inspiration, the lines coming almost too quickly for his racing pen. Here are three verses of this immortal and inspired message to those whom he loved:

> Tell me not, in mournful numbers,
>> Life is but an empty dream!—
> For the soul is dead that slumbers,
>> And things are not what they seem.
>
> Life is real! Life is earnest!
>> And the grave is not its goal;
> Dust thou art, to dust returnest,
>> Was not spoken of the soul.
>
> Let us then be up and doing,
>> With a heart for any fate;
> Still achieving, still pursuing,
>> Learn to labor and to wait.

Longfellow wrote these verses and titled his poem "The Psalm of Life." He put it aside at first, unwilling to show it to anyone. As he later explained, "It was a voice from my inmost heart, at a time when I was rallying from depression."

The immortal words of Abraham Lincoln come back for us to ponder:

With malice toward none, with charity for all, with firmness in the right as God gives us to see the right, let us strive on to finish the work we are in, to bind up the nation's wounds, to care for him who shall have borne the battle, and for his widow and his orphan, to all which may achieve a just and lasting peace among ourselves and with all nations. (Second Inaugural Address.)

The blessing to be found in pain is a right-here, right-now blessing, taking place in the very midst of suffering.

As a result of his many experiences with suffering, that great humanitarian, Dr. Albert Schweitzer, gave this advice:

> Don't vex your mind by trying to explain the suffering you have to endure in this life. Don't think that God is punishing you or disciplining you or that he has rejected you. Even in the midst of your suffering, you are in his kingdom. You are always his child, and he has his protecting arms around you. Does a child understand everything his father does? No, but he can confidently nestle in his father's arms and feel perfect happiness, even while tears glisten in his eyes, because he is his father's child.

It was a wise man who said, "We cannot banish dangers, but we can banish fears. We must not demean life, by standing in awe of death."

Remember the story of Job. After his torment his wife came to him and said: "Dost thou still retain thine integrity? curse God, and die." (Job 2:9.)

And in the majesty of his faith, Job said:

> For I know that my redeemer liveth, and that he shall stand at the latter day upon the earth:
> And though after my skin worms destroy this body, yet in my flesh shall I see God:
> Whom I shall see for myself, and mine eyes shall behold, and not another; though my reins be consumed within me. (Job 19:25-27.)

So to you who have lost loved ones, to you who know the pangs of loneliness, some of us have also gone through the fire and understand what it means. We say to you that in the faith that lifts you beyond the sordid trials of the day and points you to the glorious tomorrow that can be yours, you too, like the prophet Job, can say, "I know that my Redeemer lives."

I leave you my blessing, to bring you the peace that can come only from this knowledge and from the witness

259

that you can receive if you will put your trust in your Heavenly Father.

I know that God lives. I know that he has opened the doors to the glorious resurrection. He is biding the time when He shall come again, when the trump shall sound and those who are ready to come forth in the morning of the resurrection shall come forth to be caught up in the clouds of heaven to meet Him. God grant that we may live to be worthy to be among those who will be with Him.

# 32

# Destined for Eternity

Regardless of one's nationality, color, or creed, all are sons and daughters of God. All are searching for answers to many questions. All are, or should be, seeking for fundamentals upon which to anchor their faith. All are probably eager to challenge, but are also susceptible to counsel and improvement in their lives. Finally, all, no doubt, need someone in whom they can trust to point the way that lies ahead.

Some time ago I read an article written by a famous newspaper journalist who explained how he went about arranging for a meaningful conversation with some person whom he wished to interview. He would ask a question similar to this: "Would you mind telling me the inscription you would have written on your tombstone?" He reported that many would give answers like "have fun," "gone to another meeting," and so on. Then the journalist was asked what he himself would have written on his tombstone. He replied very quietly and sincerely, "Safely home, at last."

When the full significance of this statement is impressed upon us, we might well ask ourselves, "After all, what is life all about, and what is our hope beyond this life, believing, as we do, in a life after this one?" Almost everyone, no matter what his religious faith may be, looks forth to an existence that may be defined in various ways. If my assumption is correct, then, we would all wish to have written on our tombstones, as an epitaph to our life's work, that we were "safe at home, at last."

With these thoughts, I wish to bring to your mind some considerations with reference to what each of you, as well as myself, might conclude would be the proper course so that we might one day be safely at home in that heavenly and final abode of man.

As a central theme around which to gather your thoughts, I set forth a few simple but profound truths within the realm of my understanding. I introduce my text with a statement by an anonymous writer that appears as a panel inscription on the walls of the Memorial Chapel of Leland Stanford University at Palo Alto, California. It reads:

"An eternal existence in prospect, converts the whole of your present state into a mere vestibule of the grand court of life, a beginning, an introduction of what is to follow, the entrance into that immeasurable extent of being which is the true life of man. The best thoughts, affections and aspirations of a great soul are fixed upon the infinitude of immortality. Destined as such a soul is for immortality, it finds all that is not eternal too short, all that is not infinite too small."

In full harmony with this theme, the poet William Wordsworth directed our thinking to another great contemplation. He wrote:

> Our birth is but a sleep and a forgetting;
> The Soul that rises with us, our life's Star

> Hath had elsewhere its setting
> And cometh from afar;
> Not in entire forgetfulness,
> And not in utter nakedness,
> But trailing clouds of glory do we come
> From God, who is our home.
> —"Ode on Intimations of Immortality"

From these and other similar teachings from great minds comes that soul-searching declaration of truth. Our life did not begin with birth; our life does not end with death.

How such a faith and certainty as to the true meaning of life gives strength in meeting daily trials and tribulations is well illustrated in a letter written to a beloved brother by a twenty-eight-year-old novelist. The writer, with five other friends, had been sentenced to death during the czarist regime in Russia. While they were awaiting execution, a general came into the room and announced that their sentence had been changed and that they would be sent to Siberia for life imprisonment. In a state of mind created by the expectation of death, followed by the thought of being banished forever to Siberia, the young novelist sat down and wrote this farewell letter:

> Brother, I have not become down-hearted nor low spirited. Life is everywhere, life in ourselves—not in what is outside us. There will be people near me, and to be a man among people and remain a man forever, not to be downhearted nor to fall into whatever misfortunes may befall me—this is life; this is the task of life. I have realized this. This idea has entered my flesh and bones. (Lincoln Schuster, comp., *The World's Great Letters*.)

That writer had made a great discovery. He had his life to live no matter what circumstances would come; and even though he had been robbed of his chance to enjoy many blessings others seemed to enjoy, yet there were many opportunities for the making of new and happy discoveries within himself, to be his own happiness and advancement. Even though he had been sentenced to die, yet he would, as he had written, "remain a man forever."

As it was with that young novelist, so it is with each of us. "Man is, that he might have joy," is a saying now centuries old, but before any of us can achieve the highest of our possibilities, we must realize that the true joy of living is not attained except by him who likewise sees his life "as a beginning, as an introduction of what is to follow, the entrance into that immeasurable extent of being which is the true life of man."

It should be clear to any reasoning mind that thoughtfully ponders these matters that each of us has the responsibility of building a life, not just for the period of our mortal existence, to molder or crumble as clay into the dust when we die. Rather, we are laying the cornerstones here and now for that larger extent of being which does not end with death. Only when our lives are measuring up to the best we know, despite unfortunate and trying situations, only then have we conquered self and are realizing the joy of living which is the purpose of existence.

But, you ask, where can we find the true measure of a man as a pattern from which to develop the best within us and thus avoid the choice of that which is "too short, or too small" for that eternity for which we are preparing?

Some suppose that Jesus Christ is not the literal Son of God, but I am certain that any student of religious literature would agree that He was, without question, the greatest teacher who has ever lived. I speak of Him as a great personage whose life and teachings have endured through the years, as a guide accepted by all as the perfect example after whom all men might well pattern their lives.

He who reads the holy scriptures will remember the high standards set by Jesus Christ in the divine injunction, "Be ye therefore perfect, even as your Father which is in heaven is perfect." (Matthew 5:48.) Furthermore, in his famed Sermon on the Mount He gave us a constitution for the building of a perfect life in what is known in literature as the Beatitudes.

The summation of the perfect young manhood of the Master is expressed in these simple words: "Jesus increased in wisdom and stature, and in favour with God and man." (Luke 2:52.) O that each one of us could grow in size and stature and not lose favor with God as we try to win the honors of men.

It has been said that "a life that is founded on the principles of goodness, love, wisdom, and power that represents the Christ, has a lasting foundation and can be trusted. True life is the principles of Christ, lived. There is no other life that is true."

Jethro, the father-in-law of Moses, the great law-giver of the Old Testament, counseled him to choose able men to become judges among the people in order to avoid a physical breakdown if Moses continued his arduous labors in tending to all the small affairs of Israel. Then Jethro defined an able man as one who fears God, loves the truth, and hates covetousness. (See Exodus 18:21.)

In the life and teachings of the Master, we have an example of the perfect life and also the guiding principles by which perfection might be attained. In the definition of Jethro's able man, we have the measuring rod of a true man. Need we have more after which to pattern our eternal lives?

Let us examine ourselves to see just how some of these principles may be applied in our lives so that we may not fail of our opportunities and privileges for growth. What is meant that an able man is one who fears God? It might be better stated if we were to say that a true man is one who fears to do that which would offend God.

265

Speaking of this vital principle, the Apostle Paul asked, "Know ye not that ye are the temple of God, and that the Spirit of God dwelleth in you?" Then he declared, "If any man defile the temple of God, him shall God destroy; for the temple of God is holy, which temple ye are." (1 Corinthians 3:16-17.)

Our bodies are the temples of God! We are winged for heavenly flight! We must be prepared for split-second timing decisions to meet any competition in this world of action. On every hand we see the spectacle of those who show that they apparently fear neither God nor man because they fail to keep holy that temple of God of which Paul spoke—the human body. Those who prostitute virtue and disregard the law of chastity, who defile their bodies and waste their substance by riotous living, as in the story of the prodigal son, will learn the bitterness of having to eat husks with the swine. Nothing can ever compensate us for enfeebled minds, broken bodies, broken homes, and lost weekends, in violation of the standards of society and the laws of God, for the wages of sin are death. God will not be mocked.

I speak of another matter closely related to this same subject, the disregard of which will unfit us for that "infinitude of immortality" for which we are in training. I speak of one of the most sacred of all human relationships, marriage, and that greatest of all institutions, the home. Marriage is fraught with the highest bliss and yet attended by the weightiest responsibilities that can devolve upon man and woman here in mortality. The divine impulse within every true man and woman that impels companionships with the opposite sex is intended by our Maker as a holy impulse for a holy purpose—not to be satisfied as a mere biological urge or as a lust of the flesh in promiscuous associations, but to be reserved as an

266

expression of true love in holy wedlock. In the days of our grandparents, their great pride and joy was to rear a large and honorable family. In so doing, there was developed within the family circle an unselfishness and an individual and collective loyalty that made divorce a rare happening and therefore little thought of, in that day, as a solution for social ills.

There are those among us who think (if it can be called thinking) that having a large family of children is old-fashioned and an evidence of those who are unsophisticated and don't know better. No more pernicious doctrine than that could hardly be imagined. Those who refuse to accept the obligations of parenthood are not living up to their greatest opportunities and thereby fail to gain the sweetest joys of life with a beautiful family. The psalmist expressed it this way: "Lo, children are an heritage of the Lord: . . . As arrows are in the hand of a mighty man; so are children of the youth. Happy is the man that hath his quiver full of them: they shall not be ashamed, but they shall speak with the enemies in the gate." (Psalm 127:3-5.) Those who refuse as husbands and wives to have children are proving themselves already too small for the infinitude of God's creative powers.

There came to my attention a preface proposed for a book being written by three careful students on the subject of "Limited Parenthood or Population Control," as it is spoken of loosely. I quote from their conclusion:

Furthermore, governmental population control programs which derive from this perspective may not only solve the "wrong problem," but create other problems perhaps more serious in their impact upon human dignity and well-being than the population growth they are designed to stem. For example, in the wake of the campaign to convince people to have two or fewer children, will parents come to regard their children as less valuable than they otherwise might? What will be the consequence for a third or fourth child's concept when the people around him affirm, with strong emphasis on the mortality of the two-child norm, that his parents were remiss in allowing him to be born, or that he is a "surplus" child? Will an extended "educational" program on "overpopulation" reduce our respect for the individual human life? Will we adopt a set of values which exalt natural resources at the expense of human resources?

All are not possessed of similar talents. You may recall the story of the great painter Whistler. As a cadet at West Point Military Academy, he failed in chemistry and was dismissed from the institution, but he was at the head of his class in art. It was a sad blow, but he did not repine. Years later he remarked whimsically, "Had silicone been a gas, I would have been a major general."

But one quality in most great souls, whether they be artists or men of science and philosophy, is that if their faith in spiritual matters is not affected by their worldly knowledge, they are but showing the evidence of knowing too little about science or too little about religion or too little about both.

In an address delivered to scientists gathered in a convention of the Western Farm Chemergic Council in Omaha, Dr. Robert A. Millikin, world-renowned physicist, admonished those scientists in attendance to prove, test, and search as diligently for knowledge in the spiritual world of the unseen as they were schooled to do in their scientific fields. The Apostle Paul gave the correct answer to the critics of matters spiritual when he wrote to the Corinthians:

> For what man knoweth the things of a man, save the spirit of man which is in him? even so the things of God knoweth no man, but the Spirit of God.
>
> But the natural man receiveth not the things of the Spirit of God: for they are foolishness unto him: neither can he know them, because they are spiritual discerned. (1 Corinthians 2:11, 14.)

Lest you think this statement is unscientific, I bring you the statement of two great thinkers that bear upon this subject. Dr. Edwin W. Starbuck, professor of philosophy at the University of Iowa, remarked to a group of students in one of our western universities that "every great scientific discovery came as an intuition to the mind of the discoverer." He explained that a search of the records and his acquaintance with great living scientists revealed the fact that

> the scientist studies his problem, saturates his mind with it, puzzles over it, dreams about it, but seems to find progress impossible, blocked as it were, but a black impenetrable wall; then at last, and suddenly as if out of nowhere, comes a flash of light, the answer to his quest. His mind is now illumined by a great discovery. . . . No great discovery ever came by pure reasoning. Reason would lead to the borderline to the unknown but could not tell what was within.

Professor Albert Einstein made a similar discovery when he said:

> After all, the work of the researching scientist germinates upon the soil of imagination or vision. A hundred times you run, as it were, with your head against the wall in order to lay your hands upon and to define and fit into a system, what from a merely indefinable premonition you sense in vain, and then suddenly, perhaps like a stroke of lightning, the saving thought will come to you.

That process is no different than that by which the artist or the poet arrives at his conception.

Seemingly, then, that process as explained by the scientist is not greatly different, except it be a lesser degree, to that by which the apostle Peter, the humble fisherman, declared to Jesus in answer to the query as to who he thought the Master was. Peter declared with conviction, "Thou art the Christ, the Son of the living God." (Matthew 16:16.) That knowledge was also beyond the borderline of pure reasoning or logic. It came as Jesus declared it had, from his "Father which is in heaven." So it was with Martha, the humble friend of Jesus, at the time of the death of her brother Lazarus, when Jesus tested her faith in His divine mission. She quickly responded with the inspired declaration, "Yea, Lord, I believe that thou art the Christ, the Son of God, which should come into the world." (John 11:27.)

One is too small for a grand eternity when he, because of little learning, closes against himself the doors of the greatest of all institutions of learning, the "University of Spirituality." Someone has said that man, like every other individual, has an object and purpose to fulfill; and when he comprehends this, he will think too much of himself to stoop to any action that will bring him down from the highest position on the throne of his nature. It has also been said that every man has his price, but may I enjoin you, with all the power at my command, to be true to your ideals.

And now, the third quality of an able man, as defined by the father-in-law of Moses, is one who hates covetousness. The selfishly ambitious man is never the happy man, for always beyond his covetous grasp there lies the receding horizons that mock his ill-gotten gains. Shun evil itself, and all things with a bad reputation, and remember again the warning words with which I introduced my theme: "Destined as such a soul as yours is for immortality, it must find all that is not eternal too short, all that is not infinite too small." Never stoop to any material action that will bring you down from the highest position on the high throne of your eternal nature. May the Lord grant you the strength and wisdom so to do, I humbly pray.

# WOMAN'S
# GLORIOUS
# PURPOSE

# 33

# Woman's Glorious Purpose

*D*r. David Sarnoff, who is called the father of television and radio, is quoted as having said: "The happiest people I have known have not been the men of great worldly achievements, or accomplishments of wealth. They have been the simple people who are happily married, enjoying good health and good family life." (*Wisdom Magazine.*)

An epistle to the Church from President Brigham Young and his counselors John W. Young and Daniel H. Wells declared:

Among the many duties which devolve upon us, there is none that should receive more careful and constant attention than the education of our children. They are numerous, and if properly trained will become a great blessing to the inhabitants of the earth. Parents should take time—if not every day, at least as often as they can and not allow many days to elapse—to call their families together and interrogate them respecting their associations, their words, actions, etc., and teach them the principles of the gospel. They should send them regularly to day and sunday schools and furnish them every possible facility for gaining a sound and thorough education, and especially in the principles of the gospel and the history of the church. The teachers to whom we entrust our children for education should be faithful Latter-day Saints, sound in doctrine and thoroughly imbued with a love of Zion. In this way we can rear up a generation of men and women who shall love and maintain truth and righteousness in the earth. (July 11, 1877.)

President Joseph F. Smith, after quoting the Lord's requirement to teach the children, which is found in section 68 of the Doctrine and Covenants, said:

And if parents fail to do this and the children go astray and turn from the truth, then the Lord has said the sin shall be upon the heads of the parents. The loss of the children will be charged to the parents and they will be responsible for their apostasy and darkness. I came to the conclusion, after reflection upon this subject, . . . I do not believe that it would be possible for me to be admitted into exaltation and glory in the Kingdom of God, if through my neglect of duty my children should become the children of darkness in this regard. . . . My children must not and will not turn away with my consent. I will plead with my children; I will endeavor with all the power I possess to have them as true and faithful to this gospel as it is possible for me to be; because, without all of them in the Kingdom of God I would feel that my household was not perfect.

You will recall that the Lord called Samuel three times, and each time Samuel went to Eli and said, "Here am I; for thou didst call me." The first two times Eli told Samuel he had not called, but the third time he perceived that the Lord had called. Then the Lord, in criticizing Eli, said to Samuel: "Behold, I will do a thing in Israel, at which both the ears of every one that heareth it shall tingle. . . . For I have told him that I will judge his house for ever for the iniquity which he knoweth." Now note that he says the iniquity was "because his sons made themselves vile, and he restrained them not." (See 1 Samuel 3:3-13.) That was what caused Eli's downfall.

The importance of the teaching of the gospel in the family was expressed in the first section of the Doctrine and Covenants, and also important purposes of gospel restoration, as they apply particularly to the home, were expressed:

274

> That faith also might increase in the earth; . . .
> And inasmuch as they erred that it might be made known;
> And inasmuch as they sought wisdom they might be instructed;
> And inasmuch as they sinned they might be chastened, that they might repent;
> And inasmuch as they were humble they might be made strong, and blessed from on high, and receive knowledge from time to time. (D&C 1:21, 25-28.)

The mother's role in this vital, home-centered gospel is clear. Here are five of her prime responsibilities in the home.

1. The first counsel I would give her is this: Don't give up on the boy or girl in that insufferable state of super-egoism through which some teenagers go. I plead with you for those boys and those girls. Don't give up on the boy or girl in that impossible stage of independence and disregard of family discipline. Don't give up on him or her when they show a shocking display of irresponsibility. The know-it-all, self-sufficient person wants nothing of counsel, which to him is just a preachment of an old-timer who has lost step with youth. Knowing is not enough—we must apply. Willingness is not enough—we must do.

A harassed mother was called by a friend who asked her, "What do you think of all the riots going on in all the cities in the country?" And this mother answered, "I'm so busy putting down all the little riots in my own home that I don't have time to worry about riots elsewhere."

We had a missionary grandson in the North British Mission. He hadn't been there very long until he wrote back an interesting letter in which he said the advice of his parents now comes back to him with great force. It is like a book on a shelf that has been there for nineteen years and he has just begun to take it down and start to read it for the first time. That is your son and your daughter. You may think they are not listening. They may think they are

275

not listening, but one time yours may be the book that they will take down and read again when they need it most.

There are forces that come into play after parents have done all they can to teach their children. Such a force influenced the younger Alma, who, with the sons of Mosiah, set out to destroy the work of their great fathers. An angel, you remember, was sent, and he knocked Alma down. Alma lay as though he were dead for three days and nights, and the angel said:

> Behold, the Lord hath heard the prayers of his people, and also the prayers of his servant, Alma, who is thy father; for he has prayed with much faith concerning thee that thou mightest be brought to the knowledge of the truth; therefore, for this purpose have I come to convince thee of the power and authority of God, that the prayers of his servants might be answered according to their faith. (Mosiah 27:14.)

It was so with Nephi, whom his unruly brothers sought to destroy. He told them:

> Ye are swift to do iniquity but slow to remember the Lord your God. Ye have seen an angel, and he spake unto you; yea, ye have heard his voice from time to time; and he hath spoken unto you in a still small voice, but ye were past feeling, that ye could not feel his words; wherefore, he has spoken unto you like unto the voice of thunder, which did cause the earth to shake as if it were to divide asunder.
> . . . In the name of the Almighty God, I command you that ye touch me not, for I am filled with the power of God, even unto the consuming of my flesh; and whoso shall lay his hands upon me shall wither even as a dried reed; and he shall be as naught before the power of God, for God shall smite him. (1 Nephi 17:45, 48.)

I am remembering now a dramatic time when, at a funeral, an unruly son of a mother in whose honor we were meeting in that service asked if he might speak. And there, in great detail and with more boldness than I would have dared to have talked about him, because I knew his life, he told how, as a boy growing up, he had disregarded wholly the admonitions of his father and mother. Now, finally, with his father and mother gone, he was beginning to read, as it were, that book which had been unread for all these years, and he bore witness to the influence that the mother and father had had upon him even while he was transgressing about every law in the book.

2. The second role I would list as the responsibility of the mother is to put the father at the head of the house. A famous judge said he thought it was neglect of this duty that lay at the root of many of the problems in a delinquent home. How does mother do it? Someone said that little children soon outgrow their need for affection, but fathers never do. Wives, never, never let him feel that you don't understand him. Put father at the head of the house.

President Brigham Young said:

> I think it has been taught by some that as we lay our bodies down, they will so rise in the resurrection with all the impediments and imperfections that they have here; and that if a wife does not love her husband in this estate, she cannot love him in the next. This is not so. Those who attain to the blessing of the first or celestial resurrection will be pure and holy, and perfect in body. Every man and woman that reaches to this unspeakable attainment will be as beautiful as the angels that surround the throne of God. (*Journal of Discourses,* vol. 10, p. 24.)

Now, you sisters, polish your husbands as best you can while you have them here, and then hope that the Lord will continue the process beyond the veil.

3. Another role of the mother is to provoke her husband to honor his priesthood. Her husband has the key to the effectual door to a celestial home in the eternities for her and their children, and unless he honors the priesthood, she and the family will suffer thereby, even to being deprived of that celestial home without him. Wives, have your family prayers, even when you must take the lead. See that your husband takes the lead in that, if you can. See that he attends his priesthood meetings, that he responds

to the call to do home teaching, and then do everything you can, lovingly and patiently, to help him to perform and magnify his duties.

4. Next, I would say, enlist the aid of the priesthood in meeting what to you may be insurmountable problems. There is sometimes a tendency to bypass the bishop—to say he is too close to us, or he is too young and inexperienced, or he will not keep a confidence—which may be just an escape. I had a long-distance call early one morning, and the telephone operator said it was a collect call. She said, "The caller says she belongs to your church and she is in need of help." I said, "Well, tell her to look across the street and her bishop may be there, or the stake president may be there. That is a fully organized stake, and there is nothing that can be done from this distance that couldn't be done by the officers and leaders right there at her elbow."

The bishop has at his command all the forces of the priesthood to set in motion the necessary action, so members are just wasting time to come to the General Authorities and leap-frog over the bishop and the stake president.

I received a letter from a sweet girl whose marriage I performed some years before. It started out about the problems, and I thought, here is a temple marriage that has failed. This is what she said:

Immediately we began to have problems. We tried then and have tried since to figure out just why. There was no particular thing that consistently precipitated our difficulties. We were active in the Church and attended our meetings; we prayed; we paid our tithing; we returned to the temple regularly. We loved each other so and had such expectations from our marriage. Then we were expecting a baby and, in spite of our very great happiness in anticipating this child, things seemed to go so bad as to seem insolvable. Almost a year after we began, we knew we couldn't continue together any longer under such conditions, and I called the bishop, who was also our friend, and we went over. The three of us talked—a little. You know, I don't recall anything particular that was spoken except the questionable encouragement he offered by saying that he and his wife had had a difficult time for awhile after they were married. The inference was, we solved our problems, why can't you? But when we left the bishop's office we knew we had reached the turning point somehow. We had touched the bottom and we were on our way up. I can't explain why or what happened, but we did start up and we've been on our way up ever since.

This happy result came because they followed the counsel to see their bishop.

5. Finally, the last counsel that I shall mention is to keep the mother of your home at the "crossroads" of the home. There is a great danger today of homes breaking down because of allurements to entice mothers to neglect their being at home as the family members are coming to or going from the home. Now, I recognize the necessity of some mothers being required to earn sustenance for their family. But even here, Relief Society presidents and bishops should take care lest they fail to lend all aid possible to the mother of small children and to help her, if possible, in planning the nature of work or the schedule of time. All this lies within the province of the Relief Society working with the home.

I pray that the Lord will bless each of us, particularly our wives and mothers, that we may rise to our great opportunities. Mothers are the creators of the atmosphere in the home and do much to provide the strong foundation for their sons and daughters, to provide them with strength when they leave the influence of their homes. May we each build on that strong foundation, I humbly pray.

# 34

# *Maintain Your Place As a Woman*

Martin Luther penned a meaningful statement regarding woman's place when he wrote, "When Eve was brought unto Adam, he became filled with the Holy Spirit, and gave her the most sanctified, the most glorious of appellations. He called her Eve—that is to say, the Mother of All. He did not style her wife, but simply mother—mother of all living creatures. In this consists the glory and the most precious ornament of woman."

To be what God intended you to be as a woman depends on the way you think, believe, live, dress, and conduct yourselves as true examples of Latter-day Saint womanhood, examples of that for which you were created and made. To be thus merits the deepest respect of your sweetheart and your husband. Righteous indignation should be felt by every pure, true woman when she sees in pictures, on the screen, and in song a vulgar portrayal of a woman as something a little more than a sex symbol.

Many of you have read the righteous defense of woman's place in the world as expressed by a woman, Jill

Jackson Miller of Beverly Hills. She writes under the heading "Open Letter to Man."

> I am a woman.
>
> I am your wife, your sweetheart, your mother, your daughter, your sister—your friend.
>
> I need your help!
>
> I was created to give the world Gentleness, Understanding, Serenity, Beauty, and Love.
>
> I am finding it increasingly difficult to fulfill my purpose.
>
> Many people in advertising, motion pictures, television, and radio have ignored my inward qualities and have repeatedly used me only as a symbol of sex.
>
> This humiliates me; it destroys my dignity; it prevents me from being what you want me to be—an example of Beauty, Inspiration, and Love: love for my children, love for my husband, love of my God and country.
>
> I need your help to restore me to my true position—and to allow me to fulfill the Purpose for which I was Created.
>
> Oh, man, I know that you will find the way.

That, I think, is the plea of every true woman's heart in this day. It seems abundantly clear that to follow the extreme fashions of this day is to give credence to the efforts of some who would topple mankind from the pedestal on which we are placed in the divine plan of the Creator. The woman who is too scantily dressed, or immodestly dressed, ofttimes is the portrayal of one who is thus trying to draw the attention of the opposite sex when her natural adornments do not, in her opinion, suffice. Heaven help any woman so minded for drawing such attention. For a woman to adopt the mode of a man's dress, it is said, is to encourage the wave of sexual perversion, when men adopt women's tendencies and women become mannish in their desires.

If a woman will preserve and properly maintain her God-given identity, she can captivate and hold the true love of her husband and the admiration of those who admire natural, pure, lovely womanhood. What I am saying to sisters first of all, then, is to be what God intends you to be, a true woman.

I sat one morning with some of my brethren who are among our most prominent leaders. One of the brethren said he had recently had requests from two sisters, at different times, asking if he would give them a special blessing so that they could have children. On inquiry he found that in their earlier married life they had refused to have children, and now, when they desire children, for some reason they can't have them.

Another one of my brethren spoke up and said, "That reminds me of our own experience. We married quite young and we had our children, five of them, before my wife was twenty-eight. Then something happened and we were not able to have any more children." He continued: "If we had delayed having our family until after I had my education, which would have been about that time, we probably would have had no children of our own."

When I consider those who enter into holy wedlock in the Lord's own way and receive the divine commandments to multiply and replenish the earth, then through their own designs fail to observe the commandment, I wonder if, later on, when they are ready to have the children, the Lord might not think: "Maybe this is the time for you to do a little soul-searching in order for you to come back to the realities for which you have been placed upon the earth."

Today, strangely enough, half the world is trying to prevent life and the other half is trying to prolong life. Have you ever thought of that? Where do we brothers and sisters stand in this picture? It is when we tamper with nature that we are in trouble, for there are roles a woman plays that are natural in the divine order of things. To be a wife is one of your greatest responsibilities—true companion, a helpmeet to your husband.

A young man passed the desk of a lovely young girl. On it was a verse that caught his eye. It said "Marriage Prayer."

> I would have beauty to charm and to fire him,
> Thoughts, white as feathers, to calm and inspire him,
> Music enough to fill four little walls,
> Visions to struggle for, love over all,
> Hands not too white for the day's stern request.
> Let me know toiling and triumph and rest,
> Blessed contentment in small things and poor,
> Lifting my eyes from the world's golden lure.
> Make me forgiving of small, driftless wounds.
> Give me his heart to read, O keep mine attuned.
> Let not the years pass and leave us alone,
> Grant us thy miracle, all for our own.
> Let me be brave in the anguish of giving,
> Smiling and proud for the glory of living,
> Give me a song when the morning is cold,
> Give me a smile when toiling is old,
> Warmth in my handclasp for dusk, chill and gray,
> Prayers and a dream at the close of the day.

The young man remembered that, and when he returned home that lovely girl who chose this as her marriage prayer became his wife.

Someone spoke a profound truth when he said, "No man can live piously, or die righteously without a wife." Even God Himself said, "It is not good that the man should be alone; I will make him an helpmeet for him." (Genesis 2:18.) The Apostle Paul's statement had broader meaning than some have interpreted it, when he declared: "Nevertheless neither is the man without the woman, neither the woman without the man, in the Lord." (1 Corinthians 11:11.) He was teaching the great truth that

283

only in holy wedlock for time and eternity, in the new and everlasting covenant, can the man and woman attain to the highest privilege in the celestial world, but He may likewise have been stressing the great need of a husband and wife for each other in this world.

In defining the relationship of a wife to her husband, the late President George Albert Smith put it this way: "In showing this relationship, by a symbolic representation, God didn't say that woman was to be taken from a bone in the man's head that she should rule over him, nor from a bone in his foot that she should be trampled under his feet, but from a bone in his side to symbolize that she was to stand by his side, to be his companion, his equal, and his helpmeet in all their lives together."

I fear some husbands have interpreted erroneously the statement that the husband is to be the head of the house and that his wife is to obey the law of her husband. Brigham Young's instruction to husbands was this: "Let the husband and father learn to bend his will to the will of his God, and then instruct his wives and children in this lesson of self-government by his example as well as by his precept." (*Discourses of Brigham Young,* Deseret Book Co., 1925, pp. 306-307.)

This is but another way of saying that the wife is to obey the law of her husband only as he obeys the laws of God. No woman is expected to follow her husband in disobedience to the commandments of the Lord.

It was someone with deep understanding of married life who said that the good wife commandeth her husband in any equal matter by constantly obeying him. I will leave it to you sisters to apply that wisely in your marriage partnership. The good wife commandeth her husband in any equal matter by constantly obeying him.

284

But now there are many lovely women who have not

as yet had an acceptable offer of marriage or if married have not been able to have children, and they wonder about the doctrines that I have just now spoken about. To these President Young made a promise for which the plan of salvation provides the fulfillment. He said, "Many of the sisters grieve because they are not blessed with offspring. You will see the time when you will have millions of children around you. If you are faithful to your covenants, you will be mothers of nations." (*Discourses,* p. 310.)

I have said many times to young couples at the marriage altar: Never let the tender intimacies of your married life become unrestrained. Let your thoughts be as radiant as the sunshine. Let your words be wholesome and your association together be inspiring and uplifting, if you would keep alive the spirit of romance throughout your marriage together.

Concerning the blessings of motherhood, I came across a clipping, a quotation from an article written by Dr. Henry Link, entitled "Love, Marriage and Children."

I am convinced that having a child is the final and strongest pledge of a couple's love for each other. It is an eloquent testimony that their marriage is a complete one. It lifts their marriage from the level of selfish love and physical pleasure to that of devotion centered around a new life. It makes self-sacrifice rather than self-indulgence their guiding principle. It represents the husband's faith in his ability to provide the necessary security, and it demonstrates the wife's confidence in his ability to do so. The net result is a spiritual security which, more than any other power, helps to create material security as well.

Too much can't be said or written about woman's most important role as a mother. Napoleon is quoted as having asked Madame Campan: "What is wanting in order that the youth of France will be well educated?" "Good mothers," was her reply. The Emperor was forcibly struck with this answer. "Here," he said, "is a system in one word—*mother.*"

Over the years I have been asking mothers of large families—successful families—what did you do to make your family successful? And I recall the cardinal reply that one such mother answered to my question: "I was always at the crossroads of my home when my children were growing up." Another said, "We took great pains with our first child; then the others took that as a pattern thereafter." From my experience, I wouldn't stop at the first child. I think I would advise you to go further than that. But there is much to be said for following that counsel.

Another hallmark of true motherhood was said to me by a woman in one of the Idaho stakes. I had laid down a rather heavy criticism when I found that they were calling mothers and fathers to serve in organizations that took them both out of the home at the same time. I had spoken rather sharply, I suppose. One of the counselors was irritated and observed that they would have a wholesale resignation after that kind of a talk, so I thought I would repent. In the afternoon session I was sitting beside the stake Relief Society president, and I said, "They tell me you have a family of nine children. Would you mind taking a few minutes to tell us how you have been able to raise that successful family and still have been an active Church worker, usually presiding over organizations, all your married life." I didn't have the slightest idea what she was going to say, but I prayed that she would say what I wanted her to say.

She said, "Well, in the first place, I followed the counsel and the example of my sainted mother. I raised my children as Mother raised us." You think about that. Successful motherhood today spans the years and the eternities. If you have done well your job in your home, your sons and your daughters in the ages to come will from your example seek to do likewise.

Second, she said, "I married a wonderful companion. Daddy and I sat down together whenever we were asked to serve in a church position and decided we would both be active in the Church if we could be assigned to organizations where I could be home with the children when he was at his meetings and vice versa." Then she declared that they had done it that way all of the growing-up years of their children.

"And finally," she said, "I have an unshakable testimony of the divine mission of the Lord and Savior Jesus Christ."

I submit these teachings to you as hallmarks of great motherhood: great examples of motherhood gone by, companions who cooperate fully in the rearing of the sons and daughters, and the testimony of the divine mission of the Lord and Savior Jesus Christ. It roots the family in the things that have to be said and done while the children are growing up if we want to save our children.

Even if circumstances require mothers of families to work because of the insufficiency of their husbands' salaries, or because they have been left alone in widowhood, they should not neglect the cares and duties in the home, particularly in the education of the children. Today I feel that women are becoming victims of the speed of modern living. It is in building their motherly intuition and that marvelous closeness with their children that they are enabled to tune in upon the wavelengths of their children and to pick up the first signs of difficulty, of danger and distress, which if caught in time would save them from disaster.

This responsibility of parenthood being of the first importance was profoundly impressed upon us by our great leader, the late President J. Reuben Clark, Jr., in an address delivered years ago. This what he said:

This training work is primarily for the home, built by celestial covenant-bound father and mother, led by a righteous man bearing the Holy Priesthood of the Son of God. This home must indispensably be a house of prayer, must observe the commandments of God, be a home of unblemished sexual purity, filled with happiness; a home of law-obedience, civil and ecclesiastical, in all things big and little; a home of charity, patience, long-suffering, courtesy, family loyalty and devotion, where spirituality is dominant; a home of burning testimonies and great gospel knowledge.

We must, each of us, so build for our children if we shall escape condemnation and render the service demanded of, and reach the destiny that is provided for us.

Should there be a woman left in widowhood who has to work, she should go to her bishop and Relief Society president. Relief Society sisters should stay close to such a home and see that when that mother is away there are provided those essential elements that safeguard her home and take care of her little ones. Perchance there may be a season when her children are small that maybe there could be full enough material support so she wouldn't have to leave her children. Remember, these are days when we must think first of the welfare of the children in the home.

Within the past year a prominent speaker at a local service club dinner was quoted as saying this:

The nation has taken the wrong approach to many problems. We deal with the delinquent after he is a delinquent; the drug addict after he is an addict; the criminal after he is a criminal. We forget that we should work with our youngsters before these problems arise. There is no substitute for the family. This is where the children are brought up, where their habits are created; where they receive strength to face the world. The person who is against the 'establishment' is taking his problems out on the community because he has no communication with his parents.

This man, who was a prominent Puerto Rican official, concluded by saying, "The day we by-pass the family as the basic unit, we are going to be lost. In the typical family there is limited time between the parent and the child.

This time should be well spent in commonly enjoyed activities."

How many times have we been giving that same message the last fifty years? Now we stress it in the great program we call family home evening. We should be eternally grateful that, through inspired channels, we have been given the family home evening, and the home teaching program by which our priesthood is enjoined to encourage families in which home evening is not being held that they persist until it can be held.

Recently I walked through the foyer of the Church Offiice Building. There was a young woman with some little children around her. As we shook hands she said, "I just joined the Church a few months ago." I asked her about her husband. "No," she said, "I'm alone with my eight children." And I said, "Now don't feel alone because your husband is not with you. You stay close to your home teachers and stay close to your bishop." And she said to me with a smile, "Brother Lee, I have the finest home teachers that anybody could have, and nobody has a finer bishop than ours. We are taken care of. We have a fatherly father who is watching over us, the priesthood holder who has come into our lives."

I was invited to dinner at a home in Salt Lake City where a father had been without his wife for thirteen years. The mother in the home had passed away, and the older children had taken the mother's place. When I asked how he had been able to do without his wife's help, he took me to the window and pointed to the Highland Park Ward. He said, "You see that building? I couldn't have done it without the Church. Thank God for the plan by which the Church assists the home in taking care of their children."

Wives must strive to see that their husbands do not neglect the family. It takes planning. A statement from an unlooked-for source, Princess Grace of Monaco, emphasizes: "I am like anyone else trying to keep a home together. I must fight, I mean fight, for the time to be with my children. My husband and I spend every spare moment we have with our children in an effort to share our lives with them. And where there are no spare moments, I struggle to make them."

I now come to the teacher's responsibility. Jean Allgood, in her poem "A Teacher's Prayer," expresses these thoughts:

> My heart and mind "speak" when I behold my child
>     within my door,
> For this I know, I must respond aright—ere he doth come
>     more.
> I must needs give him help—
> Yea, more than help in course at hand:
> Help in searching, reaching, giving what's his already to
>     command.
> He has a mind—God's gift to each of us;
> He has a heart—to feel—and thus,
> He has a soul—this is my utmost care.
> So, if I reach the inmost part of this child within my door,
> Then I have taught the thing desired of me and more.

Another matter of importance we call compassionate service. My aunt, Jeanette McMurrin, told me this interesting story. She was widowed and living with her daughter. One morning her daughter came to her and said, "Mother, we don't have anything to eat in the house. My husband, as you know, has been out of work. I am sorry, Mother."

Aunt Jeanette said that she dressed and worked around the house, then closed her door, knelt down, and said, "Heavenly Father, I have tried all my life to keep the commandments; I have paid my tithing; I have given service to the Church. We have no food in our house today. Father, touch the heart of somebody so we won't have to go hungry." She said she went about with a feeling of gladness, thinking all would be right.

There came a knock at the door in a few hours, and there was a little neighbor girl with food in her arms. Choking back the tears, the widow brought the child into the kitchen and said, "Set them here, and tell your mother that this came today as an answer to our prayers. We didn't have any food in our house."

Needless to say, the little girl went back and carried that message, and in a little while she returned with still a larger armload. As she brought the bags to the kitchen table, she asked, "Did I come this time as an answer to your prayers?"

Aunt Jeanette replied, "No, my darling, this time you came as a fulfillment of a promise. Fifty years ago when your grandmother was expecting a little child, she didn't have anything to eat and she was lacking in strength and nourishment. I was the little girl who carried food into her house so that she would have the strength to bring her little baby—your mother—into the world." Then she said, "The Lord said, 'Cast your bread upon the waters, and after many days it shall return again.' This time you have been carrying back to me the foodstuff that I carried into the home of your grandmother so your mother could be born into the world." Compassionate service.

The great King Benjamin, speaking about service, said:

> . . . all you who deny the beggar, because ye have not; I would that ye say in your hearts that: I give not because I have not, but if I had I would give.
>
> And now, if ye say this in your hearts ye remain guiltless, otherwise ye are condemned; and your condemnation is just for ye covet that which ye have not received. (Mosiah 4:24-25.)

The Lord judges us not alone by our actions but by the intent of our hearts. The Prophet Joseph Smith saw in vision his father and mother and his brother Alvin in the celestial kingdom, and he marveled: How could Alvin be in the celestial kingdom since he had never been baptized, and was buried before the Church was organized? And the Lord said, "All who have died without a knowledge of this Gospel, who would have received it had they been permitted to tarry, shall be heirs of the celestial kingdom of God." (*History of the Church,* vol. 2, p. 380.) Thus, wives and mothers who have been denied the blessings of wifehood or motherhood in this life—who say in their heart, if I could have done, I would have done, or I would give if I had, but I cannot for I have not—the Lord will bless you as though you had done, and the world to come will compensate for those who desire in their hearts the righteous blessings that they were not able to have because of no fault of their own.

The most powerful weapon we have against the evils in the world today, regardless of what they are, is an unshakable testimony of the Lord and Savior, Jesus Christ. Teach your little children while they are at your knee and they will grow up to be stalwart. They may stray away, but your love and your faith will bring them back. Remember, paraphrasing what President McKay said, "No success will compensate for failure in the home."

That the Lord may help us so to do for the salvation and blessing of all our Father's children, I humbly pray.

# 35

# Three Phases of Motherhood

One of our Regional Representatives recently showed me a picture of a beautiful family of children. They looked so much alike, and when I commented about that, he said, "You'll be interested to know that all of these children are adopted. None of them are natural children. Four beautiful, lovely children!"

He said that when he and his wife realized they were to be childless and couldn't have natural children, they considered the possibility of adopting children with some anxiety and apprehension, so they sought counsel. One of the persons to whom they went for counsel said, "There are three phases of motherhood: first, the bearing of children; next, the rearing of children; and third—and perhaps the most important of all—the loving of the children."

I would like you to think about these three phases of motherhood, because you who are teachers and leaders of children are in the role of teaching children in the place of mothers, and you must always support the homes from which the children come.

Let us discuss, then, the first of these phases of motherhood, the bearing of children. Some mothers might take issue with this advice and think that other phases are more important. It suffices us to say that any woman who thinks her prime duty has been accomplished when she bears a child has a dim view of her God-given opportunities. It is the most glorious of all aspirations for womankind. Martin Luther, in commenting on Eve's role as the first earthly mother, said, "He did not style her as wife, but simply *mother*. The mother of all living creatures. In this consists the glory and the most precious ornament of woman."

Regarding the second phase, that of rearing children, someone wrote, in an old play, "The mother in her office holds the key to the soul, and she it is that stamps the coin of character and makes the being who would be a savage but for her gentle care. A Christian man! Then crown her queen of the world."

If you would reform the world from error and vice, begin by enlisting the mothers. The future of society is in the hands of mothers. If the world were in danger, only the mothers could save it. An old Spanish proverb says, "An ounce of mother is worth a pound of clergy." A man never sees all that his mother has been to him until it is too late to let her know that he sees it. I was one of those. Careless, teenage boy, warned by mother of certain and impending danger that I flicked away as not being meaningful, only to find within a matter of weeks that the danger of which she had warned me was a fact. I should have gone back to her and thanked her for it, but I guess she knew; and today I express my thanks, for, except for that counsel, I might not have been worthy of the place to which I am now called.

The task of nurturing the child has, I think, been set forth no more beautifully than by President J. Reuben

Clark, Jr., in his priesthood course of study *Immortality and Eternal Life.* This is what he said:

> But the full glory of motherhood is not yet reached when the child comes forth into this world of trial, nor is her opportunity for service passed when her creation breathes the breath of life. Still from the dust of the earth she must fabricate the food that keeps alive and nourishes the little one. She feeds not only, but clothes it. She cares for it by day and watches over it by night. When illness comes, she nurses it with that near divine love that fills her heart. She gently leads its faltering steps, till it walks alone. She helps to frame its first lisps and teaches it the full art of speech. As consciousness matures, she deftly sows into the plastic mind the love of God, of truth; and, as the years flow by and youth comes on, she adds the love of honor, of honesty, of sobriety, of industry, of chastity. She teaches, bit by bit, loyalty and reverence and devotion. She implants and makes part of the growing, virgin intellect an understanding of the restored gospel . . . She builds into the warp and woof of her creation, self-control, independence, righteousness, love of God and a desire and will to serve him.
>
> Thus to the full stature of manhood and womanhood, mother guides, incites, entreats, instructs, directs, on occasions commands, the soul for which she built the earthly home, in its march onward to exaltation. God gives the soul its destiny, but mother leads it along the way. (Melchizedek Priesthood course of study, vol. 2, 1969-70, pp. 27-28.)

What does it mean when a mother is lost and is no longer here? This touched my heart when I heard someone saying that "the loss of a mother is always severely felt." Even though her health may incapacitate her from taking active part in the care of her family, still she is the rallying point around which affection and obedience and a thousand tender endeavors to please concentrate. And dreary is the home when such a rallying point is withdrawn. A mother's heart is a child's schoolroom. The instructions received at the mother's knee, and the parental lessons together with the pious and sweet souvenirs of the fireside, are never effaced entirely from the soul.

Someone has said that the best school of discipline is the home, for family life is God's own method of training the young, and homes are largely what mothers make them.

Perhaps the most important mission a teacher can accomplish is to express love for those whom she would teach, and, more importantly, she can let them know that they are loved and, if possible, receive from them the echoing response of a child that is well loved.

Chopin said, "No language can express the power and beauty and heroism and majesty of a mother's love. It shrinks not where man cowers, and grows stronger where man faints, and over the waters of worldly fortunes, sends the radiance of its quenchless fidelity like a star in heaven."

I remember visiting in the home of a wealthy jeweler, a member of the Church, in the South. He said that he used to have a "hole-in-the-wall" kind of store where he sold what he called cheap junk kinds of jewelry. He used to walk home often because he didn't have the price of the transportation, and his route took him past a large building. As he passed it, he thought to himself, "If I could own that store, I believe I would be on my way to success."

One day as he walked home he saw a "for sale" sign on the building. He went to the owner and asked, "How much would you sell this place for?" The man replied, "Forty thousand dollars." Well, to this young man, there didn't seem to be that much money in the world. He went home and talked it over with his wife, and they sat down and did some figuring. It just didn't seem possible that they could find that much money.

That night he said, "I'll have to sleep on this, to think about it." The next morning at the breakfast table he said to his wife, "No, I can't do it. It's too big for me." She slipped her arm around his shoulders and said, "But, dear, you're a big man." "Do you mean that you think I can do it?" he asked. "Why, of course you can, because I have confidence in you."

Little children ofttimes grow away from the need for that kind of attention and love and concern, but a husband never does. Wives, don't you forget that.

A loving mother never forsakes her loved ones, no matter what may happen. Of such love, one wrote so beautifully:

A father may turn his back on his child; brothers and sisters may become embittered enemies; husbands may desert their wives and wives their husbands; but the mother's love endures through it all, in good repute, in bad repute, in the face of the world's condemnation the mother still moves on and still hopes that her child may turn from his evil ways and repent. Still she remembers the infant smiles that once filled her bosom with rapture. The merry laugh, the joyous shout of his childhood, the opening promise of his youth. She can never be brought to think of him as all unworthy.

We attended the funeral service of a great soul, a patriarch in my former stake. He had been shot down by two ruffians. What induced them to do it, no one could tell. No more innocent man or more lovely character ever lived. As we came to the sorrowing family and the sweet wife who was mourning his passing, I said, "I suppose there are two other mothers who are perhaps more sad than you who mourn here today. Those are the mothers whose sons performed this terrible deed. You can be certain that they are sad and their hearts are broken."

Dr. Lee Salk, director of psychology in the Department of Pediatrics at the New York Hospital-Cornell Medical Center, spoke impressively about this subject under the title "Mothers Go Home":

Mothers who can afford not to work should stay home with their babies for the first nine to twelve months, at least. The first year is crucial to the emotional health of the infant and the time when many emotional ills may be

297

prevented. The infant has a great capacity for learning, and there is substantial evidence that early mother-child interplay is essential to emotional and mental growth of the child.

When you get a mother-nurse and assorted others handling the baby during its infancy, there may be too many conflicting stimuli for the baby to cope with that could cause tension and insecurity later on.

Dr. Salk goes on to say that he has great confidence in the natural instincts of mothers, but he believes that scientific understanding of growth and development will help in the all-important job of bringing up emotionally healthy children.

I asked a mother how she had been able to rear a wonderful family of which she had reason to be proud. She said something very simply: "We took great pains with our first child, and the others inclined their conduct to the good example of our first son." This reminded me of the time when our first grandson was born. Naturally, he was the most beautiful grandson in all the world to his grandfather. The lovely mother said, as she looked on her firstborn infant child, "My dear little boy, what a mighty responsibility you have." Since he was the first child, the example, I always called him "Skipper," because he was the leader, the bellwether of all our family. We knew that as he went, the others would be inclined to go. To keep the family dignified and the little ones, who make little mistakes, not crushed before others—this is so important.

In the Hawaiian Islands I once visited at the home of a stake president where there was a little mishap. The dinner table was beautifully set, with everything in order, when one of the little children upset some food. Not a word was said by way of scolding, though the little child was upset. Hastily the mother helped to settle the child, and then the conversation went on just as beautifully as if nothing had happened. I said to her, "How well you handled

298

this near tragedy with your child." She replied, "I wouldn't have had him embarrassed before company for all the world."

I remember a little boyhood experience. We had pigs that were tearing up the garden, causing great mischief on the farm. Father sent me two miles to the store to get an instrument so we could ring the noses of the pigs. We had great difficulty rounding them up and getting them in the pen, and as I was fooling around with this instrument that I had been sent to purchase, I pressed down too hard and it broke. Father would have been justified in giving me a scolding right there, after all the effort and money wasted, but he just looked at me, smiled, and said, "Well, son, I guess we won't ring the pigs today. Turn them out and we'll go back tomorrow and try it over again." How I loved that father, that he didn't scold me for an innocent little mistake that could have made a breach between us.

Once we attended a dinner at the home of President and Sister Henry D. Moyle. Sister Moyle was always a gracious hostess. President Moyle, a master at carving, sat at the head of the table. Just as he started to carve the roast, apparently the table was unsteady and suddenly there was a tremendous crash as twelve beautiful, expensive china plates fell to the floor. Those who were helping in the kitchen came running out, and Sister Moyle said, "Never mind, get some more dishes and we'll go on with the meal." What a splendid example of self-control!

I contrast that experience with the girl who came to me in great distress. She confessed to wrong-doing, and I asked her about her home life. Hadn't she been taught differently in her home? She shook her head sadly and said, "In my home we had a traumatic experience once, when my angry father suddenly seized the tablecloth and pulled it and all the dishes off the table to express his wrath. That did something to me that day, and never again have I had the same regard for him." Lack of self-control in that father had a far-reaching effect, even causing character instability in his daughter.

At a stake conference in Sandy, Utah, a young woman from Brigham Young University spoke on the subject "Why I Want a Temple Marriage." She recalled lessons learned in Junior Sunday School and Primary. "The Lord is so wonderful," she began.

> He provides us with a marvelous blessing or commandment, such as temple marriage, and then gives direction to prepare us to keep this commandment. From the first time I learned the meaning of the words and could sing the song "I Am a Child of God," I have realized that the Lord has provided teachers, experiences, and lessons in our young lives to encourage us to live righteously. We have been taught correct principles by our parents and teachers and have been shown how to live them. The Lord has given us so many opportunities to prepare for temple marriage that it seems that all our living has been guided toward the accomplishment of this great goal.

As I listened to her, I thought, "Thank God for the Primary. Thank God for the Junior Sunday School. Thank God for his inspiration to the ones who wrote those beautiful songs." Please, parents and teachers, translate that into action.

The young woman continued:

> If I could have only one thing in the world, I would choose to have a testimony. I sing now, with great meaning, "I Know That My Redeemer Lives." I am grateful for how the Lord has prepared me for temple marriage, first by blessing me with wonderful parents who were married in the temple, and to whom I give credit. I hope I shall succeed in my own life and marriage. Second, I have had great friends who have always shown the same appreciation of the Church that I have and who have always been an influence for good. Third, the Lord has led me to a young man who holds temple marriage as one of his goals, a young man who knows I wouldn't marry him anywhere else—and who also wouldn't marry me anywhere else.

300     Then she closed with this challenge: "May we all have

and develop a desire to marry in the temple and let this desire work in us so that temple marriage will be a reality in our lives."

A teacher who can teach the child to see, by faith, our Heavenly Father is truly a great teacher.

I have a great teacher with whom I live in my home, one with whom I counsel and with whom I pray. Her life has been one of teaching teachers of children. She gave me a parable that to me has great meaning:

I took a little child's hand in mine. He and I were to walk together for a while. I was to lead him to the Father. It was a task that overcame me, so awful was the responsibility. And so I talked to the child only of the Father. I painted the sternness of His face were the child to do something to displease Him. I spoke of the child's goodness as something that would appease the Father's wrath. He walked under the tall trees. I said the Father had power to send them crashing down, struck by His thunderbolts. We walked in the sunshine; I told him of the greatness of the Father, who made the burning, blazing sun. And one twilight we met the Father. The child hid behind me. He was afraid. He would not look up at the face so loving; he remembered my picture. He would not take the Father's hand; I was between the child and the Father. I wondered. I had been so conscientious, so serious.

I took a little child's hand in mine. I was to lead him to the Father. I felt burdened with a multiplicity of the things I had to teach him. We did not ramble, we hastened from one spot to another spot. At one moment we compared the leaves of the different trees; in the next we were examining a bird's nest. While the child was questioning me about it, I hurried him away to chase a butterfly. Did he chance to fall asleep I awakened him, lest he should miss something I wished him to see. We spoke to the Father, oh, yes, often and rapidly. I poured into his ears all the stories he ought to know, but we were interrupted often by the wind a-blowing, of which we must trace to its source. And then, in the twilight, we met the Father. The child merely glanced at Him and then his gaze wandered in a dozen directions. The Father stretched out his hand. The child was not interested enough to take it. Feverish spots burned in his cheeks. He dropped exhausted to the ground and fell asleep. Again I was between the child and the Father. I wondered. I had taught him so many things.

I took a little child's hand to lead him to the Father. My heart was full of gratitude for the glad privilege. He walked slowly. I suited my steps to the short steps of the child. We spoke of the things the child noticed. Sometimes we picked the Father's flowers and stroked their soft petals and loved their bright colors. Sometimes it was one of the Father's birds. We watched it build its nest. We saw the eggs that were laid. We wondered, elated at the care it gave its young. Often we told stories of the Father. I told them to the child and the child told them again to me. We told them, the child and I, over and over again. Sometimes we stopped to rest, leaning against one of the Father's trees, and letting His cool air cool our brows, and never speaking. And then, in the twilight, we met the Father. The child's eyes shone. He looked lovingly, trustingly, eagerly up to the Father's face. He put his hand into the Father's hand. I was for the moment forgotten. I was content.

—Author Unknown

In the beautiful play *The Sound of Music,* the character Maria von Trapp sings: "A bell is no bell till you ring it. A song is no song till you sing it. Love wasn't put in your heart there to stay. Love isn't love till you give it away."

President Moyle and I had an experience in a stake where we were to name a new stake president. We waited and waited for the Spirit to tell us who was to be the man, and when we had talked with all of the presently serving officers, we still hadn't received that inspiration. Then a physician, the busiest man in town, was brought to us. We said to him, "We think you should be doing more to help in the Church." He replied, "Well, I'm the only physician in this town, and I'm very busy, but if you wish me to accept the call, I'll do it." And so we called him to be the stake president. The next day in the conference he bore this remarkable testimony:

Nineteen years ago the stake president asked me to be one of his counselors and I said, "Oh, I can't be a counselor; I'm too busy. I have all the responsibility for all of the illnesses, the accidents, the delivering of babies in this town. I couldn't be a counselor in the stake presidency." So he found someone else who was more obedient, more submissive, more willing. When the stake conference at which the new counselor was sustained closed, the congregation sang "I'll go where you want me to go, dear Lord; I'll be what you want me to be," and I felt like a criminal.

302

The next day I went over to the hospital, where I had a very critical operation to perform. The patient was a young mother who had several children, and her husband was a fine young man. Because the nature of the operation was so critical, and I knew it was beyond my skill, I knelt down in prayer and asked the Lord to help me. Then I heard an accusing voice say, "Oh, yes, you need me now, but what about yesterday? You didn't have time; you didn't have time." I was so shaken that I got up from my knees and walked into my office. I humbled myself and said, "Heavenly Father, you've got to help me. If I can't perform this operation, there will be a young man without a dear wife, a little family without a mother. If you will help me through this operation, I promise you that I will never again refuse anything that's asked of me in the Church."

The Lord did listen, and I performed the operation successfully. But the people in that stake took me at my word. For nineteen years I was never asked to do anything in the Church—not a single thing—because the people thought I was too busy. Now, nineteen years later, I am busier than I ever was before. I don't know how I can be your stake president, but I wouldn't dare say no.

Keep on speaking terms with the Lord. Seek ye diligently while He may be found, that happily ye might feel after Him and find Him. Though He be not far from any one of us, for in Him we live and move and have our being, we must search diligently, pray always, and be believing, and all things shall work together for our good if we remember always the covenants with which we have covenanted one with another.

Yes, a bell is not a bell until you ring it. A song is not a song until you sing it. A lesson is not taught until our teachers live it. A soul is not saved until his life is finished. Our work is not done until Satan is bound. With all my soul I bless our wonderful teachers, wherever they may be!

The Lord is moving in great power. We see evidence of His power, but we must be aware of Satan's power also. If we will put into full gear all that the Lord has given us to do, we will gain a mastery over the evil forces among us today.

I know that my Redeemer lives. I know it by witness more powerful than sight, that witness of the Spirit which bears witness to my soul. As one who has been called to be a special witness, I know as did the Apostle Paul know. I have felt the Spirit; I have known by the whisperings of the Spirit revelations I couldn't have known by seeing nor by hearing. God grant that we may all seek for that testimony, because we are living in a day when, unless we have a strong testimony, we are in danger of falling by the wayside, for the principle of revelation is on trial in this church. Those who don't believe it and haven't a testimony are going to be sorely tried; but those who believe and have faith and follow the leaders will be safe on Zion's hill when destruction shall come upon the wicked.

May each of us go forward with courage and with faith and determination to serve the Lord to the end, taking care of our Father's precious little children, I humbly pray.

# 36

# For All Eternity, If Not for Time

Shortly after I returned from my mission, I spoke at the funeral services for a devoted, faithful former missionary whom I had known as one of the most unselfish, dedicated, and effective teachers and exponents of right principles one could ever know. She died of an incurable infectious disease. As her death drew near, she had outlined in detail the memorial services that would be held following her passing. Therefore, all of those participating in that sacred service were keenly conscious that each had been chosen because he represented a different phase of her all-too-short life.

My humble offering was to remember her years as a missionary for the Church. Just before she left her home, where she had served as a teacher in the secondary schools following her graduation from Brigham Young University, a patriarch had given her a remarkable patriarchal blessing. All the specific blessings promised had already been realized except one; and the absence of the fulfillment of that one troubled me because, according to my measure, no earthly human could have lived a more nearly Christlike life than had she. Why, then, had this last promised blessing been denied her? The blessing from the Lord that came through this patriarch was that she would become a mother in Israel. She had never married; therefore in her mortal life she had not been privileged to become a mother. I spoke of this in the services and posed my unanswered question, Why?

A distraught father and mother had sought an interview to see if some light and understanding could be given them to ease their aching hearts and to bolster their faith. They had just received that ominous and tersely worded telegram from the military informing them of the tragic death of their young son. Just home from a mission for the Church, he had been inducted into military service. Before leaving, he too had received a patriarchal blessing in which he was promised that he would have a posterity of sons and daughters. Had the patriarch's words been inspired? Why did this promise fail, since, to their certain knowledge, their son had lived worthy of every blessing promised to the faithful who "live unto the Lord?"

Following my remarks at the young woman's funeral, the stake patriarch was the concluding speaker. He declared two vital principles well documented in the scriptures. He explained the doctrine that life did not begin with mortal birth and does not end with mortal death. When a patriarch pronounces an inspired blessing, such a blessing encompasses the whole of life, not just the phase we call mortality. "If in this life only we have hope in Christ, we are of all men most miserable" (1 Corinthians 15:19), the Apostle Paul wrote. Failing to understand this great truth, we are miserable and sometimes our faith is challenged. With faith that looks beyond the grave, and trusting in the Divine Providence to bring all things in

306

their proper perspective in due time, we have hope and our fears are calmed. ". . . faith is not to have a perfect knowledge of things," declared the prophet Alma; "therefore if ye have faith ye hope for things which are not seen, which are true." (Alma 32:21.)

This faithful sister, the patriarch explained, although not privileged to bear children in mortality, may through sacred ordinances in holy temples on earth, in the Lord's own time, be sealed to a worthy husband; and this sealing by divine authority, if acceptable to both, could in the world beyond this one permit a holy union in eternal wedlock, with the promise of posterity beyond the grave.

It was concerning eternal increase that the Lord, in a revelation, declared to those entering into this covenant of marriage and were faithful to the end that they would have an "exaltation and glory in all things, as hath been sealed upon their heads, which glory shall be a fulness and a continuation of the seeds forever and ever." (D&C 132:19.)

As though to further clarify this revelation, the Prophet Joseph Smith explained:

> But those who are married by the power and authority of the priesthood in this life, and continue without committing the sin against the Holy Ghost, will continue to increase and have children in the celestial glory. (*Teachings of the Prophet Joseph Smith*, p. 301.)

As Peter explained, following the Master's resurrection and as a result of the visitation of the risen Lord to the world of departed spirits, the Master preached to them "that they might be judged according to men in the flesh, but live according to God in the spirit." (1 Peter 4:6.) Explained simply, this means that for those worthy persons beyond this life who accept of the vicarious work performed by authority in the Lord's temples, such ordinances

307

performed are as efficacious as though they were living. Were this not so, as the Lord explained to Peter, to whom the keys of the kingdom were given in the meridian of times, the "gates of hell" (Matthew 16:18) would have prevailed against the church of Jesus Christ. Without this vicarious work, instituted in behalf of the faithful who "die in the Lord" (D&C 42:46), the full mission of the Master's atoning sacrifice would not have been extended to persons such as those mentioned earlier and many others that could be cited.

The loved ones of that faithful missionary sister may look forward to that glorious day for the promise of motherhood, and the parents of the faithful son who was promised a posterity need not despair. In the Lord's own way and in His own time, He will bring all things right in His own way. Thanks be to God!

Some time ago I had occasion to write some words to the many faithful sisters who had not as yet had or may not in mortal life have woman's greatest expectations fulfilled. It is appropriate that I repeat here, with some modifications, a portion of what I have said heretofore:

"You young women advancing in years who have not yet accepted a proposal of marriage, if you make yourselves worthy and ready to go to the house of the Lord and have faith in this sacred principle of celestial marriage for eternity, even though the privilege of marriage does not come to you now in mortality, the Lord will reward you in due time and no blessing will be denied you. You are not under obligation to accept a proposal from someone unworthy of you for fear you will fail of your blessings. Likewise, you young men who may lose your life in early life by accident, or a fatal illness, or in the terrible conflict of war before you have had an opportunity for marriage, the Lord knows the intent of your hearts, and in His own due time He will reward you with opportunities made possible through temple ordinances instituted in the Church for that purpose."

Do all you can to comply with the laws of God pertaining to an exaltation in the kingdom of God. The Lord will judge you too by your works, as well as by the desires of your hearts, and your reward will be assured.

# 37

# The Role of Women in Building the Kingdom

*T*he Lord declared to Moses that His work and His glory is "to bring to pass the immortality and eternal life of man." (Moses 1:39.) Since the profound declaration of Eve in the Garden of Eden after the Fall, the exalted place of women in the plan of salvation has been clearly defined. She said, "Were it not for our transgression we never should have had seed, and never should have known good and evil, and the joy of our redemption, and the eternal life which God giveth unto all the obedient." (Moses 5:11.)

Lehi explained and amplified what Mother Eve said when, apparently, his son Jacob asked for an explanation of the Fall and why evil was permitted in the world. He said:

And now, behold, if Adam had not transgressed he would not have fallen, but he would have remained in the garden of Eden. And all things which were created must have remained in the same state in which they were after they were created; and they must have remained forever, and had no end.

And they would have had no children; wherefore they would have remained in a state of innocence, having no joy, for they knew no misery; doing no good, for they knew no sin.

But behold, all things have been done in the wisdom of him who knoweth all things.

Adam fell that men might be; and men are, that they might have joy. (2 Nephi 2:22-25.)

If immortality, then, is the first step in the achievement of the Lord's work and his glory, it is readily to be understood that the process by which immortality is achieved is through the bearing of mortal offspring in holy wedlock by mortal mothers and mortal fathers. Woman's role in God's eternal plan of salvation has here, then, been reaffirmed. It would be well for mothers to consider the role of woman in the great plan of salvation as the Lord has explained it.

The woman's role involves a partnership, hopefully with a noble son of God. It was the Apostle Paul who declared this interdependence between men and women to be achieved only in holy wedlock. Here are a few of his statements: "Nevertheless neither is the man without the woman, neither the woman without the man, in the Lord. For as the woman is of the man, even so is the man also by the woman; but all things of God." (1 Corinthians 11:11-12.) ". . . but the woman is the glory of the man." (1 Corinthians 11:7.) "Husbands, love your wives, even as Christ also loved the church, and gave himself for it. . . . So ought men to love their wives as their own bodies. He that loveth his wife loveth himself." (Ephesians 5:25, 28.)

"For this cause shall a man leave father and mother, and shall cleave to his wife: and they twain shall be one flesh." (Matthew 19:5.)

The sacred nature of this partnership is nowhere bet- 311

ter explained than by President David O. McKay, who said, "Love is the highest attribute of the human soul, and fidelity is love's noblest offspring." Most, if not all, of the virtues are the natural fruit of genuine love. President McKay gave inspired counsel regarding the physical dimension of the love relationship between a man and his wife. He said:

> Let us instruct young people who come to us to know that a woman should be queen of her own body. . . .

> Second, let them remember that gentleness and consideration after the ceremony are just as appropriate and necessary and beautiful as gentleness and consideration before the wedding.

> . . . Chastity is the crown of beautiful womanhood, and self-control is the source of true manhood, if you will know it, not indulgence. . . .

> Let us teach our young men to enter into matrimony with the idea that each will be just as courteous and considerate of a wife after the ceremony as during courtship. (*Melchizedek Priesthood Manual,* 1966, p. 63.)

Companion lessons to these have been taught in Relief Society. With wives schooled in the Relief Society and husbands receiving similar lessons in the priesthood, the meeting of the two lessons brings an ideal family home evening lesson, where father and mother, with their growing-up sons and daughters, learn these fundamental principles. The curse of infidelity was also plainly set forth by President McKay. He said:

> As teachers, we are to let the people know, and warn these men—and this is not imagination—who, after having lived with their wives and brought into this world four or five children, get tired of them and seek a divorce, that they are on the road to hell.

> It is unfair to a woman to leave her that way, merely because the man happens to fall in love with some younger woman and feels that the wife is not so beautiful or attractive as she used to be. Warn him! Nothing but unhappiness for him and injustice to those children can result. (Ibid., pp. 63-64.)

Sometimes, as we travel throughout the Church, a husband and wife will come to us and ask if, because they are not compatible in their marriage—they having had a temple marriage—it wouldn't be better if they were to free themselves from each other and then seek more congenial partners. To all such we say, whenever a couple who have been married in the temple say they are tiring of each other, it is an evidence that either one or both are not true to their temple covenants. Any couple married in the temple who are true to their covenants will grow dearer to each other, and love will find a deeper meaning on their golden wedding anniversary than on the day they were married in the house of the Lord. Don't you mistake that.

The duties and purposes of women in this regard have found expression from President Joseph F. Smith, in which he emphasizes another phase of the woman's role of woman. I have spoken of the one phase of her role as a creator in company with her husband. Note what President Smith says:

I will speak of the Relief Society as one great organization in the Church, organized by the Prophet Joseph Smith, whose duty it is to look after the interests of all the women of Zion and of all the women that may come under their supervision and care, irrespective of religion, color or condition. I expect to see the day when this organization will be one of the most perfect, most efficient and effective organizations for good in the Church but that day will be when we shall have women who are not only imbued with the spirit of the gospel of Jesus Christ, and with the testimony of Christ in their hearts, but also with youth, vigor and intelligence to enable them to discharge the great duties and responsibilities that rest upon them. Today it is too much the case that our young, vigorous, intelligent women feel that only the aged should be connected with the Relief Society. This is a mistake. We want the young women, the intelligent women, women of faith, of courage and of purity to be associated with the Relief Societies of the various stakes and wards of Zion. We want them to take hold of this work with vigor, with intelligence and unitedly, for the building up of Zion and the instruction of women in their duties—domestic duties, public duties, and every duty that may devolve upon them. (*Gospel Doctrine*, pp. 386-87.)

I was startled upon one occasion to hear an announcement by a certain women's organization that one of our past Relief Society presidents had graduated from the Relief Society into another organization for women. Let there be no uncertainty in the minds of our Latter-day Saint women as to the Relief Society's being the greatest of all women's organizations. There is no greater organization on the face of the earth for the Latter-day Saint woman.

Woman's place in training her family is the third phase of this work to which I wish to refer. The Lord said:

> But behold, I say unto you, that little children are redeemed from the foundation of the world through mine Only Begotten;

> Wherefore, they cannot sin, for power is not given unto Satan to tempt little children, until they begin to become accountable before me;

> For it is given unto them even as I will, according to mine own pleasure, that great things may be required at the hands of their fathers. (D&C 29:46-48.)

What is the age of accountability and what are those great things that God requires of the fathers of children (which, by inference, means mothers as well) during this period before little children begin to become accountable before the Lord? The age of accountability, the Lord says, is eight years of age. No one can be received into the Church before he has arrived at this age. Parents are admonished to have their children baptized when they are eight years of age and to teach them the fundamental principles of the gospel. Their children shall be baptized for the remission of their sins and shall then receive the laying on of hands. They should be taught to pray and to walk uprightly before the Lord.

Great accomplishments are required of fathers and mothers before Satan has power to tempt little children. It
314 is the responsibility of the parents to lay a solid foundation

by teaching Church standards by example and by precept.

To the sisters, this means they must make a career of motherhood. They must let nothing supersede that career. They must take full advantage of the family home evening lessons each week.

I was in Cedar City, Utah, shortly after the family home evening program was provided with a full course of lessons for each week. Many persons in the Church were startled to find that we had now prepared lessons that they could teach their families. Manuals had been prepared and were placed in every home in the Church, so no one could say, "We didn't have any lessons," or "We couldn't afford a manual." At the conference in Cedar City, I was anxious to see how we were getting along with this program. I asked if the stake presidency would invite someone from a home where the lessons were being taught to speak, and they called on a young mother in the Singing Mothers chorus.

This mother said that she and her family had just begun to hold family home evenings regularly when she and her husband were asked if they would be in charge of a big dance festival. As they began to try to find a night when they could meet all the participants in the festival, they found that every night was preempted by some activity except one night—the night that had been set aside for family home evening. So they said to their children, "I guess that until the festival is over, we'll have to give up our family home evening."

So, with regrets, they went to the task of organizing the dance festival. A few nights later they came home late, weary from their exertions. They were awakened very early the next morning by the sounds of their children's voices in the living room downstairs. When they got up to see what was happening, they found the children all dressed and a

315

blazing fire in the fireplace. The night before, the fifteen-year-old daughter had engineered the children in preparing for an early morning breakfast. When the parents asked what this was all about, the children said, "Well, when you said you couldn't find a night for us to have family home evening, we counseled together and decided that hereafter we were going to have family home evening at five o'clock in the morning. We are all here now. Breakfast is ready; it will take only a few minutes. Now give us the family home evening lesson."

And as this sweet mother stood there at the pulpit, with tears streaming down her cheeks, she said, "As I sat down to that breakfast, it was the best breakfast that I have ever had in my whole life, and I resolved that never again was I going to let anything take precedence over my responsibility of teaching my family on a family home evening."

May we teach all women to do likewise! Mother's first sacrifice is to become a mother. Here is part of a letter from our oldest daughter, Maurine, when she had her first baby and was in a hospital in California:

> The miracle of all this is just slowly overwhelming me. To see that live little baby with all the intricate parts and know that it has been forming inside of my body, was more than my understanding can even possibly comprehend. I wonder that we women aren't required to undergo even more than labor pains to bring this little soul from another world into this one. It seems so right that we through pain are forced to slip for a few minutes at least half-way into another sphere to sort of bring our baby by the hand into this new life.

Our daughter Helen, at sixteen years of age, wrote this tribute to her mother:

> I'm not writing this letter to you because it's Mother's Day, or because it's your birthday—or even because I want something special! No, Mother, I've just been doing some pretty serious thinking lately, and now I want to share my thoughts with you. We've always done that, you and I, so it's not go-

316

ing to be difficult—and I thought I'd like to do it this way because it's more lasting. I love you, Mother—as I've told you many times—but I had never realized the significance of that love until just the other day when a conversation I had with one of the girls sort of prompted this serious thinking I'm talking about. I was talking with Beverly—you know, Mother, the girl with the long hair and nice eyes—and she was pretty blue because she felt she was misunderstood about something and had been all her life. But I couldn't even sympathize with her at first. I thought all mothers were just like you—understanding and easy to talk to. And then, I realized that maybe they weren't— maybe I was pretty lucky to have you who understands so well. You know, it sort of made me wonder. I thought—what about all the other mothers and daughters—are their relationships strained and difficult, or are they easy and fun like ours? And then I sort of started analyzing our situation to find out why you and I and Maurine were different from Beverly and her mother, and I've found that our closeness comes because of many things—things that are underlying in our love for one another—and I want you to know I appreciate them now more than I've ever done before.

These statements demonstrate in our own family how the great influence of mother was passed on to two lovely daughters who, in turn, have passed it on to their own children. Presumably those children, if the record is kept up, will go on and on throughout the generations, as these, my family, become part of my eternal kingdom in the world yet to come.

Pain and suffering in coming in or going out of the world seem to be a part of the plan, and mothers were promised that in pain and travail they would bring forth children. You remember Mother Eve's promise; she and her daughters would be saved in child bearing. Saved! I thought that meant protected so they would go through delivery of their babies unscathed. I'm not so sure that that's what it means now, but I know that if mothers will do their part, even though it costs their lives, then their eternal reward in our Father's celestial world will be certain.

And now, finally, a fourth role of mothers is the building of a home here and laying a foundation for a home in eternity. What is a home? Here are some rather apt quotations that indicate what I want you to learn: "Home is a roof over a good woman." (But if the roof is lacking, it isn't any home. It takes both.) "Home is the seminary of all other institutions." The most essential element in any home is God." "A man is always nearest to his God when he's at home, and farthest from God when he is away." (This could be true to a degree, if in the home there is the good influence of a true wife and mother.) "Home is the place where, when you go there, they have to take you in." (That's the boy or girl who stays out late until you've worried yourself sick and he or she comes trooping in at one, two, or three o'clock in the morning, but, after all, that's his home, that's her home.)

The First Presidency in our latter days has said:

> So far as the stages of eternal progression and attainment have been made through divine revelation, we are to understand that only the resurrected and glorified beings can become the parents of spirit offspring. Only such exalted souls have reached maturity in the appointed course of eternal life; and the spirits born to them in the eternal worlds will pass in due sequence through the several stages or estates by which the glorified parents have obtained exaltation. (Statement of the First Presidency, June 30, 1916.)

Woman has within her the power of creation in company with her legal and lawful husband here, and if sealed in celestial wedlock, she may have eternal increase in the world to come. Woman is the homemaker in her own home and an exemplar to her posterity in the generations that succeed her. Woman is a helpmeet to her husband and may render him more perfect than he otherwise would be. Woman's influence can bless a community or a nation to that extent to which she develops her spiritual powers in harmony with the heaven-sent gifts with which she has been endowed by nature. If she does not forfeit her priceless heritage by her own willful negligence, she can be largely instrumental in safeguarding democracy and downing a would-be tyrant. Year in and year out, she may cast the aura of her calming and refining influence to make certain that her posterity will enjoy the opportunities to develop to their fullest potential their spiritual and physical natures.

May God render our wives, our sweethearts, our mothers even more perfect in order to hold the bearers of the priesthood, under their influence, to a truer course of happiness here and eternal joy in the world to come, for which I humbly pray.

# 38

# Reap the Rewards of Beautiful Womanhood

I should like to address these remarks to the young women of the Church. The Lord has blessed you with beautiful figures of form and loveliness. Be sure that you keep the beautiful within you, which God only can see, as beautiful as what we can see.

If you would have the blessings of the Spirit of the Lord to be with you, you must keep your body—the temple of God, as the Apostle Paul speaks of it—clean and pure. In other words, your spiritual housekeeping must always be properly done if you would invite the Spirit of the Lord, for the gift of the Holy Ghost with which you were blessed at the time of your baptism will not be yours unless you keep your body fit to receive this blessing.

Now some of you have made mistakes and have sinned. Satan, that master of lies, would try to make you believe that because you have made a mistake, all is lost, and he will try to persuade you to continue to live the life of sin. This is a great falsehood. All sins, except the unpardonable sin (which is the sin against the Holy Ghost), can be repented of; and through the power of redemption and the gospel of Jesus Christ, all sins may be remitted, but they cannot be remitted until we ourselves who have sinned have done all we can to make right that which we have done which was wrong in the sight of God.

In one sentence, repentance means turning from that which we have done wrong in the sight of the Lord and never repeating that mistake again. Then we can have the miracle of forgiveness. Those who have made mistakes, though they have confessed their mistakes to the common judges in Israel, are always haunted by the question, "But how can I know that the Lord has forgiven me of my sin?" Here are two examples in the Book of Mormon that give you an answer. The great prophet, King Benjamin, had preached with such power that the people were pricked in their hearts and desired to have the atoning blood of the Savior by which their sins could be washed away, and they cried out that their sins had been forgiven because they had a peace of conscience. (See Mosiah 4:3.)

Another example is that of the son of Alma the prophet, the story of which is recorded in the 36th chapter of Alma in the Book of Mormon. Here is a son of a prophet who, with some sons of King Mosiah, was trying to destroy the work of their fathers. This boy was stricken dumb and endured torment and anguish when he realized the awfulness of the sins he had committed. But during the three days while he struggled in this terrible state of torment, he remembered the words of his father about the redeeming power of the Lord and Savior and he called out for forgiveness. Then there came to his soul the sweet peace when he received the assurance that through the atoning blood of the Master, his sins had been forgiven.

When you have done all within your power to overcome your mistakes and have determined in your heart that you will never repeat them again, then to you can come that peace of conscience by which you will know that your sins have been forgiven.

My plea to you, as one who loves you and through whom the Lord would desire to send blessings to you, is that I would hope that there might be instilled in your minds and in your souls the feeling of responsibility that you will have in the days that lie ahead, when you too become mothers to children yet unborn.

Within the heart of every lovely girl there is a desire for companionship with a young man. This is not an evil impulse. It comes from our Heavenly Father. There is within the breast of every fine young man a desire for companionship with a lovely young woman. This is not an evil influence. It comes from our Heavenly Father. The purpose of these feelings is to bring together at a proper time in life a man and woman in the bonds of holy wedlock, where together they may build a footpath over which heavenly spirits may be brought into mortality, into the bodies which are prepared by husband and wife.

Because these impulses are very strong, Satan tries to inflame them beyond their natural bounds. He tries to put into the mind of a young man to become ungentlemanly or to tell ugly stories to his companion; he tries to get the young woman to dress in an immodest way or to invite with unholy invitation her young companion. Satan knows that thereby these impulses might be inflamed beyond their natural bounds and cause the young people to indulge in a sin which is very serious and will destroy their ability to receive the Spirit of the Lord.

The Lord, knowing how important it is to keep from these sins, has given in the Ten Commandments a very strong commandment: "Thou shalt not commit adultery." This means, of course, to hold sacred the expression of

322

these impulses until the proper time in life, and to resist becoming immoral. A Book of Mormon prophet has said that this command is given to make one afraid to sin, which means afraid to do the things that would bring down the judgments of the Lord.

Now, you beautiful young girls, don't be as a flower by the roadside that catches the dust of every traveler by being spoiled through submitting to the handling of everyone who would invade one's beauty of loveliness. Rather, be like the beautiful flower way up on the hillside, with beauty of virgin loveliness. That is the kind of a girl that a fine boy will risk his life to possess.

My plea is that all our beautiful girls will have these thoughts in mind, and I leave my blessing and trust that these few words will kindle within them a resolution to live righteously in order to reap the rewards of beautiful womanhood.

*Section Eight*

# PERSONAL
# REFLECTIONS

# 39

# *Thoughts on Becoming a Member of the Council of the Twelve*

$S$ince nine o'clock last night* I have lived an entire lifetime in retrospect and in prospect. I spent a sleepless night. I never closed my eyes one moment, and neither would you if you had been in my place. Throughout the night, as I thought of this most appalling and soul-stirring assignment, there kept coming to me the words of the Apostle Paul, which he spoke in explanation of the human qualities that were to be found in the Lord and Savior:

> For we have not an high priest which cannot be touched with the feeling of our infirmities; but was in all points tempted like as we are, yet without sin.
> Let us therefore come boldly unto the throne of grace, that we may obtain mercy, and find grace to help in time of need. (Hebrews 4:15-16.)

One could not have listened to the soul-stirring testimony of President Heber J. Grant, in bearing testimony as to his feelings when he was called to the apostleship, or his experiences in calling others to similar positions, with-

---

*This address was given following President Lee's call to the Council of the Twelve.

out realizing that he has been close to his Heavenly Father in this experience. Therefore I shall take the word of the Apostle Paul. I shall come boldly unto the throne of grace, and ask for mercy and His grace to help me in my time of need. With that help I cannot fail. Without it I cannot succeed.

Since my childhood I have looked upon these men as the greatest men on the face of the earth, and now the contemplation of an intimate association with them is overwhelming and beyond my comprehension.

I thank God today for my parentage. My father and mother are listening, either in this great assembly or on the radio, if perchance they did not get into this meeting. I think perhaps this is my way of paying tribute to the two family names they gave me at my birth, Bingham and Lee. I trust I shall not disgrace those names. I have been blessed with a splendid father and a grand and lovely mother, one who didn't display often her affection, but who showed her love in tangible ways that, as a child, I came early to recognize as true mother love.

As just a high school boy, I went away on a high school debating team trip. We won the debate. I came back and called Mother on the telephone only to have her say, "Never mind, son. I know all about it. I will tell you when you get home at the end of the week." When I came home she took me aside and said, "When I knew it was just time for this performance to start, I went out among the willows by the creekside, and there, all by myself, I remembered you and prayed God you would not fail." I have come to know that that kind of love is necessary for every son and daughter who seek to achieve in this world: my tribute to my parents.

Last night, when I left here, as my little family with me kneeled down for our family prayers, I tested their

328

faith. I found them true. They have given me their assurance, their strength. They are willing to make the sacrifice and have accepted this as their call, along with me. I have come to know, in these last few years, in my brief service in this church, that without such help from a lovely, devoted wife, willing to sacrifice and to keep the home, no man can hold a position in this church and hope to continue to serve as he has been called. To her, likewise, as she listens this afternoon, and before you, I acknowledge her loveliness, her sweetness, her devotion and sacrifice.

For the last five glorious, strenuous years, I have labored, under a call from the First Presidency, with a group of men in the development of and the unfolding of what we have called the Church welfare plan. I felt that I should bear my testimony to you concerning that work as I close. It was on April 20, 1935, that I was called to the office of the First Presidency. That was a year before official announcement of the welfare plan was made in this tabernacle. There, after an entire half-day session, at which President Grant and President McKay were present, President Clark then being in the East—they had some communications with him, so that all members of the Presidency were in agreement—I was astounded to learn that for years there had been before them, as a result of their thinking and planning and as the result of the inspiration of Almighty God, the genius of the very plan that is being carried out and was in waiting and in preparation for a time when, in their judgment, the faith of the Latter-day Saints was such that they were willing to follow the counsel of the men who lead and preside in this church.

My humble place in this program at that time was described. I left there about noon-time, feeling quite as I do now. I drove with my car up to the head of City Creek Canyon. I got out, after I had driven as far as I could, and I

329

walked up through the trees. I sought my Heavenly Father. As I sat down to pore over this matter, wondering about an organization to be perfected to carry on this work, I received a testimony, on that beautiful spring afternoon, that God had already revealed the greatest organization that ever could be given to mankind and that all that was needed now was that that organization be set to work, and the temporal welfare of the Latter-day Saints would be safeguarded.

It was in August of that same year that, with Brother Mark Austin of the general committee, I had driven down to St. George and then back across the mountains to Richfield, for an early morning meeting. At that time there was an upturn in business, so much so that some were questioning the wisdom of this kind of activity, and why hadn't the Church done it before now? There came to me, in that early morning hour, a distinct impression that was as real as though someone had spoken audibly, and this was the impression that came and has stayed with me through these years: There is no individual in the Church who knows the real purpose for which the program then launched had been intended, but hardly before the Church has made sufficient preparation, that reason will be made manifest; and when it comes, it will challenge every resource of the Church to meet it. I trembled at the feeling that came over me. Since that day that feeling has driven me on, night and day, hardly resting, knowing that this is God's will, this is His plan. The only thing necessary today is that the Latter-day Saints everywhere recognize these men who sit here on the stand as the fountainheads of truth, through whom God will reveal His will, that His Saints might be preserved through an evil day.

I bear you my testimony that I know that God lives. I know that He has spoken in this day. I know that the work

330

that we are now advancing and unfolding has still greater potential possibilities. They will come to the extent that the Latter-day Saints will learn to do what they are told, but not until; and some of the grandest things yet to come can only come if and when we learn to listen to these men who preside as prophets, seers, and revelators.

I ask for your faith and prayers, that as the years come and go I may be the witness that one who is called to this position is expected to be. Will you pray that that might be a fruition of my activity among you. I have loved you. I have come to know you intimately. Your problems, thank the Lord, have been my problems, because I know, as you know, what it means to walk when you have not the money to ride. I know what it means to go without meals to buy a book to go to the university. I thank God now for these experiences. I have loved you because of your devotion and faith. God bless you that you won't fail, but that with this church you and it will go on to a glorious future, I pray, in the name of the Lord Jesus Christ.

# 40

# I Walked Today Where Jesus Walked

*F*or three glorious days we walked on sacred ground and felt the influence of the greatest person who ever lived upon this earth, Jesus the Christ, the very Son of the living God.

As we approached the Holy Land we read together the harmony of the four gospel narratives so beautifully put together by President J. Reuben Clark, Jr., and then as we left our room each time, we prayed that the Lord would deafen our ears to what the guide said about historical places but would make us keenly sensitive to the spiritual feeling so that we would know by impression, rather than by hearing, where the sacred spots were located.

For the first time, there in the Holy Land, I think I began to appreciate that lovely sacred refrain that has been put to music, "I walked today where Jesus walked."

I fancy, as we rode in a rented car with a competent guide the five or six miles from the walled city of Jerusalem to the town of Bethlehem, nestled among the Judean hills, we could hear again the strains of that sweet Christmas hymn:

O little town of Bethlehem,
How still we see thee lie.
Above thy deep and dreamless sleep
The silent stars go by;
Yet in the dark streets shineth
The everlasting Light.
The hopes and fears of all the years
Are met in thee tonight.

Beyond us and to our left was the field of shepherds. In our mind's eye, as we looked upon the hillside where sheep still grazed as they did way back nearly two thousand years ago, we caught the significance of the story of the shepherds.

And there were in the same country shepherds abiding in the field, keeping watch over their flock by night.

And, lo, the angel of the Lord came upon them, and the glory of the Lord shone round about them: and they were sore afraid.

And the angel said unto them, Fear not: for, behold, I bring you good tidings of great joy, which shall be to all people.

For unto you is born this day in the city of David a Saviour, which is Christ the Lord. (Luke 2:8-11.)

Presently we were, as it seemed, with the shepherds at the mouth of the cave hewn out of the rock now to be found in the basement of the Church of the Nativity. There seemed to be in this place a kind of spiritual assurance that this was indeed a hallowed spot. Down in the basement is the cave hewn out of the rock, which seemed to us to mark a sacred place.

Out beyond Jericho, the city of palms, we were to find again a wonderful spirit on the banks of the Jordan River, where the courageous John the Baptist had baptized the Son of Man. The sacred incident that took place is recorded simply:

And Jesus, when he was baptized, went up straightway out of the water: and, lo, the heavens were opened unto him, and he saw the Spirit of God descending like a dove, and lighting upon him:

333

And lo a voice from heaven, saying, This is my beloved Son, in whom I am well pleased. (Matthew 3:16-17.)

For three miles out of the walled city of Jerusalem we traversed the road to the cottage of Martha and Mary and Lazarus, where the Master found more congenial company than within the gates of Jerusalem among many of the self-sufficient of the Jews. Only a block away from the homesite of Martha and Mary is the rock-built tomb of Lazarus. As we stood there at the mouth, we remembered the drama that took place as the Savior declared, just prior to the raising of Lazarus, the significance of his great mission when He said to Martha: "I am the resurrection, and the life: he that believeth in me, though he were dead, yet shall he live: And whosoever liveth and believeth in me shall never die." (John 11:25-26.)

We fancied we could hear Martha's fervent testimony: "Yea, Lord: I believe that thou art the Christ, the Son of God, which should come into the world." (John 11:27.)

In our mind's eye we fancied we had witnessed the miracle of the raising of Lazarus, as the Savior peered into the mouth of that tomb on the whited figure of Lazarus, who had been buried for several days, and said in a commanding voice, "Lazarus, come forth." (John 11:43.) The power of this Man of God over death had asserted itself.

It was from this topmost peak that His ascension took place, and the two men appareled in white stood by and said to the multitude, as they saw Him go up into the clouds, "Ye men of Galilee, why stand ye gazing up into heaven? this same Jesus, which is taken up from you into heaven, shall so come in like manner as ye have seen him go into heaven." (Acts 1:11.)

We walked on the sacred ground in these places and again in Gethsemane. In the Garden of Gethsemane, one of 334    the deeply spiritual places, there are eight old gnarled olive trees showing evidence of great antiquity. It was here that Christ kneeled, in the vicinity of the very spot where we were standing. We fancied we could hear again the agonized words of His intense suffering, which He described in a great revelation: "Which suffering caused myself, even God, the greatest of all, to tremble because of pain, and to bleed at every pore, and to suffer both body and spirit—and would that I might not drink the bitter cup, and shrink." (D&C 19:18.)

And then He had prayed, "O my Father, if it be possible, let this cup pass from me: nevertheless not as I will, but as thou wilt." (Matthew 26:39.)

Time was now running out for us on our visit to Jerusalem. We had followed the guide through the traditional hall of judgment, where the Master was beaten and sentenced to death by a tribunal that made mockery of justice. We followed the way of the cross supposedly to the place of crucifixion and the place of the holy sepulchre. But all of this, according to tradition, we felt, was in the wrong place. We felt none of the spiritual significance that we had felt at other places, for had not the Apostle Paul said, speaking of the crucifixion, "Wherefore Jesus also, that he might sanctify the people with his own blood, suffered *without the gate*"? (Hebrews 13:12. Italics added.)

In other words, He suffered to His death upon the cross for the sins of mankind, not within the gates of Jerusalem but outside the gates, and yet the guides were trying to make us think that His crucifixion took place inside the walls. And again, what we were seeing there did not agree with John's description of the place where the crucifixion and burial took place, for John had said: "Now in the place where he was crucified there was a garden; and in the garden a new sepulchre, wherein was never man yet laid. There laid they Jesus therefore because of the Jews'

335

preparation day [the Passover]; for the sepulchre was nigh at hand." (John 19:41-42.)

There was yet another place we had to visit, the garden tomb. It is owned by the Church of the United Brethren. Here our guide took us as though it were an afterthought, and as the woman guide with her little son led us through the garden, we saw a hill outside the gate of the walled city of Jerusalem, just a short way from where the hall of judgment had been inside the city walls. The garden was right close by, or "in the hill," as John had said, and in it was a sepulchre hewn out of a rock, evidently done by someone who could afford the expense of excellent workmanship.

Something seemed to impress us as we stood there that this was the holiest place of all, and we fancied we could have witnessed the dramatic scene that took place there. That tomb has a mouth that could be sealed by a rolling stone, and there is a stone track built to guide a stone as it was rolled across the mouth of the tomb. The stone has now been removed, but the stone track is still there. Mary, after peering into the tomb, saw that He was missing, and she went out weeping bitterly.

> But Mary stood without at the sepulchre weeping: and as she wept, she stooped down, and looked into the sepulchre,
> And seeth two angels in white sitting, the one at the head, and the other at the feet, where the body of Jesus had lain.
> And they say unto her, Woman, why weepest thou? She saith unto them, Because they have taken away my Lord, and I know not where they have laid him.
> And when she had thus said, she turned herself back, and saw Jesus standing, and knew not that it was Jesus.
> Jesus saith unto her, Touch me not; for I am not yet ascended to my Father: but go to my brethren, and say unto them, I ascend unto my Father, and your father; and to my God, and your God. (John 20:11-14, 17.)

336     As we looked out that night from the veranda of our

hotel room, silhouetted against the sky was Mount Zion, and there was King David's tower marking, so they told us, the place where they say the Last Supper was held just before the Savior went down to the Brook Cedron and to His betrayal and judgment and finally to death. Here on this Mount Zion, or in America's New Jerusalem (our students of the scripture are not in agreement as to which), is to be commenced the greatest drama of the whole history of the world to usher in the second coming of the Lord. The Master himself has described this momentous event:

> . . . the Lamb shall stand upon Mount Zion, and with him a hundred and forty-four thousand, having his Father's name written on their foreheads.
>
> And it shall be a voice as the voice of many waters, and as the voice of a great thunder, which shall break down the mountains, and the valleys shall not be found. (D&C 133:18, 22.)
>
> And then shall the Lord set his foot upon this mount, and it shall cleave in twain, and the earth shall tremble, and reel to and fro, and the heavens also shall shake.
>
> And the Lord shall utter his voice, and all the ends of the earth shall hear it; and the nations of the earth shall mourn, and they that have laughed shall see their folly.
>
> And then shall the Jews look upon me and say: What are these wounds in thine hands and in thy feet?
>
> Then shall they know that I am the Lord; for I will say unto them: These wounds are the wounds with which I was wounded in the house of my friends. I am he who was lifted up. I am Jesus that was crucified. I am the Son of God. (D&C 45:48-49, 51-52.)

The next morning, as we went over the rocky slopes along the Jaffa Road to Tel Aviv and to our airport, we beheld the back-breaking work of the returning Jews to make the "desert blossom as a rose," as the prophets had foretold.

I came away from some of these experiences never to feel the same again about the mission of our Lord and Savior. I had impressed upon me, as I have never had it impressed before, what it means to be a special witness. I

337

say, with all the conviction of my soul, I know that Jesus lives. I know that He was the very Son of God. And I know that in this church and in the gospel of Jesus Christ is to be found the way to salvation.

# 41

# Have Faith in America

*I* recently came across something that I wrote in 1946 to my youngest daughter. It seemed as I read it again as though it might be something I would say to every father's daughter.

As with every day of your life, you can never relive any part of it except in memory; and if any day be wasted or misspent, that day becomes only one of regret and remorse. To live one's life to the fullest, then, becomes a daily responsibility for which you need the constant guidance of divine powers to avoid the pitfalls that make for long detours back onto the path of safety and truth. . . . One who has understanding realizes that we are always in great need of spiritual help. So it was that the Master taught, "Blessed are the poor in spirit: for theirs is the kingdom of heaven." (Matthew 5:3.) The poor in spirit are the spiritually needy who daily lean upon and trust in the arm of the Lord.

There lie yet ahead greater joys and, yes, greater anxieties than you have yet known, for remember that great love is built on great sacrifice and that a daily determination in each other to please in things that are right will build a sure foundation for a happy home. That determination for the welfare of each other must be mutual and not one-sided or selfish. Husband and wife must feel equal responsibilities and obligations to teach each other. Two of the things that today strike at the security of modern homes is that young husbands have never sensed their full obligation in supporting a family, and young wives have sidestepped the responsibility of settling down to the serious business of raising a family and of making a home.

These words were written just after her marriage. She is now the mother of six of our grandchildren. That is about half of our kingdom, and we have several great-grandchildren from that same family and from the other family.

We are living in a time of great crisis. The country is torn with scandal and with criticism, with faultfinding and condemnation. There are those who have downgraded the image of this nation as probably never before in the history of the country. It is so easy to clamber onto the bandwagon and to join the extremists in condemnation, little realizing that when they commit their actions, they are not just tearing down a man; they are tearing down a nation, and they are striking at the underpinnings of one of the greatest of all the nations of all the world—a nation that was founded upon an inspired declaration we call the Constitution of the United States. The Lord said it was written by men whom He raised up for that very purpose, and that Constitution stands today as a model to all nations to pattern their lives.

I have often wondered what the scripture meant to say that says, ". . . for the law shall go forth of Zion, and the word of the Lord from Jerusalem." (Micah 4:2.) As I was pondering that one day at the dedicatory services of the Idaho Falls Temple, I heard President George Albert Smith say in the dedicatory prayer:

We thank thee that thou hast revealed to us that those who gave us our constitutional form of government were men wise in thy sight and that thou didst raise them up for the very purpose of putting forth that sacred document.

Wilt thou, O our Father, bless the Chief Executive of this land that his heart and will may be to preserve to us and our posterity the free institutions Thy Constitution has provided. Wilt thou too bless the legislative and judicial branches of our government as well as the executive, that all may function fully and courageously in their respective branches completely independent of each other to the preservation of our constitutional form of government forever.

We pray that kings and rulers and the peoples of all nations under heaven may be persuaded of the blessings enjoyed by the people of this land by reason of their freedom under thy guidance and be constrained to adopt similar governmental systems, thus to fulfill the ancient prophecy of Isaiah that ". . . out of Zion shall go forth the law and the word of the Lord from Jerusalem." (*Improvement Era,* October 1945, p. 564.)

If ever there came into my mind, at a time when I needed it, a definition of what a scripture meant, I heard it from the mouth of a prophet when the Idaho Falls Temple was dedicated.

Some time ago the First Presidency and the Council of the Twelve were engaged in a meeting of serious import, and I said something at that time unpremeditated, but I couldn't have said it better had I taken a month to prepare it. I said:

I'm sure, brethren, that the voice of the General Authorities is a powerful influence in the world. I think we must be on the optimistic side. This is a great nation; this is a great country; this is the most favored of all lands. While it is true that there are dangers and difficulties that lie ahead of us, we must not assume that we are going to stand by and watch the country go to ruin. We should not be heard to predict ills and calamities for the nation. On the contrary, we should be providing optimistic support for the nation.

You must remember, brethren, that this church is one of the most powerful agencies for the progress of the world, and we should all bear our testimonies that we must all sound with one voice. We must tell the world how we feel about this land and this nation and should bear our testimonies about the great mission and destiny that it has. These are the subjects we should be talking about, brethren, and if we do this, we will help turn the tide of this great country and lessen the influence of the pessimists. We must be careful that we do not say or do anything that will further weaken the country. It is the negative, pessimistic comments about the nation that do as much harm as anything to the country today. We who carry these sacred responsibilities must preach the gospel of peace, and peace can only come by overcoming the things of the world. Now, we must be the dynamic force that will help turn the tide of fear and pessimism.

I remembered in the early days of the welfare program when Dr. E. G. Peterson, president of Utah State Agricultural College at that time, who was

341

on the Church Agricultural Committee, was sent out on a problem facing members of the Church in a distressed area. He came back from this assignment and said, "Brethren, I have discovered something that I am sure I always knew but was thrilled to see it in action. It is that the members of the Church are like soldiers in the ranks—all they need is for someone to give them marching orders and to show them where they are to go."

I think our people are just waiting for somebody to tell them the way to go. Our people are like soldiers in the ranks. They are waiting for us as leaders to tell them which way to go, and brethren, we must tell them in a positive way what they should be doing. This is the Lord's way, and so we should not be concerned about finding out what is wrong with America, but we should be finding what is right about America and should be speaking optimistically and enthusiastically about America.

I have since thought how important that is. There is no agency that speaks to the world that is as powerful a voice as the church and kingdom of God and the holy priesthood.

When this nation was in its infancy, we faced a terrible peril. A Revolutionary War was waged. England could have crushed this handful of colonists, but by some unseen power, France and Spain came to their aid. Why? Only the Lord knew. They joined hands with the colonists, and we gained our freedom and set up an independent nation. We survived that crisis.

When the Civil War came on because of the slavery question, there was an even greater peril, when it looked as though the nation was going to be divided. Some states were seceding from the Union. A bitter war was fought, with neighbor fighting against neighbor, family against family. We survived that. There came out of it a united nation, and the settlement movement began over the whole expanse of the United States of America, even into unknown territory. It was a tremendous task for that young nation, and yet the people proved equal to it.

We have gone through perils as a church when there was poverty, when there was slander, when there were at-

342

tempts to tear down and to malign and even to put to death the leaders of this church. Many thought that with the deaths of the Prophet Joseph Smith and his brother Hyrum, the Church would end, but the Lord knew better than that, because the Church was not founded on men. The Church was founded on the basis of the priesthood of the living God. It survived that peril, and we united as a people and moved out across a trackless waste, across deserts, across rivers, into a land that people said would never be able to grow corn and wheat; but we have seen in this intermountain country great prospering cities and towns and great peoples have been raised up here.

Today, we are faced with probably the most dangerous of all the tests of time, and that is the test of gold, affluence, and ease. When I first came into the Council of the Twelve, we had presented to us, as we went to each stake conference, a chart that showed the progress of the stake in several different categories—the percentages of those who held the priesthood who were attending priesthood meetings; the percentages of those who were paying their tithing; the percentages of ward teaching, fast offerings, sacrament meeting attendance. And as we looked at each chart showing a period of several years, up and down those marks went, showing high peaks and low peaks. Then I would say, "My, that was a wonderful record you made. But what happened in 1934?"

"Why, that was the year of the great drought."

"What happened in 1917? You were making such a fine record."

"Well, that was the time that our boys were going to war. The First World War was on, and everybody went to sacrament meeting."

During the war years everybody did their ward teaching, as we called it then; everybody paid their tithing. But    343 when the war was all over, the old story of the Book of Mormon began to repeat itself, and the people forgot what the Lord had said in warning about what would happen when people became too complacent.

The prophets said, in the time of Helaman:

> Yea, and we may see at the very time when he doth prosper his people, yea, in the increase of their fields, their flocks and their herds, and in gold, and in silver, and in all manner of precious things of every kind and art; sparing the hearts of their enemies that they should not declare wars against them; yea, and in fine, doing all things for the welfare and happiness of his people; yea, then is the time that they do harden their hearts, and do forget the Lord their God, and do trample under their feet the Holy One—yea, and this because of their ease, and their exceedingly great prosperity.
>
> And thus we see that except the Lord doth chasten his people with many afflictions, yea, except he doth visit them with death and with terror, and with famine and with all manner of pestilence, they will not remember him.
>
> O how foolish, and how vain, and how evil, and devilish, and how quick to do iniquity, and how slow to do good, are the children of men; yea, how quick to hearken unto the words of the evil one, and to set their hearts upon the vain things of the world!
>
> Yea, how quick to be lifted up in pride; yea, how quick to boast, and do all manner of that which is iniquity; and how slow are they to remember the Lord their God, and to give ear unto his counsels, yea, how slow to walk in wisdom's paths! (Helaman 12:2-5.)

Isn't that a terrible indictment, and yet that is happening before us today. We are seeing that affluence. Never was there such prosperity in this country. We have been forgetting God, and we have turned aside from His teachings, and we are paying a terrible price. It is the test that, if we survive, will perhaps take some of the punishments that this prophet said would be necessary to bring us back to our knees and seek for the Lord to guide and direct us.

Yes, we might have been close to the poverty line in the days of my youth. But out of that period came training and compensations that never could have come, I think, if we had been living in the lap of luxury. We didn't starve.

344

We had food to eat, and Mother knew how to make over the clothes for her boys. I never had what they called a "boughten suit" until I went to high school, but I always thought I was well dressed. After I filled a mission, I came back home and went to the University of Utah to get a teaching certification, and ofttimes I walked to and from school. I didn't have the money to ride because I needed the money to buy books.

Just after I passed my thirty-first birthday, I was made president of a stake of eleven wards, with a membership of 7,300. I was told that I was the youngest stake president in the Church. I wondered if the brethren had made a terrible mistake, and maybe others wondered about that too. But there I was, having been beaten down to the point where I understood the poor people over whom I had been called to preside; I understood when there was hardship.

The first Christmas after I became stake president, our little girls got some dolls and other nice things on Christmas morning, and they immediately dressed and went over to their little friend's home to show her what Santa Claus had brought them. In a few moments they came back, crying. "What in the world is the matter?" we asked. "Donna Mae didn't have any Christmas. Santa Claus didn't come." And then belatedly we realized that the father had been out of work, and there was no money for Christmas. So we brought the little ones of that family in and divided our Christmas with them, but it was too late. We sat down to Christmas dinner with heavy hearts.

I resolved then that before another Christmas came, we would be certain that every family in our stake had the same kind of Christmas and the same kind of Christmas dinner that we would have.

The bishops of our stake, under the direction of the stake presidency, made a survey of the stake membership, 345 and we were startled to discover that 4,800 of our members were either wholly or partially dependent—the heads of families did not have steady employment. There were no government make-work projects in those days. We had only ourselves to whom we could look. We were also told that we couldn't expect much help from the general funds of the Church.

We knew that we had about one thousand children under ten years of age for whom, without someone to help them, there would be no Christmas, so we started to prepare. We found a second floor over an old store on Pierpont Street. We gathered toys, some of which were broken, and for a month or two before Christmas parents came to help us. Many arrived early or stayed late to make something special for their own little ones. That was the spirit of Christmas giving—one had only to step inside the door of that workshop to see and feel it. Our goal was to see that none of the children would be without a Christmas. We would see that there was Christmas dinner in all the homes of the 4,800 who, without help, would otherwise not have Christmas dinner.

At that time I was one of the city commissioners. The night before Christmas Eve, we had had a heavy snowstorm, and I had been out all night with the crews getting the streets cleared, knowing that I would be blamed if any of my men fell down on the job. I had then gone home to change my clothes to go to the office.

As I started back to town, I saw a little boy on the roadside, hitchhiking. He stood in the biting cold with no coat, no gloves, no overshoes. I stopped and asked where he was going.

"I'm going uptown to a free picture show," he said.

I told him I was also going uptown and that he could ride with me.

346

HAVE FAITH IN AMERICA

"Son," I said, "are you ready for Christmas?"

"Oh, golly, mister," he replied, "we aren't going to have any Christmas at our home. Daddy died three months ago and left Mama and me and a little brother and sister."

Three children, all under twelve!

I turned up the heat in my car and said, "Now, son, give me your name and address. Somebody will come to your home—you won't be forgotten. And you have a good time; it's Christmas Eve!"

That night I asked each bishop to go with his delivery men and see that each family was cared for, and to report back to me. While waiting for the last bishop to report, I suddenly, painfully, remembered something. In my haste to see that all my duties at work and my responsibilities in the Church had been taken care of, I had forgotten the little boy and the promise I had made.

When the last bishop reported, I asked, "Bishop, have you enough left to visit one more family?"

"Yes, we have," he replied.

I told him the story about the little boy and gave him the address. Later he called to say that that family too had received some well-filled baskets. Christmas Eve was over at last, and I went to bed.

As I awoke that Christmas morning, I said in my heart, "God grant that I will never let another year pass but that I, as a leader, will truly know my people. I will know their needs. I will be conscious of those who need my leadership most."

My carelessness had meant suffering the first year because I did not know my people, but now I resolved never again to overlook the needs of those around me.

Then there came some tests when a loved one was taken from me and my life was crushed. A part of my life

347

was buried in the cemetery, and I wondered. Here I was struggling to help others. Why? Then I theorized that maybe this was a great test, and if I could survive it, maybe there would be no other test that I wouldn't be able to meet. Just as I was recovering from that sorrow a daughter died suddenly, leaving four little children motherless. That was difficult. It is still difficult to understand. But the ways of the Lord are righteous, and sometimes we have to go through experiences like these in order for us to be prepared to face the issues of today's world.

People frequently come to us asking why this church is growing so rapidly when other old-line churches, as they speak of them, are going in the opposite direction. I came across something that gave me an analysis. It was an article by a man who had been studying these trends, and he made conclusions that to me were true. One of the reasons, he said, was because the old-line churches, as they began to fail to attract members, started to sidetrack from the teachings of their progenitors, the teachings of the prophets; they began to substitute other means of trying to attract people—lowering standards of behavior, accepting some of the permissiveness of the world, thinking that that would attract, but it didn't, and many fell away.

But ours is a church that has held the line. When asked for reasons for our growth, we have said, "Through all of this, we are still teaching the pure, simple doctrines of the gospel of Jesus Christ. We believe in the same organization that existed in the primitive church, founded on apostles and prophets, with Jesus Christ as the chief cornerstone." Then we have added one more dimension. While the principles of the gospel are divine and do not change, the methods in dealing with the problems change to meet the circumstances, and so our methods have had to be flexible. We have adopted a welfare program. We have

348

adopted a family home evening program. We have intensified the work of our priesthood in home teaching in a more direct way to help the fathers.

We have found that we have been neglecting some of our adult members—those over eighteen who have not yet found their companions, or who are perhaps widowed or divorced. They have been saying to us, "But you have no program for us." Instead of our saying, "Sorry, we can't do anything for you except through our existing MIA or Relief Society programs," we have said to them, "We want to find out what you need. It is still the same gospel, but we are endeavoring to reach those for whom we have had no adequate programs. Man wasn't made for the Church, to paraphrase what the Master said, but the Church was made for man."

And so we have become flexible in adapting our methods in order to take care of the needs of our people, wherever they are. But we have built on a foundation laid down by the prophets, and we have not deviated from the principles and teachings of the gospel of Jesus Christ.

Sometimes there is a temptation to wonder whether or not we should perhaps give in a little bit. One man has said, "We are living in an age when we have seen black called white and white called black, and sin called good and good called sin." One example is abortion, which is contrary to all the teachings of the scriptures. It is one of the most heinous sins, and the only exception justifying it would be if it were necessary to save the life of the mother.

Another example is the eradication of prayer and Bible reading from our public school system. One atheist triumphed over the majority of the people in this country when the Supreme Court handed down its decision. In Salt Lake City a federal judge decreed that a tablet inscribed with the Ten Commandments, which had been placed on

349

the lawn of the Hall of Justice, had to be removed because it offended the sensibilities of the atheists—and we were unfair to them. We can be thankful that some concerned citizens said, "How foolish can you be! This is more than just a religious principle. The Ten Commandments are the foundation on which all law and order are founded." Through their action, the decision was reversed, and the plaque was restored.

Immorality is gripping the nation. Pornography is being distributed all over the country and affecting the lives of our young people. There is the sexual revolution, as it is called, where sex in every horrible form of perversion is being portrayed on the public screen, over television, and on the stage. There are young people rioting against any form of discipline in the home, in the schools, or on the part of the police, and many are refusing to defend their country and join the armed services.

The author I quoted previously concluded: "The great bright spot on the whole horizon today in America is the fact that there are people who do have this hunger to worship God in spirit and in truth, and places where our schools will honor the source of all wisdom and education, which is God himself." Hundreds of thousands are flocking to the churches and are taking stands on these issues, while those churches that have been against these principles and have taken the side of the atheists and the communists and the amoralists are suffering losses of membership and financial contributions. I think this speaks well for the intelligence of the American people. They are turning somewhere now where they can have a solid foundation on which to stand in these troubled times of lying, deceit, immorality, and breakdown of decency of law and order in our country.

350     Men may fail in this country, earthquakes may come,

seas may heave beyond their bounds, there may be great drought, disaster, and hardship, but this nation, founded on principles laid down by men whom God raised up, will never fail. This is the cradle of humanity, where life on this earth began in the Garden of Eden. This is the place of the new Jerusalem. This is the place that the Lord said is favored above all other nations in all the world. This is the place where the Savior will come to His temple. This is the favored land in all the world. Yes, I repeat, men may fail, but this nation won't fail. I have faith in America; you and I must have faith in America, if we understand the teachings of the gospel of Jesus Christ. We are living in a day when we *must* pay heed to these challenges.

I plead with you not to preach pessimism. Preach that this is the greatest country in all the world. This is the favored land. This is the land of our forefathers. It is the nation that will stand despite whatever trials or crises it may yet have to pass through.

The Lord will not leave His church without direction. Revelation for our guidance comes to the leadership of the kingdom of God on earth. I have a testimony regarding the modern speaking of tongues as described in the seventh Article of Faith. Many persons have wondered how the Prophet Joseph Smith was able to translate. He was an unschooled boy, and scientists have questioned how he was able to translate from unknown hieroglyphics or an unknown language into English. "How ridiculous can one be, to make such a claim," they have said.

Something happened at a recent general conference that will give you a key to how the Lord can open the mind of a man and give him spiritual understanding beyond his natural self. There were eleven translators or interpreters down in the basement of the Tabernacle translating in eleven different languages. For most of the talks they had scripts, so they could study them and, as the speakers spoke in English, they would repeat the words in the various languages for the benefit of those who were listening on earphones. One of these brethren was translating for the Swedish Saints. At the priesthood meeting I spoke extemporaneously, so he had no script to follow. But he reported that something miraculous happened. This is what he told me:

The whole conference was a spiritual experience, but at the general priesthood meeting I had an experience that I have never had before. I knew that there were some Swedish brethren attending the conference who had never been here before and perhaps would never come again. Therefore, I had a great desire that they receive everything that our prophet had to deliver. Not having a script, I commended myself into the hands of the Lord, and as you began to speak, I was startled by the fact that I knew one or two words and even three ahead of the time when you would say them. At first, I was so startled that I did not dare to pronounce them as they were given.

Usually I close my eyes and listen and then interpret as I hear the speakers deliver, but this time I was prompted to look at your face on the television screen. In this very unusual situation, I looked at you and began to translate the words as they came. However, to my amazement I did not receive just the words in my mind; with my inner eyes, I saw them emanating from the vicinity of the temple of your head and coming toward me. I did not see them actually as written on something, and yet, I saw them and how they were spelled, and I experienced the power of the Spirit as I received them.

One of the things that made it even more dramatic was that when a complex sentence was about to be delivered, I received more words so that I could reconstruct the grammar into good Swedish and deliver it at the very moment you pronounced the words. Never before had I experienced the great force with which the interpreted message was flowing as I did at that time. The same experience happened during your closing remarks on Sunday afternoon, except that I did not see the words coming to me.

I have talked with the Swedish members in attendance and they have expressed awe at what they experienced. They said they heard the interpretation and understood the interpreted message delivered at the same moment as you delivered the words in English. But the interpretation was all that they heard; the message came directly from you to them. They have all expressed that their attendance at the conference was a glorious spiritual experience, never to be forgotten.

I know that the Lord does have means of communicating with us, sending us messages that are beyond our understanding, even to translating an unknown language into our understandable language. He did it with the Prophet Joseph. He did it with King Mosiah. He has done it with others. He will do it today, as we have need. I have no doubt. My whole soul pleads that I may so live that if the Lord has any communication that He would wish me to receive for my beloved people, I will be a pure vessel through which that message might come. I do not ask for anything more than the Lord is willing to send, but I trust that I may live worthy so that I won't be a lame vessel or a broken reed that the Lord cannot use in times when He wants to communicate with his people.

I know that this is the church and kingdom of God. I know it with every fiber of my being. I, too, have been polished. Now I can see meaning in it. I thank the Lord that I have greater understanding of what the Apostle Paul meant when he said of the Master, "Though he were a Son, yet learned he obedience by the things which he suffered; And being made perfect, he became the author of eternal salvation unto all them that obey him." (Hebrews 5:8-9.)

Whatever may be necessary that I might be more refined to purge out all that which may be in me or which I have done that has not pleased the Lord, I would hope that I would stand ready to receive. Please God that I will not fail or flinch in the time of trial or testing.

I bear witness that these principles are true. Hold fast to the iron rod, which is the gospel of Jesus Christ and the power of salvation. "Stick with the old ship," as the person who was about to apostatize was told by an unseen speaker. Stick with the old ship. It will see you safely through. You may think it is out of date. It is out of date, thank goodness, as compared with some of these modern trends of permissiveness. But before you depart from those plain, simple doctrines of the gospel of Jesus Christ, be sure that you know in which direction you are going, and will listen to those who preside in authority over you. I bear you that witness and leave you my testimony.

Heavenly Father, bless thy people; take care of them; shepherd them in the folds of Thy great love and leave them not alone. Bless thy church. Care for its leaders and teachers. Bless the parents that they may watch over their little children and shepherd them from the pitfalls of evil. Father, hear my prayer, I humbly plead, in the name of the Lord, Jesus Christ. Amen.

# Appendix

The selected sermons and writings of President Harold B. Lee in this volume are adapted from the following sources:

1. "That Thy Light May Be a Standard Unto the Nations," MIA June Conference, June 29, 1969.
2. "Ye Are the Salt of the Earth," Delta Phi conference, Assembly Hall on Temple Square, March 5, 1966, and Brigham Young University, October 12, 1954.
3. "Doing the Right Things for the Right Reasons," BYU student body, April 19, 1961.
4. "Zion Must Be Strengthened," general conference, April 1951.
5. "Let Us Be As One," general conference, April 1950.
6. "Wells of Living Water," general conference, October 1943.
7. "Preparing Our Youth," *Ensign*, March 1971.
8. "The Purposes of Dating," radio address, March 20, 1960, reported in the *Church News*, March 26, 1960.
9. "The Role of Parents in the Home and Family," Mexico City area general conference, August 26, 1972, and the Munich area general conference, August 1973.

10   "Family Home Evening," *Improvement Era,* January 1967.

11   "Plain and Precious Things," *Ensign,* August 1972.

12   "The Gospel Teacher," *Children's Friend,* February 1951.

13   "The Mission of the Church Schools," address to institute and seminary teachers, Brigham Young University, August 21, 1953.

14   "Education for All," inauguration of President Dallin H. Oaks, Brigham Young University, November 1971.

15   "Seek Learning by Study and Also by Faith," general conference, April 1968.

16   "And the Spirit Shall Be Given You by the Prayer of Faith," article prepared for the Teacher Development Committee, May 1971.

17   "Strengthen the Stakes of Zion," general conference, April 1973.

18   "The Church in the Orient," general conference, October 1954.

19   "The Work in Great Britain," general conference, April 1960.

20   "The Spirit of Gathering," general conference, April 1948.

21   "True Patriotism—An Expression of Faith," Church of the Air, April 13, 1941.

22   "A Time of Decision," general conference, April 1972.

23   "Remaining Steadfast," general conference, October 1943.

24   "Salvation for the Dead," World Conference on Records, October 3, 1969.

25   "The Temple Endowment," *Instructor,* July 1961.

26   "God's Kingdom: A Kingdom of Order," *Ensign,* January 1971.

27   "Spiritual Rebirth and Death," general conference, October 1947.

28   "If a Man Die, Shall He Live Again?"—memorial service for President John F. Kennedy, Salt Lake Tabernacle, November 25, 1963.

29   "Easter Morning—A Newness of Life," Church of the Air, April 12, 1941.

30   "Faith to Surmount Life's Inevitables," Church of the Air, April 6, 1953.

31   "From the Valley of Despair to the Mountain Peaks of Hope," Memorial Day address, May 30, 1971.

32   "Destined for Eternity," Weber State College, Ogden, Utah, June 2, 1972.

33   "Woman's Glorious Purpose," *Relief Society Magazine,* January 1968.

34 "Maintain Your Place As a Woman," *Ensign,* February 1972.
35 "Three Phases of Motherhood," Primary Conference, April 3, 1970.
36 "For All Eternity, If Not for Time," *Relief Society Magazine,* October 1968.
37 "The Role of Women in Building the Kingdom," Relief Society Conference, September 29, 1966.
38 "Reap the Rewards of Beautiful Womanhood," Mexico City area general conference, August 26, 1972.
39 "Thoughts on Becoming a Member of the Council of the Twelve," general conference, April 1941.
40 "I Walked Today Where Jesus Walked," *Ensign,* April 1972.
41 "Have Faith in America," Ricks College, Rexburg, Idaho, October 26, 1973, and *Improvement Era,* December 1968.

# INDEX

YE ARE THE LIGHT OF THE WORLD

Moses, counsel to, from Jethro, 265
Mosheim, Johann, 91
Mosiah, sons of, 276
Motherhood, three phases of, 293-304;
 letter from daughter on, 316
Mothers, role of, 275-79; reports from
 successful, 286-87; not to work, if
 possible, 279, 287-88; to teach
 children, 295-96, 314. (See also
 Parents)
"Mothers Go Home," 297-98
Mount Zion, saviors on, 207
Moyle, Henry D., 299, 302
Mysteries revealed in temples, 210-11

Napoleon, 103, 285
Nephi, filled with power of God, 276
New Guinea, servicemen in, 58
Nibley, Hugh, 212
Nova Scotia, 169

"Ode on Intimations of Immortality," 263
"Open Letter to Man," 281
Ordinances are administered through the
 Church, 49
Orient, Church in, 149-57

Parable on teaching, 301-302
Parents, to teach children in home, 64-65,
 273-74; role of, in home and family,
 74-80; to hold family home evening,
 81-84. (See also Mothers)
Patriarchal blessings concerning marriage,
 305-306
Patten, David W., 164
Paul, Apostle, on sinning against Christ,
 21; advice of, to Timothy, 63; on
 learning through Spirit, 123; on
 combating evil, 189; on baptism, 202;
 on resurrection, 229; before King
 Agrippa, 247-48
Penrose, Charles W., 82
Perfection, working for, 265-66
Persecution of Saints, 223
Peter, loyalty of, 247
Peterson, E. G., 341
Petting, 68-70
Philippines, 20, 150-52
Philosophy, teaching of, 105
Phocian, prominent Athenian, 13
Pigs, boyhood experience with, 299
Pioneer Stake conference, 121

Pioneers, 173, 176, 177-178, 178-80, 228
Plural marriage, 34-35
Plutarch, 13
Political philosophies, 183-92
Politicians who are hypocrites, 29
Population control, 267-68
Pork, not mentioned in Word of Wisdom,
 32-33
Pratt, Parley P., 149
Prayer for wounded serviceman, 220-21;
 answers to, 257, 290-91
Preparation for second coming of
 Messiah, 40
"Present Crisis, The," 234
Presidency of the United States, 184
Pretenders, beware of, 9
Pricks, kicking against, 222-23
Priesthood, honoring, 22, 277-78; quorums
 to disseminate truth, 56; power of,
 203; on local level, 278-79
Primary general board member, 76
Prophecies, of Isaiah and Micah, 3; of last
 days, 137-40, 343-44
Protection promised to Church
 leaders, 8
"Psalm of Life, The," 258
Public officials, responsibilities of,
 188-90
Publications, Church, 46
Publications committee, 108
Publicizing private worship, 30
Puerto Rican offical, 288
Pure in heart, meaning of, 31-32

Reader's Digest, 6, 217
Relief Society, 279, 288, 312, 313, 314
Religion writer's impressions of Church,
 4-5
Repentance, 320-23
Restraints of gospel, 222
Resurrection, 204-205, 228-29, 238-41, 244
Revelation, criticism of professor about, 7;
 on restoration, 142-43; in modern
 days, 217-18
Revolutionary War, 342
Richards, Willard, 51, 158
Roberts, B. H., 121-22
Robertson, President and Sister Hilton A.,
 149
Roosevelt, Theodore, 233
Royal House of God, member of, 22
Russell, Isaac, 158